Learning in the Museum

George E. Hein

First published 1998 by Routledge
2 Park Square, Milton Park, Abingdon, Oxon, OX14 4RN

Simultaneously published in the USA and Canada
by Routledge
270 Madison Ave, New York NY 10016

Reprinted 1998,1999, 2000

Transferred to Digital Printing 2005

Routledge is an imprint of the Taylor & Francis Group

This project was supported, in part,
by the
National Science Foundation
Opinions expressed are those of the authors
and not necessarily those of the Foundation

Typeset in Sabon by Keystroke, Jacaranda Lodge, Wolverhampton

British Library Cataloguing in Publication Data
A catalogue record for this book is available from the British Library

Library of Congress Cataloging in Publication Data
Hein, George E., 1932–
Learning in the museum / George E. Hein.
p.   cm. — (Museum meanings)
Includes bibliographical references (p.   ) and index.
1. Museums—Educational aspects. 2. Museum exhibits—Educational
aspects. 3. Museum attendance—Educational aspects. 4. Museum
techniques—Educational aspects. 5. Constructivism (Education)
I. Title. II. Series.
AM7.H44   1998
069—dc21   97–26899
                          CIP

ISBN 0–415–09775–4 (hbk)
ISBN 0–415–09776–2 (pbk)

Learning in the Museum

Over the last twenty years, museum professionals have become increasingly aware of the educational role of museums and have begun to re-evaluate the relationship between museums and their visitors. Museum visits tend to be brief, infrequent events requiring less time and effort than most other educational activities. Can adults and children alike learn anything from such fleeting exposure, let alone find the experience profound and meaningful? *Learning in the Museum* confronts these issues and shows how research in visitor studies and the philosophy of education can be applied to facilitate a meaningful educational experience in museums.

Learning in the Museum begins with a brief history of education in public museums, and a rigorous examination of how the educational theories of Dewey, Piaget, Vygotsky and subsequent theorists relate to learning in the museum. A survey of the wide range of research methods employed in visitor studies is illustrated with examples taken from museums around the world. George Hein concludes that visitors can best learn when knowledge is actively constructed in their own minds, in exhibitions which are physically, socially, and intellectually accessible to every single visitor. He shows how museums can adapt to create this kind of environment, to provide what he calls the "Constructivist Museum."

As well as providing a meaningful theoretical basis to museum education, this volume serves as a practical guide for all museum professionals on how to adapt their museums to maximize the educational experience of every visitor. It will be essential reading for all educators interested in learning in the museum.

George E. Hein is a Professor at Lesley College, Cambridge, Massachusetts. He is co-author of *Active Assessment of Active Science* (1991) and a leading authority on museum education.

Museum Meanings

Series editors

Eilean Hooper-Greenhill

Flora Kaplan

The museum has been constructed as a symbol in Western society since the Renaissance. This symbol is both complex and multi-layered, acting as a sign for domination and liberation, learning and leisure. As sites for exposition, through their collections, displays and buildings, museums mediate many of society's basic values. But these mediations are subject to contestation, and the museum can also be seen as a site for cultural politics. In post-colonial societies, museums have changed radically, reinventing themselves under pressure from many forces, which include new roles and functions for museums, economic rationalism and moves towards greater democratic access.

Museum Meanings analyzes and explores the relationships between museums and their publics. 'Museums' are understood very broadly, to include art galleries, historic sites and historic houses. 'Relationships with publics' is also understood very broadly, including interactions with artifacts, exhibitions and architecture, which may be analyzed from a range of theoretical perspectives. These include material culture studies, mass communication and media studies, and learning theories and cultural studies. The analysis of the relationship of the museum to its publics shifts the emphasis from the museum as text, to studies grounded in the relationships of bodies and sites, identities and communities.

Also in this series:

Museum, Media, Message
Edited by Eilean Hooper-Greenhill

Colonialism and the Object: *Empire, Material Culture and the Museum*
Edited by Tim Barringer and Tom Flynn

To Emily,
with love and appreciation

Contents

Illustrations

Figures

Tables

Introduction

A generation ago I changed academic fields. I left chemistry, the discipline in which I had received my training, to enter education. For years I struggled to master the content of this new domain. A major frustration was always the lack of a solid, well indexed and well documented research literature. What was actually known about how humans learn, about effective practice in education, and about the conditions of learning? These questions became no easier to answer when I turned my attention to learning in the museum about fifteen years ago.

In chemistry, I could always rely on bibliographical resources to provide me with access to relevant literature. *Chemical Abstracts*, *Beilstein*, and specific *Annual Reviews*[1] were sure to lead to the sources that would describe what was known from research in the field. I could also be sure that, with some exceptions, I would be able to trace the development of a topic from early work through to current research to appreciate how current research was built on previous work and incorporated it, and how all of it was relevant to my own research. There are exceptions, of course, striking examples of work over-looked, or a generally accepted concept overturned by a new idea. Sometimes previous work may even have shown the inadequacy of a concept long before it is overturned. But, by and large, what is known is both known by all and accepted by most people in the field.

I have never achieved such certainty in education, whether in the literature about school learning or learning in the museum. In fact, I believe that it is not possible to arrive at such certainty. There is continual conflict about all the significant issues surrounding learning. Heraclitus' dictum that we cannot step into the same stream twice applies to education in a way that it does not apply to chemistry. It's only recently that I've come to realize just why this is true, and what insight this difference provides us with about educational practice and educational research.

In chemistry, molecules and the forces that govern their behavior do not change over time. Although explanations and theories evolve, the phenomena remain the same. The amino acids that Emil Fischer, my professional great-grandfather, studied are the same as those studied by his student Max Bergmann in the

1920s and 1930s and by Bergmann's student Carl Niemann in the 1960s when I had the privilege of working with him. Alanine, now as then, dissolves in water; phenylalaninamide, now as then, is a substrate for chymotrypsin. But the same consistency of phenomena cannot be applied to data about visitors to museums. Higgins's emigrants in Liverpool in 1884 are not the same people as Melton's immigrant children in Buffalo in the 1920s, and neither group is identical to the families we observe now in Boston's Museum of Science. Nor can we assume that what they learn, and even the way they learn – so dependent upon culture, social values and personal attributes – is the same today as it was a hundred years ago. We cannot build a totally hierarchical literature when variables not only increase but actually change with time.

Thus, the subject and conditions of educational research constantly change. Older work, although valuable, needs to be interpreted and translated before it can be applied to today's settings. To say that the meaning of objects is dependent on culture is hardly profound. The consequences of a constantly changing culture on research about that society – research, which is itself culture-bound – is profound, as has been pointed out frequently by social scientists. This issue adds a layer of ambiguity to past findings, so that they are not necessarily a good guide for current research and may be the reason that educational research has a poor reputation among natural scientists. The latter would like us to isolate variables, define a problem, and then solve it, once and for all. But educational practice and descriptions of how learning takes place are more likely than natural science to include schools of belief each buttressed by their own selective view of the relevant supporting research and none completely refuted by the evidence.

I have attempted to learn what has been written about learning and to understand both the historical literature and current efforts. There are strikingly different ways of looking at the world, and these overarching world views determine our positions about both theories of education and theories of research. The consequences of these choices lead to several well documented, consistent literatures about learning. I do not pretend to be neutral in this discussion. I favor a constructivist view of education for museums and a naturalistic approach to studying visitors. How these are related and why I support them will, I trust, become clear in the subsequent chapters.

In this book, I first delineate the relationships between different world views about learning in the museum and illustrate the evidence that supports these. I emphasize constructivism, the particular perspective that I think is both the most promising for explaining the complex interaction between visitors and museums, and which is most compatible with my general world view. I hope the chapters provide material in support of a consistent, reasonable, and persuasive thesis. Given the position I support, I cannot claim that they present the truth about learning. But I hope that readers will see these arguments as reasonable.

Many people have assisted me in completing this book. My debt to them is enormous. At every stage I asked people to read drafts of chapters, completed chapters and, finally, a bulky, clumsy manuscript. If it has risen to the level of a coherent and useful document, this is largely because of the careful reading and sound advice I have received. I'm appreciative of the assistance, large and small, from Mary Alexander, Ted Ansbacher, Laurie Beckelman, Gina Cobin Brenda Engel, John Fuller, Janette Griffin, David Ellis, Elsa Feher, Eilean Hooper-Greenhill, Sabra Lee, Paulette McManus, Laura Martin, Caryl Marsh, Robin Mello, Emily Romney, and Debra Smith.

In addition, it is a privilege to acknowledge the institutions that have assisted me. First and foremost, the Informal Science Education Program of the National Science Foundation, which awarded me a grant, NSF 9552584, that allowed me to spend a semester away from home. During that time I was generously accepted as a visitor in the Department of Museum Studies, University of Leicester. More recently I had the good fortune to spend two months as a Howard Hughes Medical Institute Visiting Scholar at the CalTech Precollege Science Initiative (CAPSI) in Pasadena. Both the time there and the opportunity to teach a short course on learning in museums were invaluable; I thank my hosts and the students in that course. Lesley College granted me leaves for these activities. Finally, all my colleagues at the Program Evaluation and Research Group at Lesley College always provide stimulation, companionship and support. Any shortcomings and errors in this book are my responsibility.

The Heraclitian river flows on. As Catherine Bateson has reminded us (Bateson 1962/1987), "a book is also affected by the passage of time; its intellectual meaning changes as its readers change." I hope the current is kind to this volume, that it lands in congenial hands and that it can be useful for some time to all my professional colleagues who work so diligently and imaginatively to make museums vital, living institutions.

1

The significance of museum education

This is educational for everybody. The fathers are always quieting
their sons saying, "Listen to this," as the Sergeant Major pats the
barrel of the howitzer and tells his little story about Fallen
Timbers. The women and the girls hang around the kitchens and
out near the bower down by the river, where the ladies from the
fort do the laundry. Sometimes people will help weed the plots of
vegetables or churn butter. They'll add a few stitches to the quilt.

The college kids work here for credit, I think. Or write papers.
Something.

Everyone who visits is interested in sanitation.

I take people around to the privies, point out the chamber pots,
tell them how it was a real problem in the previous fort during the
war and the siege.

"Here is the gutter that Major Whistler, my father, had dug around
the parade ground for the water to run off." I've learned a lot too
about history and speaking in front of people. I like talking about
things and having people listening. I like it when they nod and
whisper to each other. The little boys look at what I'm wearing.

Kids my age will try to trip me up, asking about hamburgers or the
Civil War. But I haven't made a mistake once. Well, once I did, but
the guy who asked didn't know I did, so it was all right.

I'll be a senior next year at North Side High School, which is up
the banks of the St. Joe near the site of a French fort . . . My
teachers think this will be good experience. They wrote good
recommendations for me. My own father isn't so sure, but he is
happy I have a job and that I work outside.

To him, it's a summer job, that's all.

(Martone 1984: 40–1)

Introduction

Museums are extraordinary places where visitors have an incredible range of experiences. It is not unusual for visitors to describe epiphanies in recounting their own history with museums. I can remember vividly my own childhood visit more than 50 years ago to the silent streets of Pompeii; I have stood transformed in front of a painting as its scope and meaning grew and grew for me the longer I focused on it; I once spent an hour on a misty, raw November morning in a native American bark-covered dwelling talking to a staff member at Plimoth Plantation while she tended a cooking pot over an open fire. After a few minutes, only our conversation, the smell of the wood fire, the wooden seats and blankets inside and the natural sounds of the brook and dripping water outside existed. When I left and looked back in the cool, shrouding mist to see my informant emerge from her home to fetch more water in this Arcadian woodland setting, I felt not only privileged, but overwhelmed at the opportunity given me to enter, if only for a moment, a lost world.

Millions of visitors have memories of such experiences; ones that John Dewey would call educative. Dewey, who strongly stressed the value of experience for education, was also clear that not every experience is indeed educative.

> The belief that all genuine education comes from experience does not mean that all experiences are genuinely or equally educative. Experience and education cannot be directly equated with each other. For some experiences are mis-educative. Any experience is mis-educative that has the effect of arresting or distorting the growth of further experience. An experience may be such as to engender callousness; it may produce lack of sensitivity and of responsiveness . . . a given experience may increase a person's automatic skill in a particular direction and yet tend to land him in a groove or rut . . . An experience may be immediately enjoyable and yet promote the formation of a slack and careless attitude . . . Each experience may be lively, vivid, and "interesting," and yet their disconnectedness may artificially generate dispersive, disintegrated, centrifugal habits. The consequence of formation of such habits is inability to control future experiences. They are then taken, either by way of enjoyment or of discontent and revolt, just as they come.
>
> (Dewey 1938: 13–14)

Dewey makes two points here that are relevant to the power of museum experiences to change us. First, routine experiences that do not challenge and stimulate us may not be educative. This idea is now frequently enunciated in the phrase that in order to be educative, experiences must be not only "hands-on" but also "minds-on." Second, it is not sufficient for experiences to be "lively, vivid, and 'interesting'"; they must also be organized to be educative.

In order for visitors to grow and learn from their museum experiences, we need to understand these experiences sufficiently so that we can shape them. We need to understand what meaning visitors make of their museum experiences. How, exactly, do their ordinary responses to visits, as well as the occasional, powerful, epiphanies affect our visitors? How can the educative value of experience be enhanced?

The need to consider what meaning visitors make of their museum experience comes from two different sources: one is the increasing importance of the educational role of museums; the other is the increasing pressure on museums to justify their existence. The latter pressure is mainly (but not exclusively) addressed through market research; it manifests itself in efforts by museum staff to know who their audience is, to develop exhibitions that will be popular and that will increase attendance. Other providers of entertainment, such as the Disney enterprises and other theme parks, have greatly advanced our under-standing of public responses to leisure-time options. Much can be learned from these efforts about crowd control, what makes a site appealing, how to attract various audience segments, and how best to market any leisure "product."

But exploring the educational value and potential of museums is more complex and deserves to be analyzed at some length. Dewey's criteria of "lively, vivid, and 'interesting'," along with good accessibility and ample amenities, may be sufficient for entertainment. They are necessary, but not sufficient for education. To make them educative represents the fundamental challenge of museum exhibitions and programs: how to transform the obvious enthusiasm of visitors into connected, engaging, integrated activities that lead to growth.

A brief history of museum education

Education as a crucial museum function has been recognized as long as there have been public museums. The public museum as we know it – the display of objects for the edification and entertainment of the public – is a product of the eighteenth century, with a major expansion of museums into significant public institutions occurring in the nineteenth century. Museums developed approximately parallel with the advent of the nation-state in response to recognition that the welfare of citizens was the responsibility of government. Public museums grew as knowledge spread beyond a very limited class. Hudson (1975) attributes to René Huyge, a French scholar, the observation that museums and encyclopedias appeared at about the same time.

> Both were an expression of the eighteenth-century spirit of
> enlightenment which produced an enthusiasm for equality of
> opportunity of learning . . . The theory behind these movements was a
> simple one, that collections which had hitherto been reserved for the
> pleasure and instruction of a few people should be made accessible to
> everybody.
>
> (Hudson 1975: 6)

In the early part of the nineteenth century, newly opened museums – although with limited access for the public – primarily demonstrated the wealth and power of governments. They displayed imperial conquests, exhibited the exotic material and treasures brought back to Europe by colonial administrations and private travelers or unearthed by increasingly popular excavations, and generally awed those fortunate enough to be allowed to enter and observe the splendor of a nation's wealth.

The Museum of Napoléon at the Louvre displayed the booty of imperial conquest; every new campaign necessitated opening a new gallery to house the material shipped to Paris after the battles. The Congress of Vienna supervised the return of many treasures to their original owners, much to the dismay of the curator of the Louvre (Wittlin 1949: 233–4).

Museums that contain material from places other than the home country are restricted to the imperialist nations. Only in imperial nations in Europe and North America can one find large *international* collections of paintings or natural history objects. Museums in most other countries house primarily *national* collections. Museums of Greece have few northern European (or Asian) objects; Chinese museums do not have Occidental departments to match their Oriental counterparts in England or the United States.

In the latter half of the nineteenth century, as industrialization progressed, populations moved to the cities, and science and industry reshaped life, governments also increasingly took responsibility for social services and education. Museums were viewed as one type of institution among several that could provide education for the masses. Henry Cole, the influential director of the new South Kensington Museum "was engaged on a massive experiment in public education" (Anderson 1995: 15). Museums were included among the agencies available to help people better themselves and to appreciate the value of modern life. Museum exhibitions, for example, were mounted in support of public campaigns for health education; to show off magnificent developments in industry or advances in technology; or to exhibit curiosities, marvels, and wonders for public entertainment. All the approaches to education still used today, as well as many of the controversies surrounding them, were first introduced by pioneering staff members a century ago: didactic labels of varying length and complexity, lectures and other events for the public, special courses and programs for school groups, deliberately didactic exhibitions, and in-house and outreach programs for general and specific audiences.

The public school movement in industrialized countries developed at the same time. Schooling, not common for the majority of the population at the beginning of the nineteenth century, began to provide a uniform educational base for the labor force. School attendance became mandatory during the nineteenth century, but most children went to school only for a few years, and often only after completing a full day's work. Children in cities worked 10–12 hour days, and farm children were often absent from the school population. As late as the 1940s, only about 50 per cent of children in the United States went on to secondary school.

Schools, like public museums, were part of the developing system of public expenditure for the masses. But, unlike museums, they quickly developed an accountability system – inspectors, tests, and standard curriculum as well as public discussion of what schools were for, how they should be run, and whether they were doing their intended job. By the late nineteenth century, the increasingly universal school system included an assessment system, as well as evaluations of schools and school systems. Museums, although equally public institutions in most countries, did not establish similar approaches to assessing impact on their clients. It was assumed that people would learn, be enlightened, and be entertained by their visits to museums without any reference to the study of visitors' experiences. The attitude that the response of the museum's audience is irrelevant still exists in many museums.

By the end of the century, schools had so eclipsed museums' public educational function that it was necessary to argue that museums could support the educational work of schools. In a lecture delivered in 1853, Professor Edward Forbes had argued that curators "may be prodigies of learning and yet unfit for their posts," if they do not know anything about pedagogy, if they are not equipped to teach people who know nothing (quoted in Greenwood 1888: 185). Thirty-five years later James Paton, Superintendent of the Glasgow Art Gallery and Museums, is quoted as saying:

> We are now on the threshold of other important changes in connection with scientific and secondary education; and in the efficiency of all these educational movements the museum of the city should be an important factor. It ought to be the centre around which educational institutions cluster, the storehouse whence they could draw the material examples and illustrations required on the lecture table and in the class-room.
> (Glasgow Art Gallery and Museums n.d.: 5)

As Hooper-Greenhill (1991) points out:

> During the nineteenth century, education had been the prime function of the museum. The ideal museum was understood to be "the advanced school of self-instruction", and the place where teachers should "naturally go for assistance". Although many museums and galleries were unable to achieve this ideal, this was a firmly held view. By the 1920s this conviction, held so strongly by nineteenth-century thinkers in so many areas of intellectual and political life, was under attack. A new generation of curators was less interested in the public use of museums, and more interested in the accumulation of collections.
> (Hooper-Greenhill 1991: 25)

Similarly in the United States, the educational function of museums was acknowledged early (Roberts 1997) but, despite some notable exceptions of school museums in the late nineteenth century, the public school movement and educational work in museums diverged. Only recently has interest in the contribution that "informal" education can make to the overall educational efforts of schools extended beyond a small group within either museums or general education.

One common, retrospective criticism of museums as educational institutions is that nineteenth-century museums were torn between their educational goals and a more elitist, exclusive tradition. Proponents of this argument cite the limited access and restrictive practices (dress codes, concern about entry for the "masses," etc.) of early museums. Although there has been a long tradition of criticism of museums for not making a more serious effort to fulfill their social obligations (see Low 1942, Wittlin 1949, Hudson 1975), it is hardly appropriate to hold museums of 1850 or 1900 to the standards of democracy we embrace today. The United States is considered a democracy, even though its original formulation disqualified more than 50 per cent of its residents, and it took two constitutional amendments, the most recent ratified within living memory, to give the vote to African-Americans and women. As Orosz (1990) suggests, in the United States at least, museums have always been

> direct products of the American democratic culture and developed in synchronization with the evolution of the general cultural climate . . . the great majority had serious and egalitarian aspirations.
>
> (Orosz 1990: 3)

The significance of education in museums

Although the educational function of museums is venerable, the last three decades have witnessed a shift in both the definition of education and its relative importance within museums and within the museum profession. The modern world has changed the social and cultural structure in which this function is taking place. Indeed, the very nature of education, both what we mean by the term and what we expect of educational institutions, has changed.

Definitions of education

One major factor contributing to this change in definitions of education is our current, more sophisticated approach to education, which will be discussed more fully in later chapters. Learning is now seen as an active participation of the learner with the environment. This conception of learning has elevated experience (as distinct from codified information contained in books) to a more important place in the effort to educate. Museums focus on the "stuff" of the world. They specialize in the objects representing both culture and nature and, therefore, become central to any educational effort when the focus shifts from the written word to learners' active participation through interaction with objects.

Although the writings and teaching of Comenius (Piaget 1967), the philosophy of John Dewey, and the developmental psychology of Piaget all recognize the significance of learning from experience, our society has yet to accept this principle fully. Critics continually argue that education is a matter of "learning" facts and that valuing experience is not only unnecessary, but also detrimental. There is no important role for museums in the "back to basics" education movement.

Formal and informal education

Some writers have attributed all progressive educational ideas to the education that takes place in museums, contrasting the "informal" education that takes place in museums – self-directed learning, use of materials, respect for all learners – with "formal" education in schools, depicted as dull, content driven, and highly didactic. It is important to recognize that interest in museum education is and has been part of a continuing effort to make all educational institutions relevant for the entire population.

In this book the terms "formal" and "informal" are reserved for a description of settings and the presence or absence of a formal curriculum. Schools provide primarily formal education; they teach a specific, hierarchical curriculum, and they usually have rules about attendance, time spent in classes, classmates, and requirements for successful completion. Museums, even when overtly engaged in education, usually offer informal education; they do not have a set curriculum that progresses from lower to higher levels, usually do not require attendance, and do not certify mastery of specific knowledge at the conclusion of a visit.

The terms do not distinguish between possible characteristics of the education that takes place in the two institutions. Both formal and informal settings (i.e. both schools and museums) can be places where learning is facilitated through the use of objects, the opportunities to learn are based on the learners' interests, education includes discovery and/or construction of meaning, and students take responsibility for their own activities. "Formal" and "informal" adequately describe the administrative attributes of educational settings; the terms should not be used to describe pedagogic qualities. Classrooms in progressive schools, committed to a developmental–active learning philosophy, may look very much like a discovery gallery in a science museum. Conversely, there are museum programs that place the participants in isolated classrooms with a lecturer in front of the group, and these may share many attributes with a traditional school.

Education within the museum profession

A second influence on the need for thoughtful consideration of the visitor's experience in the museum comes from the changing importance of the educational role of museums within the profession. Three major reports on the status of museums in the United States published in the past 25 years illustrate this shift in how museum educators view their own role. The first, *The Belmont Report* (American Association of Museums 1969), arose from the museum profession's desire to be included in and contribute to the social programs that originated during the Johnson administration. *The Belmont Report* warns of the increasing pressure on museums to serve the public and the need for resources to carry out the museum's mission. In response to the mandate to answer the following three questions

1 "What is [the museums'] present condition?"

2 "What are the unmet needs of America's museums?"
3 "What is their relation to other educational and cultural institutions?"
                            (American Association of Museums 1969: xi)

the authors define the mission of the museum as

> two-fold: the advancement and diffusion of knowledge, and the
> enhancement of that awareness which affords pleasure and delight.
>   (American Association of Museums 1969: 1)

The report then goes on to discuss the functions of museums as research
institutions, as educational institutions, and as potential collaborators in the
national effort to provide "education for disadvantaged children in slum areas"
(American Association of Museums 1969: 13).

In 1982 the American Association of Museums convened the Commission on
Museums for a New Century

> to accomplish this formidable task: to study and clarify the role of
> museums in American society, their obligations to preserve and interpret
> our cultural and natural heritage, and their responsibilities to an
> ever-broadening audience.
>   (American Association of Museums 1984: 11)

The Commission sought the public's view of museums and their appropriate
positioning within communities through a series of forums with museum
professionals listening to community leaders. The Commission's *Museums for
a New Century* (American Association of Museums 1984) included a chapter
highlighting the necessity for museums to interpret their collections for the
public. In that chapter, "Learning in Museums," the Commission acknowledged, once again, the importance of education to museums, and went on to
suggest that "Museums have not realized their full potential as educational
institutions" (American Association of Museums 1984: 28). The general tone
of *Museums for a New Century* is that the educational function of museums is
not only important, but is as important as other aspects of museum professional
practice.

Only a few years after this publication, the American Association Of Museums
convened a group of professional museum educators and directors to specifically address museum education issues. *Excellence and Equity: Education and
the Public Dimension of Museums* (American Association Of Museums 1992)
restated the profession's commitment to education, or museum learning, and
returned to the theme of community service as essential to museum practice.
In this report, education has risen even further in significance. The report
summary states

> The community of museums in the United States shares the
> responsibility with other educational institutions to enrich learning
> opportunities for all individuals and to nurture an enlightened, humane
> citizenry that appreciates the value of knowing about its past, is
> resourcefully and sensitively engaged in the present, and is determined to

shape a future in which many experiences and many points of view are given voice.

(American Association of Museums 1992: 25)

In Britain, the introduction of a national curriculum in 1989 gave rise to publi-cations (Moffat 1996, School Curriculum and Assessment Authority 1995, Yorath 1995) that discussed the use of museums to support state-mandated education goals. Museum staff have worked closely with local educational authorities to assure that exhibitions and programs mesh with the school cur-riculum. Unfortunately, museums that happen to have collections on topics that fall outside the main themes of the required topics must struggle to justify the educational value of their possessions. A recent report acknowledges both the past potential and the present opportunity to create "the museums that will be needed if they are truly to serve society and its learning needs in the new century" (Anderson 1997: iv).

> Museums in the United Kingdom have always been seen as educational institutions. Yet this is the first comprehensive report to examine their educational role in full. Its publication reflects a renewed awareness of the contribution that museums make to lifelong public learning, and the even greater contribution that they could make in future if their work was coordinated at local, regional and national levels.

(Anderson 1997: iv)

Interpretations of culture

Additional socio-political forces have also brought interpretation to the fore-ground in museums. As other major institutions in our society – state religion, schools, political parties, and social organizations – have declined in importance, the role of museums as interpreters of culture has increased.

History museums have taken on the burden of reinterpreting their displays and collections to reflect modern re-examination of national and local history. Colonial Williamsburg added slave quarters (and even a provocative slave auction!) to its public exhibitions and programs; Liverpool Museum has included an exhibition on the slave trade in its coverage of the growth of that city; the interpretation of the Little Bighorn Battlefield has dramatically changed since it began to include the Native American side of the story. Some of these aspects of wider interpretation or reinterpretation also result in controversial exhibitions, such as the presentation of the Enola Gay, the plane that dropped the first atomic bomb on Hiroshima, at the Smithsonian Air and Space Museum. The role of museums in interpreting culture has become public enough to attract the attention of social theorists (see Macdonald and Fyfe 1996), who discuss both how museums interpret culture and how studying museums as social institutions may inform us about our culture.

> First, [this volume] is concerned with museums as sites in which socially and culturally embedded theories are performed. The interest here is in the stories museums tell, the technologies they employ to tell their tales,

9

and the relation these stories have to those of other sites, including those of social and cultural studies. Second, the volume is concerned to highlight ways in which museums may be theorized within social and cultural studies. What stories can we tell, and what devices can we employ, to make sense of museums?

(Macdonald 1996: 3)

These issues are all concerned with the overt as well as the hidden, implicit educational roles of museums.

Museums in a changing world

Such recognition of the primacy of interpretation and education in museum practice is particularly evident in museums in newer, emerging countries (Eoe 1995), although it also surfaces in developed countries as all embrace a wider range of ethnicities among their residents.

If there is anything that museums should be proud of, it is the Museum's contribution to the issue of "national identity" at least this is true for many developing countries and it is certainly true of Papua New Guinea.

(Eoe 1995: 15)

How should a new (or changing) nation-state define its museums, and how can these help to define the culture of the nation?

Such problems are frequently discussed at international museum education conferences where speakers illustrate the immense diversity of educational activity and the significance of museums for national cultures in dozens of countries. For example, at the 1993 annual conference of the Committee for Education and Cultural Action (CECA) of ICOM in India, S. K. Bagchi (1993) cited the example of direct intervention of a district science centre in rural India to support socio-cultural development in a poor district. As a result,

In 1984, the District Science Centre got fully involved with socio-economic development . . . About 45 Kheria villages were motivated to dig tube wells and ponds for harvesting and providing drinking water . . . The Kheria women were taught to make marketable products from bamboo and leaves. The science centre helped in maintaining these products. As literacy was extremely poor, non-formal schools were arranged and stipends given . . . the Science Centre developed visual exhibitions on malaria and diarrhoea.

(Bagchi 1993)

Other reports at the same conference stressed the outreach efforts to communities in Bangladesh (Hague 1993), cross-cultural programs for children in Israel (Gino 1993, Shilo-Cohen 1993), museum efforts to assist social integration (Mukhopadhyay 1993) and environmental protection (Dekvar 1993) in India, expanding educational cooperation between schools and the National Museum in Kenya (Maikweki 1993), and a program to encourage Bengali women living in England to visit and utilize the Victoria and Albert Museum (Akbar 1993; see also Akbar 1995). What is striking is the overt political-social purpose of these programs, with or without cooperation from the national authorities, to change the societies in which they take place through museum-related educational activities.

Museums as active preservers of culture

Just as museums have taken on major educational roles in many countries through programs and exhibitions intended to benefit various segments of the population, they have also become active preservers of (often vanishing) cultures, not just passive collectors of cultural artifacts. This function was discussed both at the CECA meeting in India and the subsequent 1994 meeting in Cuenca, Ecuador (Astudillo 1996). In industrial societies with their influx of diverse cultural groups this function involves expanding the museum's role (amid controversy!) and making decisions about what to include in its collections. In post-colonial countries with disappearing ways of life this aspect means going out to local and remote communities and actively working to preserve cultural artifacts and cultural production. In all countries, active collecting is required and involves aggressive search for cultural components that are disappearing for a variety of reasons. Memories of Holocaust survivors, neighborhoods uprooted by urban renewal, or quickly forgotten, obsolete technologies require immediate attention so that they can be included in museum exhibitions.

The dramatic political changes in the world since 1990 have brought to the fore the significant role of museums in helping to redefine new nations and reinterpret the history of these same states under former regimes. Groys (1995), discussing this role for museums in the modern world where "there is no fixed, metaphysical, eternal order any more," suggests that

> Therefore, in the modern age, an artificial memory, a cultural archive, a museum would have to be created in which historical memories are recorded in the form of books, pictures, and other historical documents. Modern subjectivity has no other way to define itself in the world than by collecting, by creating an archive of objects which would be saved from the destruction through time by the technical means of conservation.

> (Groys 1995: 8)

Although these expanded social functions of museums involve the traditional roles museums have always played – collection, preservation, documentation, research, and education – they particularly acknowledge and require the educational activities of museums. The crucial decisions concern what is to be included in the museum and what meanings are to be attributed to the contents of museums. These activities illuminate the significance of the *interpretation* of objects and their use by and with the public (i.e. the work of museum education).

11

Conclusion

For a variety of reasons, ranging from changing definitions of learning and pressures on museums to justify their existence to expanding socio-political roles of museums in increasingly self-conscious societies, museum education is increasing in significance. What is learned in museums and how learning takes place is more than a matter of intellectual curiosity. Learning in the museum and understanding visitors' learning has become a matter of survival for museums.

This rise in the importance of education in museums, and education's increased role in shaping the mission of museums (and museum associations), requires that we study and understand learning in museums. The intent of this book is to examine possible theories of education, as well as theories of research about visitors, how these theories determine our definitions of learning, and how they are applied to exhibitions and programs.

In Chapter 2 I develop a framework for understanding educational theories, classifying them according to their positions on two main elements, theories of knowledge and learning, and developing an educational policy. The analysis of theories is a necessary component of educational practice but it is not sufficient. A complete educational program consists of more than a theory; it requires application of that theory through a specific pedagogy. It also includes an educational policy: what is the aim of the education? to whom is it directed? how does it relate to other social and political institutions? Later chapters will include such considerations as learning in the museum is discussed from a broader perspective.

Visitor studies has a 100-year history, culminating in the current thriving enterprise involving hundreds of professionals and generating an increasing practical and theoretical literature. In Chapter 3, I briefly summarize the history of the field, and point out contrasting traditions that emerged. These traditions illustrate contrasting theories in social science. In Chapter 4, I discuss the experimental–design ("quantitative") and naturalistic ("qualitative") styles of social science research, the emergence of program evaluation as a professional field, and the relevance of both of these to visitor studies.

Educational theories and research theories do not exist independently of each other but share common conceptions of how the world works; they arise from similar "world views." In Chapter 5, I discuss this relationship, especially as it applies to museum education and visitor studies research.

The field of visitor studies has developed a broad range of methodologies derived from the methods used generally in social science. These methods have provided us with our current (inadequate) knowledge about visitor behavior and learning in museums. In Chapters 6 and 7, I discuss first the methods that have been employed and then the kinds of insights they provide into what visitors do and what they may learn in museums.

Finally, I believe that focusing on visitors, the meanings they attribute to their experiences, and their understandings, is the most useful way to develop exhibitions and programs that will allow visitors to have satisfying museum experiences and allow museums to maximize the inherent potential of objects to contribute to human growth and learning. My views on the constructivist museum are presented in Chapter 8.

2

Educational theory

The history of educational theory is marked by opposition between the idea that education is development from within and that it is formation from without; that it is based upon natural endowments, and that education is a process of overcoming natural inclination and substituting in its place habits acquired under external pressure . . . The solution of this problem requires a well thought-out philosophy . . .

(Dewey 1938: 1, 9)

The necessity of educational theory

Human beings are enormously complex. We have confounded any attempt to describe our behavior in terms of simple, or even complex, theories. But models that attempt to describe human behavior are, nevertheless, useful; for they provide a rational basis for discussing behavior and organizing educational situations. This chapter outlines a theoretical structure that encompasses any educational theory and then relates that model to museum practices that would follow rationally from the various theories. The model developed here is not a description of how people learn, but an outline of a set of theories required to form a "well thought-out philosophy" of education.

In Chapter 1, I argued, following Dewey's lead, that not all experience was educational. Museum experiences, almost always rich and often involving novelty for the visitor, are bound to contain an educational potential, regardless of the intentions of either the museum staff or the visitor. Museum staff increasingly argue that the educational role of the museum is significant. Yet just what the educational intention of the museum might be, how the institution considers education, how it believes that people learn, and what education consists of, are frequently vaguely defined if defined at all.

To pursue an intentional educational role successfully and efficiently, museums need to have a conscious educational policy. If no conscious effort is made to adopt a theory of education, the museum's exhibitions, layout, and general atmosphere will still express a point of view about education and visitors will still receive powerful educational messages, but these may be mixed and/or contradictory and visitors may be confused. I once evaluated a program in an art museum intended to increase its community outreach activities to schools. The program provided opportunities for high school students to become "junior curators," and interpret galleries for younger students. At the same time, the museum's library barred all high school students from using its resources. The net result of the program was far less than could have been achieved if an overall, overt consistent educational policy had been formulated for the entire museum and deliberately pursued.

An analogy can be made to parenting. All parents educate their children; all have a parenting style and approach. In most families the theory on which their actions are based is not conscious, it is deeply embedded in the cultural and social network of the society in which the parents live and its characteristics are part of a more general cultural landscape. Our culture is the sea in which we swim, as transparent to us as the ocean is for the fish that live in it.

For anyone from outside the culture, or for an anthropologist or sociologist studying parenting, the peculiar child-shaping practices of parents become evident: the particular choice of words, the decisions to punish or reward, to ignore or single-out some behavior, time spent with the children, activities carried out as a family – all serve to describe a particular parenting mode. These acts can be classified and described as matching categories of behavior.

Similarly, our educational practices in museums follow some pattern, adhere to some theory, and reflect the beliefs of the staff and the larger culture in which they are embedded. Following the lead of the anthropologist, we can make the effort to think through the underlying principles on which we base educational activities and shape the general educational stance of the museum according to these principles, or we can follow an unexamined collection of policies and practices that, taken together, present to visitors an educational position which may or may not conform to our desires.

Parenting consists not only of the conscious acts of parenting – the educational family trip, the specific training of children, the fostering of communication with other relatives – but also of casual acts, usually quite unconscious – listening to or ignoring children's stories, taking children along on errands (or leaving them at home), responding to crisis situations (where the child may be quite forgotten, but is still "learning" from observing the adults' activities and words), and the thousands of other deeds and words that parents initiate and children absorb. Sometimes these acts send confusing, mixed messages to children. Similarly, everything that the visitor experiences contributes to the educational role of the museum. The architecture of the museum, the arrangement of the galleries, the style of the signage welcoming visitors (or the lack of orienting devices!), the composition of the staff, all contribute to communicating a museum's educational policy.

Confused messages are not useful in parenting; they are equally unproductive in museum practice. In the following sections and in subsequent chapters, I lay the

15

groundwork for examining beliefs about education and visitor studies so that museum staff can adopt and implement an examined, deliberate educational policy.

Components of any educational theory

In order to develop an educational theory, three kinds of issues, two theoretical and one more practical, must be addressed: an educational theory requires a theory of *knowledge* (an epistemology); it requires a theory of *learning*; and, finally, a theory of *teaching*, the application of the conceptions about how people learn and what it is they learn. The first two represent the theoretical underpinning of what a museum does as an educational institution. The third determines how the theories are put into practice.

A theory of education requires a *theory of knowledge*. What do we think knowledge is and how is knowledge acquired? Closely related to epistemology is our position on the status of the knowledge that is acquired through education – the ontological status of the content of museums. Do museum exhibitions show the world "as it really is," do they represent convenient social conventions, or do they provide phenomena for the visitors to interpret as they will?

The second issue that needs to be addressed is a consideration of a *theory of learning*. Without a fairly clear notion of how people learn, it is not possible to develop a coherent educational policy. Do we believe that learning consists of the incremental addition of individual "bits" of information into the mind or do we think that learning is an active process that transforms the mind of the learner?

The third issue, dependent on the other two, concerns *pedagogy*; how we should teach. Teaching styles and the organization of material to be taught require different methods for some epistemologies than for others, and the methods also differ depending on our psychology of learning. What pedagogic activities are appropriate for any particular educational theory? If we believe that people learn in a particular way, what does that suggest for our exhibitions and programs? It is even possible to argue that teaching is not required for learning to take place, a position that is more consistent with some educational theories than with others.

Theories of knowledge (epistemologies)

The question, "What is knowledge?" has puzzled humans for the full history of recorded philosophy. Does knowledge exist externally, independent of individuals, or does it reside only in our minds? Any position on this topic raises problems. If knowledge is external, how do we come to know it? If it resides in our minds, how can we share it? There is no simple solution to this philosophical dilemma; any answer suggested has been found inadequate by critics. We can get along quite well in our daily lives without worrying about our epistemological preferences, but if we want to reflect on our work and pursue it thoughtfully and deliberately we need to consider our beliefs. What is unavoidable is that an educator takes *some* position about what the "it" is that people learn.

Epistemological theories can be classified on a continuum between two extremes. One whole set of theories claim that the "real" world exists out there, independent of any ideas about it that humans may have. Such views are called "realism." The classic realist position is that taken by Plato, who argued that our perceptions of the world were only poor imitations of the real ideas and that dialog and reason (not experimentation and interaction with nature) could bring us closer to an understanding of these true ideas. Plato's famous story of the cave – that our knowledge in comparison to the true nature of ideas is like that of people shackled in a cave who see only the shadows on a screen as compared to what they would see if they looked at actual objects in true sunlight – sharply illuminates his belief that the world of our experiences is limited in contrast to reality. A recent expression of realist views is formulated by Harré (1986) and has been used to criticize constructivism in science education by Osborne (1996). Osborne argues that it makes no sense to consider scientific knowledge as only constructed by individual minds, since scientific knowledge must correspond to the behavior of "real" objects in the world. Thus he advocates a "modest realist position" which acknowledges the existence of a relatively stable body of objects of scientific investigation, as distinct from the humanly constructed and changing body of theories and theoretical constructs.

The opposite extreme epistemological position is the one labeled "Idealism" by philosophers. According to this view knowledge exists only in the minds of people and does not necessarily correspond to anything "out there" in nature. There can be no ideas, no generalizations, no "laws of nature" except in the minds of people who invent and hold these views. A famous proponent of such a view was the British philosopher George Berkeley. To demonstrate his position that the sensations of the world depend on human minds for their existence, he argued that there would be no sound of a tree falling in the forest if there was no one there to hear it. More generally, he argued that there was no absolute existence of physical constructs. Recently the more extreme statements of this position have been made by some constructivists, most notably von Glasersfeld, and called "radical constructivism." He argues that we should

> Give up the requirement that knowledge represent [*sic*] an independent world, and admit instead that knowledge represents something that is far more important to us, namely what we can *do* in our *experiential world*, the successful ways of dealing with the objects we call physical and the successful ways of thinking with abstract concepts . . . I have never denied an absolute reality, I only claim, as the skeptics do, that we have no way of knowing it. As a constructivist, I go one step farther: I claim that we can define the meaning of *to exist* only within the realm of our experiential world and not ontologically.
>
> (von Glasersfeld 1995: 6–7)

The philosophical subtleties of epistemological positions need not be debated among museum staff, but some consideration of the ontological status of the "stuff" that is contained in museums is necessary. Either extreme position raises problems. If we take a realist position the immediate philosophical problem is to come up with an answer to the question of how individuals come to have this knowledge, how can the real picture, the real concepts – the world as it really is – become part of our own knowledge? If we take the opposite position there is a problem in reaching any agreement, among a small social group or universally, about the contents of individual minds.

We can illustrate these positions by referring to a continuum, as illustrated in Figure 2.1. Other possible epistemological positions take intermediate positions along this continuum. John Dewey (1929/1988) criticized not just Plato, but *all* philosophies that searched for certainty. He argued for a position where knowledge depended more on practical experience and the application of ideas to action, than to a verbal description of "truth." Thus, he opted for an active definition of knowledge, one that would place him towards the right-hand side of the continuum, but not at the extreme. Similarly, Berkeley's attack on Newton, and his opposition that there could not be any "absolutes" in science, can be seen (Popper 1968) as a precursor of modern criticisms of positivist science (a view that experimental methods would reveal the "truth" about nature).[1] That is, an attempt to avoid the extreme right-hand side, rather than a conscious choice of a position on the extreme left of the diagram.

An example of an epistemological position in education that involves the learner in determining the meaning of what is learned is Paulo Freire's idea of *conscientização* (critical consciousness), a conception that knowledge includes an active learner. Critical consciousness represents

> things and facts as they exist empirically, in their causal and circumstantial correlations . . . critical consciousness is integrated with reality . . . It so happens that to every understanding, sooner or later an action corresponds. Once man perceives a challenge, understands it, and recognizes the possibilities of response, he acts. The nature of that action corresponds to the nature of his understanding. Critical understanding leads to critical action; magic understanding to magic response.
>
> (Freire 1973: 44)

He contrasts his view with "Our traditional curriculum, disconnected from life, centered on words emptied of the reality they are meant to represent, lacking in concrete activity" (Freire 1973: 37).

Figure 2.1 A continuum of theories of knowledge

For Freire, as for Dewey before him, knowledge cannot be divorced from its circumstances, nor can it be separated from action. Freire also supports an active-mind position on learning theory. The quotations above, however, refer to the ontological status of knowledge, *not* to how it is acquired.

For any theory of museum education, epistemological positions, whether articulated or tacit, determine how a museum decides what it is that is contained within its walls, and how it should be displayed. Does the museum take the view that its mission is to impart truth, independently of the particular previous experiences, culture, and disposition of its visitors? Does the museum take the position that knowledge is relative, influenced by culture and needs to be explained and interpreted, depending on purpose, use, and situation? Museums that take a more realist position – that knowledge exists independently of the learner – will, if they are consistent, focus their exhibition policy on the structure of the subject they are displaying. For example, many of the world's older science museums were designed to illustrate the "true" structure of science – they are arranged by science subject, chemistry, physics, biology, geology, etc. – and thus are designed to elucidate both the wonders of science and "correct" descriptions of the laws of the universe. Louis Agassiz designed the Museum of Comparative Zoology at Harvard University to illustrate the true organization of species, in contrast to what he believed to be the false position of Darwin about evolution (Gould 1981). The museum was intended to refute Darwin by showing nature as it really is. Agassiz not only intended to illustrate the preformist view of biology – that animals belonged to distinct species, each of which was formed independently of every other – but also that this was the true description of nature. His son, who followed him as director, preserved the museum as conceived; this display mode appears to be retained to this day.

History museums may be organized to depict the "true" history of a country, or era. Much recent writing critical of traditional museum display practices challenges older, implicit or explicit realism of museum displays, often those in history museums. As Peter Vergo (1989) writes, arguing for a more relativist view of the status of museum objects,

> Whether we like it or not, every acquisition (and indeed disposal), every juxtaposition or arrangement of an object or work of art, together with other objects or works of art, within the context of a temporary exhibition or museum display means placing a certain construction upon history, be it the history of the distant or more recent past, of our own culture or someone else's, of mankind [*sic*] in general or a particular aspect of human endeavor. Beyond the captions, the information panels, the accompanying catalogue, the press handout, there is a subtext comprising innumerable diverse, often contradictory strands, woven from the wishes and ambitions and preconceptions, the intellectual or political or social or educational aspirations and preconceptions of the museum director, the curator, the scholar, the designer, the sponsor – to say nothing of the society, the political or social or educational system

which nurtured all these people and in so doing left its stamp upon them.

(Vergo 1989: 2–3)

The suggestion that history museums portray history "as it really is" may seem odd, given the recent controversies about many historical exhibitions, and the obviously diverse views about what "story" should be exhibited. A similar argument can be made about the content of science museums; is what is depicted "true" or is it a story invented by one set of human beings for specific purposes? Much recent literature in the philosophy of science discusses this issue. The point for our discussion is not whether a specific exhibition, whether science, history, anthropology or art, is in fact depicting the real world (it could be mistaken, it could contain errors) but whether the *purpose* of the exhibition is to depict "truth."

A common organizing principle in art museums is to hang pictures chronologically, or to place together pictures of a similar type or style with at least the implicit indication that they "naturally" belong together. Again, the realist position would argue that such placements, impressionists in one room, Italian Renaissance painting in another, is not only a matter of convenience, but reflects some absolute characteristic of the structure of the field.

One consequence of the great nineteenth-century explosion of academic knowledge under the umbrella of positivist views of knowledge, was the development of textbooks. Traditionally, texts were organized (and still are to a large extent) around the nature of the subject. The simplest or most fundamental ideas are presented first, and then the subject is built up, bit by bit, until the highest or most advanced elements are reached in the later chapters. The subject is analyzed in terms of its *logical* structure. Further, from a realist perspective, this structure is considered an essential component of the subject itself, not an arbitrary organization of knowledge determined by human mental activity.

The same principles have often been applied to museum exhibitions, although there can be considerable disagreement about what constitutes the structure of a subject. Simplest may refer to fundamental, the basic ideas upon which all others are presumed to rely. Alternatively, simplest may refer to those defined by the curator or other exhibition developer as least complex, requiring the least mental effort, most readily accessible to visitors. In either case, the definition of simple refers only to characteristics determined by the properties of the material to be presented. It is not determined by how viewers respond to the material.

Although epistemology and learning theory are independent in principle, they are still closely connected. The paragraph above illustrates the almost inevitable intermingling of the two. If "simplicity" (defined as "requiring the least mental effort") is considered only as the outcome of a logical analysis of content, then it refers exclusively to theory of knowledge; if "simplicity" is defined with reference to a theory about how the mind of the learner works, then it slips over into learning theory.

The important point for this argument is that in a realist epistemology, the focus of the museum content is guided by the material being displayed, by the *nature of the subject.* It is not organized with a primary concern for the viewer's interest, or the meaning the viewer might make from the material. In contrast, the idealist curator believes that meaning of an object (or of an entire exhibition) derives not from some external reality, but arises from the interpretation it is given, either by the curator or by the viewer. Thus, a curator who ascribes to an epistemology towards the right of the continuum might more likely consider showing multiple perspectives, or arranging an exhibition so that it allows visitors to draw various conclusions from their interactions with it.

Theories of learning

Theories of learning can also be organized on a continuum with two clear contrasting positions at the extremes. One end of this continuum consists of the transmission–absorption notion of learning: people learn by absorbing information that has been transmitted to them. They do it in small pieces, step-by-step, by adding individual items to their storehouse of information. A classic description of learning of this style is provided in the opening scene of Dickens's *Hard Times*, where

> The speaker, and the schoolmaster [Mr Choakumchild], and the third grown person present, all backed a little, and swept with their eyes the inclined plane of little vessels then and there arranged in order, ready to have imperial gallons of facts poured into them until they were full to the brim.
>
> (Dickens 1854/1964: 2)

The image of the vessels to be filled has also been used by a number of educational writers to describe transmission–absorption theories of learning. An article in a professional newsletter titled "Psychology's input leads to better tests" uses an illustration that shows a teacher lifting the top of the cranium off a child to peer at the knowledge contained inside (American Psychological Association 1994).

Anyone who attends schools or universities today can testify that the image of the vessels to be filled still dominates practice. Schooling has not changed significantly in over a hundred years (Cuban 1993). Also, consider Jane Smiley's Prof. Lionel Gift in the novel *Moo* (Smiley 1995), contemplating an increase in class size due to budget cuts.

> It touched him, it really did, the imparting of knowledge, the initiation of a whole new group of customers into the domain of truth . . . this sense in the room of knowledge pouring out of his mouth and being soaked up by their eyes and ears and note-taking hands was intoxicating. How much more intoxicating, how loaves-and-fishes-like it would be when the same amount of knowledge poured out and was soaked up by three times as many customers!
>
> (Smiley 1995: 143)

21

Toward the opposite end of the continuum is a constellation of learning theories based on the belief that people construct knowledge. Much of recent educational theory, following the writings of John Dewey, the empirical work of Piaget and his followers, and the socially situated theories of learning of Vygotsky and others, emphasizes the active participation of the mind in learning, and recognition that the process of learning is not a simple addition of items into some sort of mental data bank but a transformation of schemas in which the learner plays an active role and which involves making sense out of a range of phenomena presented to the mind. Roschelle (1995) provides an excellent review of this work in the museum literature.

An excellent example of this view of learning applied to practice is the shift in reading instruction in the past twenty years from a focus on individual skills to a more holistic, "whole language" approach. Traditional didactic approaches to reading required the teacher to spend most of the time breaking down reading instruction into a set of individual skills to be learned, with children progressing through a series of carefully selected graded readers, each devised to provide slightly more complex tasks as the students' skill levels increased. Whole language reading instruction, although recognizing that there are skills involved, focuses much more on reading as a task of constructing meaning from text. Emphasis is also placed on the activity of reading itself rather than on preparation for reading. Learners are introduced to books as aesthetic and cultural artifacts. There is more opportunity than in traditional pedagogy for the emerging reader to select from a range of printed materials – those that connect with and build on the reader's previous experience. In learning to read, children are encouraged to balance the various cueing systems – syntax, semantics (meaning) and graphophonics. Phonics, the practice of learning word components based on their sounds, is seen as only one of several available strategies for making meaning of print. Although books are still arranged in some order of increasing complexity, the selection of books is based more on literary quality and interest to the reader than on their specific skill level.

Most recently, the debate about reading instruction, and formal education in general, appears to be swinging back with critics favoring a more skills-based approach, as a reaction to the intense constructivist stance of some whole-language advocates. Proponents of "back-to-basics" movements usually favor a heavy emphasis on instruction of individual skills presented in sequential order. Disputes about how students learn will continue (see Anderson *et al.* 1996, 1997, and Greeno 1997).

The continuum of learning theories is illustrated in Figure 2.2. As in the case of epistemologies, educators' views on learning theory will determine the focus of their attention. Acceptance of a transmission–absorption view of learning requires placing major focus on presentation of the subject in units appropriate for learning. If learning is assumed to be incremental, then the subject needs to be broken down into small, discreet steps and arranged in the order appropriate for the items to be learned. Again, as in the case of theory of knowledge, the focus is primarily on the subject to be taught. In contrast, active, developmental

Figure 2.2   A continuum of learning theories

learning theories require that much more attention be paid to the learner. One consequence of the current acceptance of these active learning theories is the emergence of various typologies of learners. If learning is an active process, determined by the individual, then what are the characteristics of learners? Psychologists have developed a range of typologies to describe different types of active learners. Some of the most common are depicted in Figure 2.3. Although derived from different theoretical approaches for analyzing learning, all these formulations share the common feature that they focus on the qualities of the *learner*, rather than on the subject to be learned. Presumably, "field-independent" learners, "global" learners, or learners who favor a bodily–kinesthetic mode use their preferred style independent of the subject that is to be learned, although certain kinds of learning activities lend themselves more readily to one learning style or another.

Theories of knowledge and theories of learning

The two continua described above are independent of each other; an educator may have either a more realist or idealist epistemology and still believe that learning is a passive process of assimilation; it is also possible to consider learners as either passive recipients of information or active creators of knowledge and view the knowledge created as either existing externally or residing primarily in the learners' minds. For example, most chemistry teachers teach the balancing of equations as a simple mathematical exercise, with the students first being exposed to the simplest types of equations and then gradually learning to juggle the numbers to accommodate more complex molecular interactions. This decidedly step-wise, transmission–absorption mode of teaching does not commit the teacher to any belief that atoms and molecules exist elsewhere than in our minds. Balancing chemical equations can be viewed as a mental game and nothing more. A whole generation of scientists in the early twentieth century argued that entities such as atoms and molecules had no physical counterpart, that they were only convenient mental constructs. Thus, a transmission–absorption approach to learning can be adopted while espousing either a realist or idealist epistemology. Similarly, epistemological positions can accommodate either kind of learning theory: two teachers who both believe that there is a true history of the United States, independent of individual learners' experiences, can still choose to teach that history differently. One could transmit information bit by bit, starting with the simplest "facts," while the other might give students primary source material from which they would be expected to draw the "correct" conclusions.

23

Binary:

- *Analytic / Global*
- *Field Independent / Field Dependent*
- *Left Brain / Right Brain*

Fourfold:

- *Learning Style Inventory (Kolb)*

  Accommodator, Diverger, Converger, or Assimilator,

  based on four basic learning modes:

  Concrete Experience, Reflective Observation,

  Abstract Conceptualization, and Active Experimentation
- *4MAT System (McCarthy)*

  Innovative, Analytic, Commonsense, Dynamic

Multiple Intelligences (Gardner)

Linguistic

Musical

Logical / Mathematical

Spatial

Bodily / Kinesthetic

Intrapersonal

Interpersonal

Myers–Briggs Type Indicator[†]

Extroversion / Introversion (EI)

Sensing / Intuition (SI)

Thinking / Feeling (TF)

Judgment / Perception (JP)

Figure 2.3 Learner typologies*

Notes: *See Schmeck 1987.

† The Myers–Briggs Type Indicator is not actually a learning categorization, but a personality inventory. It has been widely applied, although severely criticized (Pittenger 1993).

We can use the possible combinations of the two extremes of each of the continua to develop a set of four families of educational theories.

Educational theories

I have suggested (Hein 1994a, 1995b, 1996b) that the two continua described above can be juxtaposed on each other orthogonally to create four domains, each of which describes a particular type of educational theory. Each theory takes a position on both epistemology and on learning theory, and any two theories share a common view on either epistemology or learning theory. This diagram is illustrated in Figure 2.4.

Didactic, expository education

Ask most people to describe what happens in "school" and they will usually describe traditional, didactic, expository education. The teacher organizes a lesson, based on the structure of the subject, and then "teaches" (that is, presents what is to be learned in a rational sequence) the students. The teacher

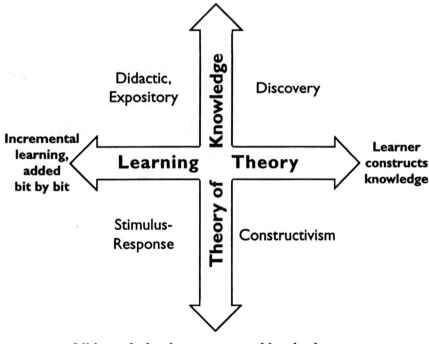

Figure 2.4 Education theories

presents principles, provides examples to illustrate these principles, and repeats to some extent to implant the material in the learner's mind. Of course, the "teacher" need not be a human being – text, programmed instruction, a tape, a museum exhibition, or any material deliberately constructed to provide a "lesson" can teach. This form of education can also include any number of combinations of these delivery modes.

From the perspective of our diagram, the epistemological challenge for the teacher who subscribes to the views contained in this quadrant is to represent the "true" content in an orderly fashion, going from the simplest to the most complex, and for the material to be divided into small enough units so that it can be learned.

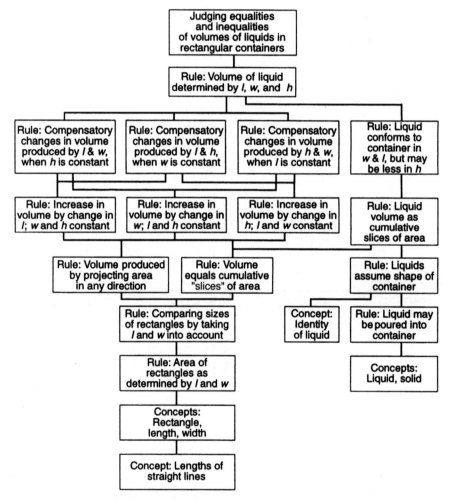

Figure 2.5 Learning hierarchy: concepts of volume. *Source:* After Gagné 1968. Copyright 1968 by the American Psychological Association. Reprinted or adapted with permission.

Science a Process Approach, the science curriculum developed by the American Association for the Advancement of Science in the l960s, provides a good example of this approach. The curriculum was based on the educational theories of Robert Gagné (1977) and included detailed hierarchical diagrams that showed the steps necessary to develop individual concepts. Figure 2.5 provides the diagram for the teaching and learning of "equalities and inequalities of liquids in rectangular containers," and Figure 2.6 provides a partial learning sequence for a slice of a social studies curriculum, also developed by Gagné (1967). The diagrams describe the individual steps required for understanding, and these steps are arranged in a necessary sequential order. It is the responsibility of the teacher to present each of these skills in the appropriate sequence and not to go on to the next until the previous one is mastered.

Figure 2.5 is particularly significant because it illustrates Gagné's effort to provide an alternative to the Piagetian notion that learning is active and involves the internalization of a complete "schema" rather than a sequential step-by-step process. Piaget came to his conclusion about the learning of volume from experiments such as those in which children are shown two identical glasses of orange juice. The contents of one glass are then poured into a taller, narrower glass and the child is asked whether the new glass and the unchanged one contain the same amount of orange juice or whether one has more in it than the other. In his typical manner, Piaget illustrates that children of different ages (and developmental stages) can be classified into three groups. The youngest children (below about 7 years of age) are certain that the two glasses hold different amounts of juice, while the oldest children are equally certain that pouring the juice from one glass to another does not change its volume; they have learned the principle of "conservation of volume." Between these two is a group of children who provide contradictory answers; they are in transition from one stage to another. The transition appears to be holistic, not step-wise. Gagné (1977) takes a different approach:

> The cumulative learning theory proposes a conception of "what is learned" . . . which differs from Piaget's theory . . . a specific intellectual skill of "identifying equal volumes given compensatory changes in length and width, height remaining constant," is acquired through learning. In addition, and at approximately the same time, the child may acquire a number of other intellectual skills such a those shown in Figure 6.3 [2.5 in this chapter]. If the necessary specific capabilities are learned, perhaps by being taught in some systematic fashion, the child will be able to perform the conservation task.
>
> (Gagné 1977: 149)

Museums organized on didactic, expository lines will have:

- exhibitions that are sequential, with a clear beginning and end, and an intended order;[2]
- didactic components (labels, panels) that describe what is to be learned from the exhibition;

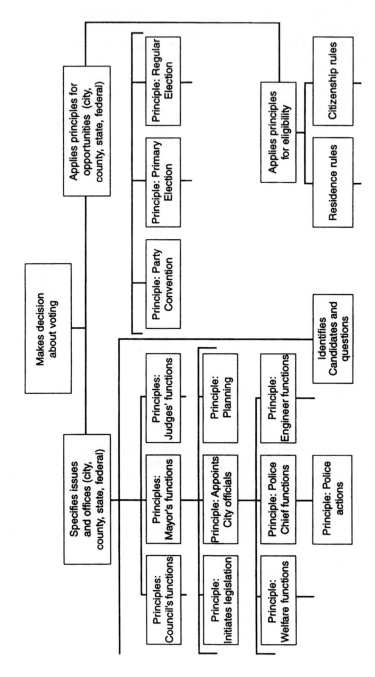

Figure 2.6 *Learning hierarchy: citizenship (partial). Source: After Gagné 1967. Copyright 1967 by the American Educational Research Association. Reprinted or adapted by permission of the publisher.*

- a hierarchical arrangement of subject from simple to complex;
- school programs that follow a traditional curriculum, with a hierarchical arrangement of subject from simple to complex;
- educational programs with specified learning objectives determined by the content to be learned.

In addition to "telling a story" with a beginning and an end – a story with a specific theme – didactic exhibitions make some claim that the story they are reporting is "true"; it is the way things really are. Thus, they would not be likely to include panels that suggest that this is only one interpretation of the historic event and that there might be others, they are not likely to refer the visitor to an alternative explanation, or indicate explicitly or implicitly that this arrangement is arbitrary, to be replaced by a different intellectual scheme at a later date or in another gallery in the museum.

Stimulus–response education

The bottom-left quadrant of Figure 2.4 represents an educational position that shares a learning theory with the didactic, expository approach, but makes no claims for the objective truth of what is learned. Educational theories that focus primarily on training usually fall into this category. If the educator is concerned only with method, and not with what is taught, the approach may fall in this quadrant.

Stimulus–response formulations of learning are at the heart of early behaviorist psychology, although more recent formulations stress more complicated relationships. One of the earliest behaviorist experiments, performed by Watson (1930), was to instill in an infant a fear of cuddly animals by making a loud noise behind a six-month-old baby when he was shown a white rat. Watson demonstrated that he could cause averse responses to many stimuli, but made no claims about the "true" nature of the child's fear.[3] In fact, he delighted in pointing out that some future Freudian analyst might puzzle over the child's condition and attribute it to various causes, all of which would be false. Stimulus–response theory refers only to the outcome from a specific stimulus.

Museums organized on stimulus–response lines will be characterized, as are didactic, expository exhibitions, by:

- didactic components (labels, panels) that describe what is to be learned from the exhibition;
- exhibits that are sequential, with a clear beginning and end, and an intended order for pedagogic purposes.

In addition, behaviorist exhibitions would have reinforcing components that repeatedly impress the stimulus on the learner and reward appropriate response. Some exhibits do this by providing a positive written or computer screen response ("Yes, that's the right answer!") when a visitor pushes the correct button, lifts the appropriate flap, or arranges items in the correct sequence.

29

But in the Behaviorist Museum this lesson-oriented approach will not be able to legitimately make a formal claim to presenting "truth." Of course, there are few museums that would accept this position. Museums that follow this approach are usually apparent only to their critics, to those who hold a different conception of truth; they are not advertised as such by their proponents. Western critics of socialist ideology often claimed that museums in socialist countries were full of "propaganda" intended to indoctrinate rather than to educate; their methods were based on behaviorist learning theory, but, according to their critics, these museums certainly were not transmitting objective truth. Conversely, many left-wing critics have argued that museum presentations in industrialized nations often assume such concepts as manifest destiny, white, male, capitalist hegemony, and other incorrect ideas ingrained in our capitalist society.

Discovery learning

The shift from the left-hand side of Figure 2.4 to the right-hand side represents a dramatic change in orientation. The difference is epitomized by the language used to describe the two sides; for example, it is common to talk of expository *teaching* and discovery *learning*. This shift in language emphasizes that on the right side of the diagram attention is focused on the learner as well as, or rather than, on the subject.

The diagram refers to the theory underlying educational practice. What actually takes place is inevitably more complex. Observing educational settings provides ample evidence that even in strictly didactic, expository educational situations, individual learners discover things. Students have epiphanies – they suddenly understand some idea or concept, regardless of the instructional method to which they are exposed. Conversely, in situations structured along the lines of active learning, the student may still respond by literally memorizing the instructions, simply reproducing the situation at a future time, or not participating actively. As an unnamed discussant at a conference pointed out

> Just because teaching is inductive, it does not follow that the learner is discovering. Conversely, simply because the teacher is instructing didactically, discovery experiences on the part of the learner are not precluded.

> (Shulman and Keislar 1966: 28)

Discovery education approaches have accepted the idea that learning is an active process, that learners undergo changes as they learn, that they interact with the material to be learned more fundamentally than only absorbing it, that they somehow change the way their minds work as they learn. Learning includes more than piling facts and concepts into the warehouse of the mind. As people learn, their capacity to learn expands; the shape and volume of the mind's warehouse is transformed by the process of grappling with the new information.

Active learning is often translated into physical activity associated with learning;

thus the common reference to "hands-on" learning. Physical interaction with the world, with the requirement that the learner take an active part in the process, whether it is building something, solving a puzzle, handling objects, or otherwise engaging with the "stuff" of the world, can lead to situations that offer a range of options, which require the learner to think. But the "activity" referred to in these theories is *mental* activity, which may or may not be stimulated by physical activity; the two are certainly not synonymous. Monotonous repetitive physical activity, or "mindless" actions are not particularly conducive to mental changes associated with this form of learning, and recent literature has stressed the need for "minds-on" as well as "hands-on" engagement by learners.

A common image invoked by advocates of active learning is the Chinese proverb about teaching someone to fish:

> Give me a fish and I eat for a day
> Teach me to fish and I'll eat forever.

The term "Discovery Learning" has been applied to all of the education that takes place on the right-hand side of Figure 2.4; it has been used as a synonym for any form of education that attributes active participation to the learner. Many science and youth museums include a space called a discovery room, usually a resource room filled with materials of all sorts that visitors can explore and examine, often under the guidance of a staff member. Usually the emphasis is on exploration – asking questions and being able to have experiences with materials – rather than on arriving at conclusions or learning something in particular. In terms of our definitions, such discovery rooms would fall under the heading of constructivist education facilities.

The top right-hand quadrant, which suggests a more restricted meaning for discovery, offers some specific opportunities and dilemmas for the educator. Proponents of discovery education take a particular perspective on active learning. They argue that by engaging learners in activity, specific desired educational outcomes can be achieved; the learners will learn those things we wish them to learn. If people are exposed to raw data, to the phenomena of the world, they will arrive at the correct conclusions; they will reach the generalizations that describe the world as it actually is. Thus, in science, if students are given pendulums and weights they will be able to induce the inverse square law that governs the motion of pendulums; in history, if students are given the materials developed by the founding fathers of the United States, they will come to realize the advantages of the United States constitutional system.

The linking of active learning with a realist position on knowledge, the combination of the opportunity for the learner to discover truth by "finding out for herself," to "learn through doing," is appealing to all of us who have been exposed to the recent decades of educational theory. Since museums, unlike schools, value objects and learning from objects, discovery learning seems a natural approach for these institutions. Further, it is satisfying to think that our knowledge – the history we feel passionate about, the aesthetics we espouse, or the science we have learned as universal truths – can be taught (and learned) by allowing visitors to explore and use their minds.

But there are serious problems with the theory described in this quadrant. Having abandoned the psychology that there is one systematic way to present information to the learner and that the logical structure of the subject should guide our pedagogy, we are left with the position that learners can learn by actively constructing, but should come to conclusions determined by others. The inherent difficulty of this approach is obvious. The farther we move to the right on the learning theory continuum, the less likely it will be that we can expect learners to reach predetermined outcomes, if these are associated with some criterion independent of any references to learners.

Some writers (see Cronbach 1966) have made the distinction between "big D" discoveries and discovery in general. The former refers to big ideas, the great concepts of our civilizations, such as the law of gravity, the inverse square law, etc. Discovery learning is not expected to lead to these generalizations. It is presumptuous or naïve to expect that students on their own, with a few bits of string, pendulum bobs, and weights should reproduce conclusions that required the reflections of Galileo to conjure up after they had eluded the best efforts of thoughtful scientists for centuries. Or that the study of original documents for a few weeks would allow teenagers to formulate the United States Constitution. Any attempt to have the learner figure things out on her own raises the possibility that what will be figured out will not be what is expected. But advocates of discovery learning argue that the appropriate combination of materials will allow, perhaps even make it extremely likely, that learners will gain insights that move them in the direction of deeper understanding of traditional concepts in physics, history, or aesthetics.

Another issue that needs to be addressed in discovery learning approaches is whether learners or visitors will pay attention to those aspects of situations presented and materials available that are actually relevant to what we want them to learn. Children may "discover" that the hymn sung in church has the words "Gladly the cross-eyed bear" because that's the meaning they make of the words they hear. The "obvious" way to use materials provided for a science experiment may not be self-evident for the learner who doesn't already know the intention is to measure the change in acceleration of objects rolling down the inclined plane as it is tilted at different angles. For students who should discover this regularity, differences in color of materials used, in the nature of the blocks that hold up one end of the board, or other "extraneous" variables may draw their attention. Their experiments may be instructive to them about variables that don't make a difference, but may not lead them to discover what they were intended to learn. Often, to know what is relevant requires that the learner already have the knowledge the situation is intending to impart!

Proponents of discovery learning sometimes structure situations so that the desired outcomes will be obtained. The producers of a particular kind of computer-based microlaboratory (IBM 1990) boast that their equipment is so error proof that it will assure that students engage in discovery learning since:

> When you want your students to discover that the laws of science have
> predictable effects – that water at sea level boils at 100 degrees Celsius,

for example – you don't want the laboratory equipment to show any inconsistencies in measurement.

(IBM 1990: 2)

So by using this equipment students can discover the laws of science without having to worry about getting misleading data; the brochure goes on to say that

> Discovery learning is a very effective way to teach. When students learn a scientific principle by observing it for themselves – such as seeing the effect of gravity on a falling object is constant regardless of the object's weight – science becomes a lot more than just something your students read about in textbooks.

> Science becomes a natural extension of their world, something your students can see, hear, touch, record, categorize, interpret, understand and use.

(IBM 1990: 1)

But can an "experiment" be an experiment if there is no chance of getting any but the correct results? An essential quality of science is that in fact things can go wrong, that you can be done in by nature. It is only by sorting through data and finding a regularity that is not self-evident that it could be claimed that something is "discovered." We cannot claim that someone has discovered something when there was no chance for error (see Glaser 1966). Being able *not* to discover the appropriate conclusion would seem to be a necessary minimum condition to make discovery learning different from didactic, expository education in any subject.

Nevertheless, discovery learning has its appeal. Museums organized on discovery learning lines will have:

- exhibitions that allow exploration, probably including going back and forth among exhibit components;
- a wide range of active learning modes;
- didactic components (labels, panels) that ask questions, prompt visitors to find out for themselves;
- some means for visitors to assess their own interpretation against the "correct" interpretation of the exhibition;
- school programs that engage students in activities intended to lead them to accepted conclusions;
- workshops for adults that offer expert testimony and other forms of evidence for contemplation and consideration, so participants can understand the true meaning of the material.

Exhibits in a gallery designed on discovery lines may or may not be arranged linearly, with a beginning and end. If the entire exhibition is intended to lead the visitor to appropriate conclusions, the placement of exhibit components may provide such guidance. If the discoveries at each station were more or less independent, then there would be no reason to have a specified path through the exhibition.

Constructivism

The fourth quadrant in Figure 2.4 describes education theory that postulates that learning requires active participation of the learner in both the way that the mind is employed and in the product of the activity, the knowledge that is acquired. Despite the vast literature on constructivism (Fosnot 1996b; Steffe and Gale 1995), there has been little written that emphasizes that both an epistemological and a learning theory component are required for a constructivist position. The personal construction of knowledge has been stressed by various writers, to the extent that a radical constructivist position (von Glasersfeld 1990) holds that knowledge resides only in the minds of individual learners. Many other writers focus on the collection of developmental learning theories that lead to constructivism, especially those derived from the work of Piaget and Vygotsky, to emphasize the learning aspect of constructivism.

Constructivist learning situations require two separate components, first a recognition that in order to learn the active participation of the learner is required. Therefore, the constructivist classroom or exhibition includes ways for learners to use both their hands and minds, to interact with the world, to manipulate it, to reach conclusions, experiment, and increase their understanding; that is, their ability to make generalizations about the phenomena with which they engage. Experiments are crucial for constructivist learning, whether in science or other subjects. An experiment, as distinct from a demonstration, is a situation in which a range of results are possible *and acceptable*.

Second, constructivist education requires that the conclusions reached by the learner are *not* validated by whether or not they conform to some external standard of truth, but whether they "make sense" within the constructed reality of the learner. The validity of ideas according to constructivists does not depend on their match to some objective truth, which has an existence separate from any learner or group of learners. Rather, validity arises from the value of the concepts in leading to action (use) and in the consistency of the ideas one with another. Thus, while traditional educators talk about learners' *misconceptions*, constructivists will talk only about *naïve*, *personal*, or *private* conceptions.

In the constructivist vocabulary, "mistake" and "error" are terms reserved for conclusions that don't correspond to the evidence at hand, that differ from what a learner might reasonably conclude from all the information available to her at the time she reaches that conclusion. This is different from judging an answer with reference to an external standard of truth based on the structure of a subject.

The inevitability of constructivism If we accept modern theories of learning, then we inevitably need to accept the constructivist position on theory of knowledge at least to some degree. That people make their own meaning out of experience appears to be a phenomenon of nature (not just a theoretical construction). There is overwhelming research evidence to back up our common-sense knowledge that exposure to any set of phenomena leads people to different conclusions. All of us interpret nature and society differently, depending on our own background and experience. I hear my favorite politician speaking sensibly; my neighbor hears her as a liar. The evidence on the relationship between diet and health leads people to differing conclusions (not to mention to engage in different behaviors!), and significant course work in science does not mean that even successful students (who pass the courses) accept the canonical theories of motion or gravity, any more than successful completion of an official state curriculum means that citizens accept the truth of the state's version of history.

In short, if we take the position that it is *possible* for people to construct personal knowledge then we have to accept the idea that it is *inevitable* that they do so, regardless of our efforts to constrain them. It is not unusual in the museum world for exhibit designers to put up an exhibition with a specific theme and to have visitors give it a completely different interpretation. In an interesting article based on interviews with visitors to the Holocaust Museum, a journalist (Gourevitch 1995) concluded that

> My conversations in Washington suggest that . . . [visitors'] diverse reactions reflect the beliefs and attitudes they brought to the museum as much as anything they discovered within its walls.
>
> (Gourevitch 1995: 45)

Among many groups he observed making their own meanings, he gives the example of a fundamentalist Christian school group that goes through the exhibit and sees it as evidence for their view that the Jews received punishment for their failure to accept Jesus Christ as their savior. Evaluation of *The Peopling of London*, an exhibition on the role of overseas settlement in populating London (Selwood *et al.* 1996), provides similar results.

> While the exhibition encouraged the majority of visitors we spoke to, to reconsider their perceptions of Londoners, it served to reinforce the opinions of a small minority of others – as evidenced by the racist remarks made in the comments book.
>
> (Selwood *et al.* 1996: 30)

A constructivist exhibition, like one based on discovery learning, will provide opportunities for visitors to construct knowledge. But in addition, it will provide some way of validating visitors' conclusions, regardless of whether they match those intended by the curatorial staff. Thus, a constructivist exhibition:

- will have many entry points, no specific path and no beginning and end;
- will provide a wide range of active learning modes;
- will present a range of points of view;
- will enable visitors to connect with objects (and ideas) through a range of activities and experiences that utilize their life experiences;
- will provide experiences and materials that allow students in school programs to experiment, conjecture, and draw conclusions.

The constructivist exhibition would be likely to present various perspectives, validate different ways of interpreting objects and refer to different points of view and different "truths" about the material presented. This is in sharp contrast to a traditional view of museum exhibitions. For example, the eleventh edition of the *Encyclopaedia Britannica*, published at a time when the idea of independent truth was generally accepted, incorporates this concept into the definition of a museum:

> The ideal museum should cover the whole field of human knowledge. It should teach the truths of all the sciences, including anthropology, the science which deals with man and all his works in every age.
>
> (Holland 1911: 64)

Theories of teaching

An epistemology and a learning theory are essential for any educational theory, but they are not sufficient. They represent the theoretical background for the educational work to take place. In addition, a theory of instruction – a plan for how to carry out the educational activity as described by the theory – is required. If we believe that people learn incrementally, what is the pedagogic strategy that will make this happen? If we believe that people construct meaning, what is the educational task required to allow them to do so? Constructivism, an educational theory that deals primarily with meaning and knowledge and says little about teaching, especially requires detailed elaboration of the pedagogic activities appropriate for it.

If an educator believes that the nature and structure of a subject exists by itself, then an appropriate question in developing any educational program (or any exhibition) is to ask, how does my project relate to the nature of the subject? How is this subject structured, what is its "true" structure? A long educational tradition argues that in order to teach, it is important to understand the organization of the material from its simplest to its most complex aspects, from the fundamental ideas to the more peripheral ones, from the basic tenets to the elaborations, and that this is essentially all that a teacher has to know. Note that the emphasis here is all on the subject, not on the learner. It is the structure of the material that is important.

The focus on the subject and its organization also makes educators, in museums or elsewhere, ask questions about the visitors or learners in terms of their *formal* exposure to the subject. If knowledge is the acquisition of something external to the person, then the most important issue is the extent to which visitors have been exposed to this material, since this will determine their level of knowledge. Has the visitor had high school chemistry? A college education? Do visitors need a degree in art history to appreciate the exhibition?

On the other hand, if museum staff have an idealistic view, the source of information about what visitors bring to the exhibition is the mind of the visitor and his or her personal experiences. If people construct knowledge, then we have to ask: what knowledge resides in their minds, regardless of the formal structure of the subject? It becomes much more important to look at the learner, and to ask: what ideas does the learner have, regardless of formal education?; what are visitors' previous *personal* experiences?

An example of this latter approach applied to developing museum exhibitions is illustrated by research on visitors' ideas about "prehistory" at the Museum of London. The exhibition opens with a panel that depicts popular images of prehistory – cavewomen and dinosaurs – and indicates that the exhibition will challenge these conceptions (Cotton and Wood 1996). At the Franklin Museum in Philadelphia, Minda Borun and coworkers (1993) asked visitors about their personal conceptions of gravity and then devised an exhibition to challenge these beliefs. A contrasting approach would be to decide that an exhibition was intended for people who had not attended any higher education courses on mechanics and to provide models and explanations that would provide the information usually included in such courses. But as dozens of investigators have noted in recent years, providing experiences and explanations that allow people to come to understand the canonical view is not sufficient; learners will persist in maintaining the views they already have despite instruction. What is needed is first to find out what personal knowledge (Polanyi 1958) they bring with them and to start from that basis.

Pedagogy for expository–didactic education

The focus here is exclusively on the subject. The way to teach something is to analyze it, and then to present it. The pedagogic challenge associated with this epistemology is to find the essential structure of the subject; the challenge from the learning theory is to find the individual units that can be most easily learned. Much of the work in experimental psychology over this century has been based on this educational theory and therefore there is an enormous literature on how to teach using this educational approach.

Pedagogy for stimulus–response education

As indicated before, the learning theory challenge for Stimulus–Response (S–R) education is the same as for Expository–Didactic education, but the epistemological challenge has been removed; it is important only that the teacher have a clear idea of what should be learned. The focus is on method, not on the congruence of what is learned with an externally validated canon. S–R approaches are often favored by generic trainers and by organizations that want to instill uniform behavior in trainees without encouraging employees or students to challenge authority or to ask too many questions. The approach is called brain-washing or indoctrination by its critics and can be adapted to such purposes.

Examples of S–R teaching, in the sense that the lessons taught are completely arbitrary and the instructors focus exclusively on method and not at all on the value of what they teach, are rare if they exist at all. But a substantial educational literature exists that concentrates exclusively on methodology of teaching, with little consideration for the topic taught. Objectives for each hour of teaching; systematic, short-term learning goals; and highly sequential programs are common in schools for all subjects, although their integrity is often compromised by the realities of classrooms and the independence of teachers. Educators often use behavioral objectives to develop lessons, and many believe that children learn by responding to specific stimuli. For example, Mager's (1975) *Preparing Instructional Objectives* assumes identical processes would apply to different subject matter ranging from military training to music appreciation.

In the museum field this kind of pedagogy includes descriptions of exhibit content that focus on linear, sequential structuring of exhibit components, defining specific learning objectives and reinforcement models, in which methods dominate without reference to epistemology and are assumed to apply to any subject areas. To consider methods independent of what is to be learned, independent of the context of their application, is to operate in the behaviorist quadrant.

Pedagogy for discovery learning

Discovery learning requires an active learning situation in which learners have the opportunity to manipulate, explore and experiment. It is important to stress, however, that unless the mind is also engaged, unless activities challenge ideas, lead to cognitive uncertainty, and stretch the beliefs held previously, hands-on by itself does not lead anywhere. The challenge discovery learning theory poses is to provide the appropriate environment for individual learners to be both challenged and stimulated and to partake in experiences that will move them towards the desired goals. The epistemological challenge, alluded to above, is to provide sufficient openness so that learners can discover something while also structuring the learning environment so that they will reach desired conclusions. Discovery pedagogy has to include reference to the ideas and concepts that are intended to be taught; activity and insight that do not lead to these goals would not be desired.

Pedagogy for constructivism

As with discovery learning, the pedagogic challenge is to find experiences that stimulate and challenge. Constructivists, with their concern with the schemas and ideas that are already in learners' minds, will be more likely to ask whether the environment is one with which the learner can make any connections. Is there a familiar reference, object, idea, or activity that will allow the learner to engage with the issue?

But a constructivist museum education policy will also take a unique view of how the museum is to be used to teach. The model for the museum as an educational resource will be an encyclopedia or a catalogue, not a textbook. The organizing principles will inevitably permit visitors to pick and choose what subject they want to pursue, or even what branch of the subject. The idea that a topic can be arranged linearly, like a text, will not even be considered.

An example of a component of exhibitions that could be more or less constructively organized is the familiar audio tours available in many museums. For years, visitors to a museum exhibition could rent a portable audiocassette which allowed them to enjoy a recorded message about some selection of works in an exhibition. Until recently, these audio tours necessarily provided a *linear* guided path through an exhibition. Visitors were instructed to proceed to the "next" picture or object that would be discussed, and then heard a message concerning that selected item. The order of the tour had to be predetermined by the person who recorded the tape. Recent advances in technology, and museums' awareness of the desires of visitors to structure their own sequences, have led to a new form of audio guide that permits random access to channels on the hand-held guide. This allows visitors to select their own path through the exhibition, to go back to previous stations described on the audio guide and listen to the descriptions again, or even to call up a description of an object viewed at the other end of the gallery, simply by pressing the appropriate button on their hand-held device. Traditional educators might still wish to guide visitors through an exhibition in a particular order; constructivist pedagogues can only welcome this release from necessarily following a predetermined sequence.

An extreme constructivist theory of teaching would postulate that learning takes place without teaching and that experience is the best (and only) teacher. However, I believe that constructivism places more, not less, demands on the teacher to provide rich and rewarding environments in which learning can take place. What these learning environments might be and how they can be organized in museums will be discussed more fully in Chapter 8.

Conclusion

This chapter has provided an overview of different categories of educational theories. Every education theory requires both a theory of knowledge and a theory of learning, and these can be combined to provide, in principle, four different kinds of educational theories. In addition, in order to have a working theory of education, a style of pedagogy needs to be elucidated that is consistent with the particular combination of theory of knowledge and learning theory selected.

The discussion stressed the contrast between traditional approaches to education and constructivism as examples of two differing ways to think about education. These theoretical differences come from very different views of human beings and how they behave. What appears to be sound practice under one approach is considered heretical in another; what is considered systematic and thorough under one view, appears random or arbitrary under another.

How learning is defined is also theory dependent, as we shall see in more detail in later chapters. The very vocabulary we employ is governed by our perspective on these issues. For example, for some educators "subjective" has a pejorative connotation, for others it is a purely descriptive term.

Ways of studying learning in museums, how we carry out research and evaluation, and what we consider appropriate goals for such study are also theory dependent. Chapter 4 analyzes some of the debates between proponents of differing research styles, using a perspective similar to the one presented here. There is, furthermore, a thread that connects some kinds of theories of education with particular types of theories about research. This relationship is discussed in Chapter 5.

3

Early visitor studies

*The introduction of exhibits of illustrative materials from the
public school museum has met a much-felt want in our urban
teaching. There are a few extremists in pedagogical theory who still
maintain that it is useless to afford children specimens of natural
or artificial life which are not directly involved in their own
experiences. This principle would narrowly restrict the educational
field, eliminating much that is taught and intelligently grasped in
geography, natural science, and history . . . It is precisely because
many children can not go forth and experience at first hand many
of the interesting facts of nature and life that the museum is "put
on wheels" and carried to their own classroom.*
(Opinion cited as evidence for the value of the St Louis Public
School Museum; Rathman 1915: 52)

Introduction

In this chapter I will briefly survey the history of visitor studies in museums and
point out that visitor studies arise out of the educational role of museums. Since
its inception, visitor studies has illustrated different assumptions about learning
and how to study it in museums. In the next chapter, I will discuss how this
history is reflected in more recent visitor studies research.

Approaches to assessing the results of formal education are relevant for visitor
studies. Traditionally, questions about the results of formal schooling have been
addressed in three different ways:

1 Student assessment – specific examination of what individual participants
   (or groups) in the educational system have learned, what they can demonstrate as a result of their interaction with the educational program.
2 Evaluation of the activity itself – examination of schools and school systems
   to see if they are "doing their job." This endeavor has ranged from thoughtful research on the impact of schooling on large populations to journalistic
   exposés of the failures of schools.

3 Research on how people learn in general and application of the results to school learning.

All three of these approaches are relevant to assessing the results of the educative function of museums. The field of visitor studies has addressed each of these three components, although not with equal intensity. Because visitor studies is a relatively new specialization within the larger domain examining the outcomes of education, some areas have only recently received attention.

There has been considerable "testing" of visitors to ascertain what they have learned by attending exhibitions in museums. There are also many evaluations of the impact of exhibitions, in addition to attempts to measure their cognitive effect on visitors. This work is essentially the museum equivalent of program evaluations of school-based programs. Considerably less is known about the nature of learning in museums, although a few generalizations are beginning to emerge from the research to date. Until the past 50 years, visitor studies consisted primarily of efforts to examine individual visitors' behaviors in the museum.

Early work, 1900–50

There are almost no published studies of visitor experiences in museums before 1900. The only nineteenth-century study I know was of visitors to the Liverpool Museum.[1]

> I have long been convinced that a series of observations on the constituents of this irregular procession of visitors, combined with overtures suitable for inducing them to make remarks on the objects exhibited – in a word, the application of the inductive method to the examination of human elements *in transitu* through a museum – might lead to much valuable information.
>
> (Higgins 1884: 185)

Higgins classified visitors as Students (1–2 per cent), Observers (78 per cent), and Loungers (20 per cent). His purpose in doing this work was to further the educational value of the museum.

He also recognized another group which, although small, was significant. He describes them in rich Victorian prose while evoking the great northern European migration to North America at the turn of the century.

> One other class, however, deserves distinction; and it is gratifying to mention the admission, year after year, of streams of German and Scandinavian emigrants, who, after seeing their packages piled up at the railway station, seem to pass almost immediately to the Museum or the Gallery of Art. In the midst of the distractions of the most important crisis of their lives, these strong-hearted men and women find time and inclination to increase their stock of knowledge; and, though they are

unable to understand the explanatory labels, their conduct strikingly indicates respect towards the institution and its purpose.

(Higgins 1884: 186–7)

The lack of systematic work continued despite the fact that, generally, museums were recognized by their supporters as important educational institutions. During the first 50 years of this century – a time during which the entire psychometric testing system was developed and, in the United States, adopted as an integral part of formal education, when extensive experimental work on learning and perception was carried out by academic psychologists in growing educational psychology departments, and the domain of developmental psychology was initiated by Piaget and others – almost no research was carried out on visitors to museums. The entire *oeuvre* of work up to the Second World War consists of less then three dozen articles, scattered in education and psychology journals.

Some influential museum pioneers, especially in the United States, argued that museums should exist primarily for pleasure and aesthetic satisfaction, while others argued that museums should be used for specific educational purposes (Alexander 1983). But even the opponents of a more formal educational role for museums, such as Benjamin Ives Gilman of the Boston Museum of Fine Arts who argued that the museum experience should be mainly aesthetic, supported an educational function for museums. Gilman hired docents (he first applied this German academic term to museum staff), established a lecture room, published an educational handbook, instituted educational tours, and carried out one of the first visitor studies.

At the same time, the connection between schools and museums was reinforced by the development of museums within school systems (Rathman 1915) and the establishment of children's museums and other museums in association with school activities (Coleman 1939).

Progressive educators were well aware of museums and their importance to education. For example, Dewey recognized the value of the museum. In *The School and Society* (Dewey 1900/1956: 87) he develops diagrammatic representations of the ideal school. He depicts it as a two-story building with the more practical connections to learning – shop, dining room, kitchen and textile industries – on the ground floor, and the more intellectual pursuits – art, music, physical and chemical laboratories and biological laboratory – on the floor above. On each floor the pursuits are linked by a central room; the library on the ground floor and the museum connects those above. In Viennese schools, which after the 1918 revolution and the establishment of a socialist government became world renowned models of progressive education (Hein 1975), museums played a vital role in teaching local history and new school subjects, such as economics.[2] Despite this recognition of the importance of museums for learning, both for the general public and as an adjunct to the school, there was little study of their efficacy in this process.

Early practitioner research

Among the few works on visitor reactions to museums written before 1950, two by practitioners stand out for their relevance to current work.

One of the earliest papers on the visitor experience, "Museum Fatigue" by Benjamin Ives Gilman (1916), is an imaginative study of the physical problems associated with viewing exhibits that are awkwardly placed in galleries.

> A series of simple questions was devised relating to certain objects mostly installed at higher or lower levels and in cases; and an observer was photographed in the act of answering them. The observer, an intelligent man with good eye-sight, and well accustomed to museums and their contents, was instructed to answer the questions with the least possible exertions and to hold the positions he needed to assume for the purpose until he could be photographed.
>
> (Gilman 1916: 62)

The questions were simple requests, such as to read the label on a pedestal, to describe a design on a piece of sculpture, or to identify one of the figures in a painting.

Gilman's paper includes 30 photographs showing his observer bending to various degrees, "half" crouching and crouching, kneeling, stretching and looking up, even climbing on a ladder in his effort to view the objects. Gilman concludes

> These pictures indicate that the principal sources of that part of museum fatigue which comes from muscular effort to see objects well are two: (1) low installation in upright cases; (2) broad installations in flat or desk cases.
>
> (Gilman 1916: 63)

He goes on to recommend that museums exhibit fewer objects, divide their collections between exhibition and study areas, and include changing exhibitions. Loomis (1987) has pointed out the forward looking and far reaching qualities of Gilman's study and his progressive approach to museum exhibition.

A second early study by a museum curator is also highly informative as a model for current practice in visitor studies. Alma Wittlin (1949) published a history of museums which culminated in a call for the expanding educational role of museums. She spells out her agenda in the preface

> Two considerations have prompted the writing of this essay. First, the conviction that the unsettled conditions which have been and are still developing increasingly in contemporary society will not find a balance until general education, both as to its content and its method, has been radically revised and adjusted to existing reality, and, secondly, the belief that the museum – the method of communicating information and experience by the visual means of the exhibition and the appeal of the three dimensional object – holds special potentialities for the fulfillment and the furtherance of educational requirements.
>
> (Wittlin 1949: xiii)

In a long appendix (Wittlin 1949: 236–51) she described her own experiments, carried out from 1942–3 to "observe the reactions of people to two different manners of selection and presentation of specimens in exhibitions" (Wittlin 1949: 236). Within the University Museum of Archeology and Ethnology in Cambridge, England, she set up experimental galleries and tested visitors' reactions to two different forms of presentation of an exhibition on money, a topic she felt would be popular.

> The Old Exhibition (OE): a cubicle that contained several hundred specimens of currency of communities of primitive culture . . . which were housed in upright cases lining the walls almost from the floor to high up, far above eye-level . . . The labelling was limited to a minimum.

> The New Exhibition (NE): the principle of arrangement was an evolutionary outline from barter trade to token money in the form of coin. A few specimens of current British currency, together with charts illustrating the working of money in a modern community, formed the beginning of the presentation. Each type of currency was represented by a single specimen. Photographs showing the people who produced and used some of the exhibited types of currency were added to the objects. All objects were shown at eye level and were well spaced. Information was offered in captions and in more detailed descriptions . . .
>
> (Wittlin 1949: 237)

Her experimental study involved 96 selected visitors, including roughly equal numbers of adults with and without university education, undergraduates, and high school students (all female). Single visitors were asked to view one exhibition or the other for 20–25 minutes. They were observed during their visit, an informal interview was conducted with each using a set of questions prepared beforehand but not shown to the visitors, and some of the visitors "supplemented their verbal statements by one or more sketches illustrating their reminiscences of the exhibition" (Wittlin 1949: 237).

Wittlin provides us with the questions she asked, as well as numerous excerpts from her interviews. Based on her questions, she groups her findings under three headings: what visitors think about museums, the reactions of people to specific features of exhibits, and a comparison of responses to the two types of exhibitions they viewed. She concludes that, on the whole, visitors find museums stimulating and exciting, that in reference to traditional functions of museums (listed by her earlier in the volume) visitors condemn "hoarding" and "boasting" as museum functions, they express loyalty to humanity as a group, express a desire to acquire knowledge, appreciate the emotional experiences offered by exhibitions, and prefer "syntheses" arrangements to miscellaneous groupings of objects.

She goes on to note that visitors especially appreciated the inclusion of modern objects into an historical exhibition, were better able to remember the theme of the NE than the OE, and that it appeared to help their logical thought processes and encouraged more emotional responses.

Visitors to the NE expressed their alertness at the end of their visit to the NE by asking questions, asking for literature, and by their general mood.

The adverse effects of the OE may be best illustrated by some quotations from statements made by people. [This is followed by quotations that demonstrate] *Decrease in alertness . . . Irritation . . . The confusing effect . . . The depressing . . .* effect . . . Two visitors expressed their mood by leaving the Old Exhibition.

(Wittlin 1949: 244)

Wittlin carried out a second, similar experiment with school children, which, unfortunately, she describes in less detail. She exposed 118 children (ages not given) to two forms of an exhibition on "*How Things Began*' (Early Civilization)."

There were again, two presentations of the subject in two separate rooms of the museum, each containing an almost equal number of exhibits (the Old Exhibition (OE) contained 68 specimens; the New Exhibition (NE) 35 specimens and 29 pictorial exhibits, photographs and drawings). The OE recapitulated on a small scale the "miscellaneous" presentation known from many museums, with prehistoric implements, African basketry and Roman pottery, following each other without much coherence or explanation. The NE was arranged on principles chosen by the experimenter and aimed at presenting the exhibits in a coherent sequence of evolution, with each single object well visible and all together combining to a pleasing pattern. One feature of the NE was a table covered with a sheet which the children themselves were asked to remove when they reached this part of the exhibition. On the table part of the objects were exhibited. Some of the captions of the NE were in the form of questions. ("What would YOU do if you found yourself without shops in which to buy food, clothes . . . ? – "Can you think of any other important first inventions?")

(Wittlin 1949: 245)

Again, she observed children, interviewed them (in groups of five), gave the older ones questionnaires to fill out, and had them make drawings. She reports that her results support her findings from the first experiment.

Both her approach to the New Exhibition as well as her evaluation methods are remarkably similar to current practice. She recognized the importance of context, of including familiar, modern objects among the ancient museum pieces; the need for an explicit exhibition theme; and the use of a range of modalities and presentation methods.

Her evaluation strategies also recognized the need to get beyond simple behavior in an attempt to understand the significance of the exhibition for her visitors.

Early behavioral research

Another, quite different, contribution to visitor studies from before the Second World War is the systematic work of Robinson and Melton and their collaborators sponsored by the American Association of Museums, supported by the Carnegie Foundation and carried out in several US museums. Professor William S. Robinson and his student, Arthur W. Melton, academic psychologists at Yale, applied the current methods of their discipline to look at the behavior of museum visitors. This work has also been thoroughly reviewed by Loomis (1987: 21–3), and two of the major studies have been reprinted by the American Association of Museums (Melton 1935/1988, Melton *et al.* 1936/1988). A few examples of their methodology and conclusions will serve to contrast their approach to the work of Gilman and Wittlin.

One of the reprinted volumes describes several studies of the behavioral characteristics of adults in different science and art museums; the other focuses on children's learning during school group visits to museums. In the 1935 study, large samples of adult visitors are timed and tracked during their visits to art and natural history museums, with some experimental work also carried out in an art museum. The study is the first detailed, published report of tracking, a representation of visitors' paths through a gallery. The data consists of reports of total visitor times in a gallery (room time), time devoted to individual exhibit objects (object time) and, in some instances, number of stops by visitors.

Much of the monograph is devoted to defining the behavioral parameters and justifying the data collected as valid and reliable. Interviews are rejected as a less valid measure of visitor interest than observed behavior.

> The number of objects that a visitor examines and the time he spends before each object are all we can know about his interest without importuning him with requests for subjective reports and even though these subjective reports were obtained, we would still insist that the spread and duration of his attention to museum objects are kinds or dimensions of interest which have inherent validity. As long as one holds to a definition of interest which makes it an observable phenomenon of everyday life, and thus avoids a definition which relegates interest to the realm of transcendental phenomena, the number of exhibits examined and the time spent in examining them will be taken as *the* interest of the visitor rather than as fallible expressions of his interest.
>
> (Melton 1935/1988: 6–7)

For the statistical summaries and conclusions only data from single visitors are used since they are easier to track and time than groups, although they represent only 10 per cent of all visitors in his studies. Melton acknowledges that data from couples, for example, is qualitatively different, but the data for single visitors is taken as representative of all visitors because the *average* times for single visitors and groups do not vary significantly.

There are, of course, serious problems with drawing conclusions from such a small fraction of the total sample; at best one can only generalize about that segment of the total museum population. The overwhelming majority of museum visitors then and now come in groups, not as single visitors. For example, Korn (1995) reports 6 per cent of visitors as "adults alone" in a study conducted at two natural history museums and two science centers. Hughes *et al.* (1995) observed approximately 15–20 per cent single visitors at three different exhibitions at an art museum.

These studies of the behavior of adult visitors have provided definitions and a baseline for understanding visitors in museums that have influenced most visitor research performed since. Some have argued that the reliance on these early studies has misled the field. The limitations of this approach will be discussed in subsequent sections and chapters.

The most enduring findings from this work were the definitions of *attracting-power* (to what extent visitors stopped to look at an object) and *holding-power* (how long visitors stay looking at an individual object or an entire gallery), first defined by Robinson (1928), and their discovery of the tendency of visitors to turn right rather than left when entering a symmetrical gallery with only pictures along outside walls.

Equally significant was their finding that the overwhelming majority of visitors spend very little time in any gallery, on the order of a few minutes, and only brief seconds examining any individual object. They noted that an exit competed successfully with exhibits in attracting visitors, and increasingly so as a visit progressed. They recognized that most visitors remain only a short time in any gallery with a smaller percentage remaining longer, and that this can be depicted graphically as a steady decline of visitors remaining when numbers are plotted against time. Melton called these "J" curves. They are now plotted as "visitor decay" or "visitor survival" curves.

They also carried out some experiments with different exhibit arrangements. For example, they demonstrated that visitor time in a gallery of an art museum – both time spent looking at individual pictures and total time – increased as the number of pictures increased from six to twelve to eighteen. However, as additional pictures were added, total time did not increase (visitors looked at more pictures, but shortened the time they looked at each) and in some instances, as gallery walls became more crowded with pictures, total time actually decreased.

Melton's further studies, many carried out at the Buffalo Museum of Science with the cooperation of the Buffalo School Department, examined children's learning as a result of school visits to the museum. The data collected is exclusively children's performances on "objective" tests, mostly multiple-choice and true-or-false questions of factual material corresponding to the subject matter of the museum lessons, administered to the children before the visit and again at its conclusion or in the school after a period of days or weeks. The experiments examine such variables as the effect of a 15 vs. 30 minute lecture on the test scores, the effect of various forms of preparation for the visit, the use of discussions vs. lectures (and their comparison to no preparation or no intervention by docents) as the educational method in the museum, and other, similar experimental variations.

The research exemplifies the prejudices of that time, both about the virtues of tests, including IQ scores, and the inheritance of intelligence. Much is made of the equivalence of the various experimental groups on the basis of comparison of IQ scores of the children, and allowance is made for the fact that many classes consist primarily of "Polish" or "Italian" children. Children are defined as such if their *fathers* were born in either country. In 1933–4, the time of this study, 42 per cent of the school population of Buffalo consisted of children of foreign born fathers, the majority of Italian and Polish descent. The mother's nationality is not listed and no distinction is made between children who are themselves foreign born and children of foreign born parents. Ascribing hereditary significance to patriarchal lineage only was common in studies that attempted to link intelligence with heredity.[3]

Unfortunately, the authors never used a control group of children who did *not* participate in the museum visit. They state:

> It is obvious that a considerable portion of the questions which were asked at the end of the sessions concerned with subjects such as *Birds*, *Vertebrates*, *Earth Science*, or the *Story of Man* – these were the major subjects of study for pupils of the fifth, sixth, seventh, and eighth grades respectively – probably could have been answered correctly by the pupils even though no museum visit had occurred. Therefore, we have been forced to judge the relative effectiveness of any two ways of conducting the museum visit in terms of the *relative* amounts of information possessed by the groups of pupils instructed in the different ways. The absolute scores of the pupils on the information test do not represent how much was learned during the museum visit. They represent both prior knowledge and knowledge gained during the visit. Although it would have been of some value to have determined the absolute increment in knowledge which resulted from the museum visit, it was not feasible to subject the pupils to prior examination.
> (Melton *et al.* 1936/1988: 17–18)

Since the differences in test scores for the various "treatments" are relatively small compared to the absolute scores, it is difficult to arrive at valid conclusions about the impact of variations in educational experiences on the children's learning.

A striking feature of all these studies is the large sample sizes – timing studies of adults used samples up to almost 2,000, and the children's studies involved hundreds of children, usually all the children in a grade level in Buffalo. At the time of these studies, the school population of Buffalo was over 70,000.

At approximately the same time and in a similar manner, Gibson (1925) was testing children in the public schools of Cleveland and examining the educational value of their visits to the Cleveland Museum of Art.

Discussion

The experiments by Gilman and Wittlin and the studies by Robinson, Melton and colleagues (and others) illustrate two very different approaches to understanding learning in museums. In modern terminology, they represent naturalistic, "qualitative" research and experimental-design, "quantitative"[4] research. They can serve to illustrate and introduce a more general discussion of the possibilities for visitor research in museums.

Common attributes of early work

Despite the differences in approaches, these early studies all share a number of important attributes.

First, the writers mentioned above all claim to provide evidence about the educational function of museums. Gilman (1916: 74) argues that only by minimizing museum fatigue can museums fulfill their function as "expositors of the treasures committed to their charge," and Wittlin argues that museum exhibitions need to be more effective in order to serve the educational purpose of museums. Melton's study of adults, which describes only data on time in the museum and the paths taken by visitors, is introduced with the sentence

> The conception of museums as educational institutions serving the
> general public has become more and more popular during the present
> century and has been used increasingly as a basis for judgments of the
> value of museum practices in installing and labeling objects for display.
> (Melton 1935/1988: 1)

Second, both kinds of studies are justified by their authors as scientific, experimental work. Wittlin (1949: 236) introduces her work with the statement, "In the present writer's view, attempts at devising new manners of presentation of museum specimens are likely to bear reliable results only if based on controlled experiments." Melton described his work as follows:

> judgments regarding the educational effectiveness of the many, and often
> conflicting, museum practices have leaned heavily on *a priori*
> generalizations regarding the psychological capacities and characteristics
> of the museum visitor, who is to be the supposed beneficiary. The
> pattern of a science of museum education built on knowledge of the
> behavior of the museum visitor was first sketched in 1928 by Edward S.
> Robinson and since that time there has been an ever increasing effort to
> discard all *a priori* generalizations, to replace them with generalizations
> founded on direct observation, and to resort to rigidly controlled
> observations and experiments for the empirical determination of the
> reactions of visitors to different museum situations.
> (Melton 1935/1988: 1)

Third, both provide significant new information about the audiences they studied, and both have contributed to the furthering of our knowledge about what constitutes a better educational experience in a museum. Yet there is still a considerable gap between their (and others') research methods and findings and much museum practice.

Fourth, at the time of these studies, the term "evaluation" was seldom used in social science literature, and the distinction between evaluation and research, now frequently debated, was not discussed. These early authors describe their work as "science" and "research." Evaluation, as a professional activity associated with applied social science studies on the effect of educational interventions on learners, did not exist.

Finally, both Wittlin and Melton generalize beyond their data, bringing in additional information and appeals to other work, published and unpublished. They make categorical statements to buttress their arguments.

Contrasts between Wittlin and Melton

There are also dramatic differences between the two kinds of studies.

First, they differ in their definition of what it means for visitors to interact with an exhibition. Melton and coworkers solve the problem of what exhibits may mean to people by defining "interest" in terms of a simple, behavioral variable – time in the exhibition. Wittlin has another set of concepts she believes are important in defining "interest" and addresses them by asking people open-ended questions and interpreting their answers as well as their drawings.

Second, although both groups use observation methods, they employ very different approaches. Melton provides a precise, detailed description of his definition of observation, using time as the determining variable, while Wittlin summarizes her observations and describes them in qualitative terms.

Third, the kinds of arguments the authors provide to support conclusions are qualitatively different. Melton relies on numbers and statistics, while Wittlin relies on selected samples of the raw data. For instance, Wittlin provides nine examples of visitors' responses to an interview question to document her point that visitors "expressed a desire to acquire knowledge." She provides the actual words of the visitors, not an averaged numerical scale based on their responses. Individual visitors are not present in the Melton reports, and Melton (1935/1988: 8) takes pains to explain that the reports discuss an imaginary "representative or average visitor, since this imaginary person reflects the behavior trends of all museum visitors" (Melton 1935/1988: 8).

Finally, Melton and coworkers spend an extraordinary amount of time standardizing their experimental methods, trying to find possible challenges to the generalizability of their data, and trying to account for all the possible variables that may interfere with this generalizability. Wittlin devotes less time to this effort and relies more on the immediacy of her work, as well as the use of multiple methods, to convince the reader.

These differences are characteristic of two qualitatively different approaches to research and evaluation in museums, which will be discussed more fully below.

The post-war period, 1950 to early 1960s

The immediate post-war period, a time of amazing growth in museums and in museum education, appears to have been a low point in systematic empirical visitor studies. According to Shettel (1989) the ten papers published by Robinson and Melton in the period from 1928 to 1936 were followed by only nine total publications by various authors in the entire twenty-year period from 1940–59. De Borhegyi and Hanson (1968) list a somewhat more extensive bibliography for this period, but the dearth of publications during this time is evident. Academic researchers spent little time in museums and most museum staffs also turned their attention elsewhere.

Yet this was a time when the museum profession underwent staggering growth in size and quality. Many new museums were started and museum practice itself became a thriving profession. The International Council of Museums (ICOM) was a product of the post-war period of renewed and new international connections, and the Committee for Education and Cultural Action (CECA), the professional museum educators' group within ICOM, has held annual international meetings since 1978. In the United States, the Education Committee (EdCom) was recognized as a standing committee of the American Association of Museums (AAM) in 1973, although educators gathered informally much earlier. The current British Group for Education in Museums (GEM) was originally established in 1948 as the Group for Educational Services in Museums (Hooper-Greenhill 1991: 56). All of these official, professional bodies developed out of informal groups concerned with education that began to meet after the Second World War.

During this post-war period, only a few guiding spirits carried out any significant visitor studies work. Centers of such work were the Royal Ontario Museum and the Milwaukee Public Museum. As late as 1980, a meeting of the still informal Visitor Studies Committee of the American Association of Museums might attract a score of interested participants, while the educators' group, EdCom, a recognized standing committee of AAM, would attract hundreds to a parallel session.

As Table 3.1 illustrates, interest in visitor studies expanded dramatically in the 1960s, coincident both with increased government spending on a wide range of social services and increased application of social science research to examine these activities. The rise of visitor studies is closely associated with the rise of program evaluation in formal education. This growth is described in the next chapter. The increased examination of both visitor behaviors and the meaning visitors make of their museum experiences has resulted in the robust, multifaceted activities now carried out by academics, museum employees and eager students. Its contribution to improving museum exhibitions and programs will be discussed in Chapter 7.

Table 3.1 Number of papers on visitor studies in the twentieth century, by decade

	De Borhegyi*	Shettel[†]	Screven[‡]	Hein[§]
<1920	1	1	1	3
1920s	2	1	4	5
1930s	10	9	15	20
1940s	9	4	5	13
1950s	31	5	8	26
1960s	48	36	58	
1970s		99	143	
1980s		225	335	

Notes: *Data from De Borhegyi and Hanson (1968) citing literature through 1965.
[†] Data from Shettel (1989) citing literature through 1988.
[‡] Data from Screven and Shettel (1993). This bibliography includes some non-museum evaluation literature.
[§] Hein (1996a). A listing of US and British papers published before 1960.

4

The countenance of visitor studies[1]

Science is doing your damnedest with your mind, no holds barred.
(P. W. Bridgman)

Perhaps the simplest rule for method in qualitative case work is this:
Place the best brains available in the thick of what is going on.
(Stake 1994: 242)

Introduction

The same forces that generated progressive social action in the 1960s also contributed to expanded intellectual activity. Western prosperity, increased social consciousness, and greater acceptance of diversity were paralleled by expansion in methods and applications of the social sciences. As has been the case for the past hundred years, progressive political action influenced social science research (Hamilton 1994).

What had been a small, marginal group interested in examining museum visitors and studying learning in museums grew. Some of these new colleagues were drawn to the field by intellectual curiosity; more were thrust into the "business" of evaluating programs and exhibits as increased external funding, especially government funding, led to requests – then demands – that museum education be effective and that its outcomes be evaluated.

The emergence of program evaluation

In the United States, a significant development for all research on the outcomes from educational activities, including visitor studies, was the passage of the Elementary and Secondary Education Act (ESEA) in 1965, one component of President Johnson's ambitious anti-poverty, social program. The first entry of the federal government into education had come about as a result of the 1958 National Defense Education Act, a cold war initiative to bolster education in the face of Soviet successes. Now, the federal government assumed an even stronger role, initiating new educational strategies, including Follow Through and Title I through IX (later, called Chapter I–IX) Programs supporting arts education, bilingual education, programs to address race and gender discrimination, etc. A crucial component of the ESEA legislation was the requirement that federally funded programs have an evaluation component. Recipients of funds – local school departments, state agencies, academic institutions and newly created non-profit centers and consortia – were *required* to spend significant funds (usually 5–10 per cent of total budget) on evaluation of the effectiveness of the educational intervention.

Although application of this requirement varied a great deal, with some programs (e.g. Title I reading program) developing a nationwide, standard evaluation plan while others never completed any evaluation, the concept of accountability and evaluation was established and has remained and increased in influence. Evaluation spread from the United States Office of Education (USOE) to other offices of the Department of Health, Education, and Welfare,[2] to programs funded by the Department of Justice as well as to other agencies. In some instances, evaluation dominated the programs and determined their fate (Stake 1986).

Shortly after passage of the ESEA legislation, social scientists and program practitioners developed new evaluation methods and established professional associations to discuss their work and legitimize their activities. The profession of program evaluation emerged as more than a minor activity within applied sociology or one specialization among many for educational psychologists. The Evaluation Network was founded in 1974 and merged with the Evaluation Research Society to form the American Evaluation Association in 1986. Although academic work on program evaluation occurred before the mid-1960s, including the studies of visitor behavior in museums described in the previous chapter, the application of the term *program evaluation* to a standard aspect of educational activity, at least in the United States, was a direct result of President Johnson's anti-poverty programs.

Gradually, the influence of this growing profession spread to the United States museum community. As the Education Directorate of the National Science Foundation increased its support for exhibitions and programs in science museums, it also began to suggest that funds be spent on exhibit evaluation. In the 1980s National Science Foundation (NSF) officials became more insistent. They required that an evaluation plan be included in proposals. In science museums, at least, the evaluation mandate evolved as part of the NSF-funded exhibit development process. Other funding agencies, including private foundations, followed the same path. Many museums entered the arena of visitor studies only because they were forced to carry out visitor studies as a requirement of their funding sources, but enter it they did.

The British experience, without the specific goad of a federal mandate, was somewhat different. Much of the early work stems from the efforts of Roger Miles (Miles *et al.* 1988) and his colleagues at the Natural History Museum (see Hooper-Greenhill 1994), who followed the lead of United States evaluators active in the 1970s to develop exhibition policy based on visitor studies.

Whatever the motivations, visitor studies as a professional activity has grown rapidly. At the time of writing, one can no longer count studies carried out in even a year, let alone a decade. The earlier growth of publications in this field is shown in Table 3.1 in the previous chapter. As late as the 1960s, the number was a few hundred for the decade; now they number at least in the hundreds if not over a thousand annually.

Similarly, the field has produced professional museum evaluators, some working within individual museums and others thriving as independent contractors. Finally, there now exist professional organizations of museum researchers. In the United States, the Committee for Audience Research and Evaluation (CARE) was recognized as a standing committee of the American Association of Museums in 1989 and the Visitor Studies Association, founded in 1990, had more than 350 members in 1997.

Some major achievements of the growing professional practice of program evaluation relevant to visitor studies in museums are discussed below.

Evaluation and research

Academics as well as practitioners have long debated whether distinctions exist between "research" and "evaluation" or between "pure" research and "applied" research. Increased program evaluation activity accentuated potential differences between these activities.

Typically, program evaluation, both formative (for the purpose of improving an actual program) and summative (passing judgment on the extent to which the program has achieved its goals) is carried out with constrained, specified means and limited time-frames. Although there have been efforts to expand program evaluation beyond these constraints, such limits have repeatedly reasserted themselves.

Consequently, although methods used by both researchers and evaluators – observation, interview, document review, etc. – are identical, the two enterprises can be differentiated. Evaluation cannot be divorced from judgment; it is carried out in response to a need to make decisions in a practical situation. The questions it asks are usually about specific processes or outcomes – whether a program or exhibit does or does not meet specifications. These questions are not framed primarily to maximize their contribution to expanding the store of human knowledge. Evaluations can be successful even though they have no application beyond the particular exhibition or program that is their subject.

In contrast, research is carried out for the sake of increasing knowledge, with no particular outcome required. Questions that begin with "I wonder if . . . " can be perfectly acceptable research questions; such questions make little sense as evaluation questions. The latter usually are about whether something "works," meets some standard, or does what it claimed to do. Some form of generalizability or rich description is a requirement for any research study, whether behavioral or naturalistic.

Both evaluation and research can be rigorous, exploratory, or, of course, poorly designed. The difference is that evaluation studies, although often limited by the project or exhibition goals they must evaluate, time and resources available for the task, and the knowledge and experience of the staff, may still improve a particular exhibition. Research studies that are underfunded and not carefully thought out are not likely to contribute significantly to better understanding of museum visitors.

A few years ago we developed a detailed research design for evaluation of a new exhibition at a science museum. We decided to compare visitor response to the new interactive exhibition to visitor interaction with some similar, but more traditional, exhibitions. We also planned to study visitors in several phases; first, after some of the newer exhibit components were installed individually, and again later, when the entire gallery was completed. Early in our study, we demonstrated that visitors spent more time and engaged more with the newer exhibit components than they did with the older methods of presentation. Before we could study visitors in detail in an adjacent older gallery, the exhibit designers completely transformed that older gallery so that its exhibit style was similar to the approach used in the new one. The change was appropriate for them: it made sense from what they had learned, and it was done most conveniently and economically by working in both galleries simultaneously. We were not able to carry out our research plan, since we had no baseline data on visitors to the older gallery. Our plans to carry out a study that could be generalized (to do research), were thwarted but we were gratified that our findings were of use to the museum to improve its offerings to the public.

Miles (1993) distinguishes between the purposes and approach of evaluation and research. Evaluation is practical, intended to solve specific problems; pragmatism is the guiding principle for carrying out studies rather than (necessarily) attempting the rigor of research. Miles seems to extend the distinction beyond what is necessary in stating that, "it is always wrong to treat a piece of evaluation as research, but not necessarily wrong to treat a piece of research as evaluation" (Miles 1993: 28).

While it is probable that evaluation studies, focused on practical problems, are less likely than research to expand general knowledge about a situation, there is no inherent reason why they cannot. For example, the exhibit evaluation literature contains examples of pre/post-test studies that conform to Campbell and Stanley's criteria (1963, also see below) for a true experiment and are indistinguishable from many academic research efforts. Also, *collections* of evaluation studies may make a contribution to more generalized knowledge.

Summative, formative, and front-end evaluations

In 1967, early in the history of the evaluation profession, Michael Scriven (1967), one influential founder of the new profession, developed the distinction between formative and summative evaluation. *Formative evaluation* refers to work that is carried on while a program is developing, that is used to change that program and, if possible, to improve it. *Summative evaluation* refers to any study that looks at the impact of a completed program.

Summative evaluations attempt to describe what happened as a consequence of a program or exhibition. In carrying out a summative evaluation, it is important to describe both what the intervention (program or exhibition) actually consists of, and what its impact, intended or unintended, has been. By definition, summative evaluations can only be carried out after a program has been implemented or an exhibition opened to the public. In the case of formal educational programs, these requirements often create considerable difficulty, since it is not always clear that programs – curricula, teaching methods, or administrative reorganizations – have actually been carried out as proposed. Just because a school claims to introduce whole language instruction doesn't mean that is what actually occurs in classrooms. First, activities may differ from those proposed. Second, it may be difficult to describe the intended program and almost impossible to describe the range of practice. What do teachers actually do in the classroom while they are supposedly teaching inquiry? What does it mean to "facilitate cooperative learning?" Thus, a number of summative evaluations of educational programs are flawed. They studied outcomes without adequately describing what activities were presumed to correlate with observed outcomes or without confirming that the program being evaluated actually happened.

This problem of defining the subject of summative evaluations is of less concern in the evaluation of exhibitions, since these can usually be described with some accuracy. Either the exhibition opened and a summative evaluation can be carried out, or there is no exhibition to evaluate. However, since visitors so often spend very short times engaged with the exhibitions subjected to summative evaluation, the extent to which any changes noted can be attributed to the exhibition is a particularly acute problem in museum settings.

An even more perplexing problem in museum evaluations is that visitors may interact with an exhibition in ways that bear little relationship to what the exhibition designers may have intended. A newspaper report of an exhibition at Boston's Museum of Science included the following anecdote:

> This is what the display is designed to do: recreate Galileo's famous experiment of dropping different weights from the top of the Leaning Tower of Pisa, proving that objects of differing weights fall at the same speed . . . Here's what the kid was doing instead: Figuring out the mechanism that stopped the buckets from rising whenever he opened the little doors that let users put weights in the buckets. Having figured that out, he was testing his reaction time by seeing if he could open the door fast enough, after the weights started falling, to catch them before they hit the bottom.
>
> (Chandler 1996: 33)

Formative evaluation – modification of an exhibition as it is being developed – has blossomed into a wide-ranging activity in museums. Increasingly, museum exhibit designers make some effort to gauge visitor reaction to exhibit components before they are permanently installed. These efforts range from informally trying out prototypes on the floor or asking a few visitors what they think about an exhibit component, to elaborate research studies, in which successive waves of exhibit components are subjected to relatively rigorous examination by visitors.

A third category of visitor study, front-end evaluation (Screven 1986), or preliminary assessment, to use an informal term more appropriate for the activities often carried out, is also effective in developing exhibitions. *Front-end evaluation* refers to visitor studies carried out in the early development of a program or exhibition concept intended to ascertain the desirability of a particular plan of action. What do the intended visitors know about the subject of the exhibition? What does the name "Africa" conjure up for visitors? What do people know about gravity? Would they be interested in an exhibition on India? What do non-visitors think an art museum is? These are all questions that actually have been asked of visitors, or potential visitors, during the planning stages for various activities before museum staff had made any decisions about how exhibitions should look or what topics to include. Most of the methods for visitor studies discussed in Chapter 6 can be applied to all three categories of evaluations.

Front-end, formative, or summative evaluations can be formal processes, with considerable planning and large scale research designs. The terms are also applied to quite informal processes, just finding out anything about visitor preferences and how something works when visitors actually view it or use it. Summative evaluations – the attempt to find the impact of a program or exhibition on the audience – usually require formal design and execution if they are to yield useful information.

For improving exhibits, even informal, short, and *ad hoc* formative evaluations can provide useful information to museum staff. It's better to ask a few people what they think a term means than to ask no one; to try out an exhibit component on a few visitors than on none. Some museum evaluators have stressed the power of even brief field-testing of exhibits. MacNamara (1987) argued that by carefully developing specific questions and requiring a small number of visitors to engage with a model for an exhibit for a considerable length of time (in her example, evaluators hid all the labels) she was able to get more useful information from ten visitors than she would have from less intrusive observation and interviews with a much larger, random sample of casual visitors.

Especially in formative evaluations, the process is most useful when it is iterative; something is tried out, modified, and tried again. If the process corrects the most egregious errors, and modifies the most unsuccessful components – those no one understands or those some visitors totally misinterpret – a better exhibition will result. If these corrections are made, it matters little if the visitor group did not represent the total museum population, or that the text would have offended only one small audience segment. If an exhibit component or a whole exhibition can be demonstrated to be more accessible for some visitors, it is likely to be more accessible to all; if a potential cause for complaint or for a frustrating experience for even a small fraction of visitors is eliminated, a major problem for the museum may be avoided.

For situations where summative evaluations are required, for example, if the impact of an exhibit on the total museum audience is to be assessed, it becomes especially important to assure that a representative audience sample is included and all possible impacts are studied. If visitors are observed only during school vacation days, family groups will probably be over-represented; if the study is carried out exclusively on weekday mornings, seniors and single visitors may be over-represented instead. Also, visitors may react differently when the museum is crowded than when it is relatively empty. Summative evaluations not only require a carefully thought out, formal plan of coordinated evaluation studies, they also require some policy decisions about what is to be evaluated and who will be the intended subjects for evaluation.

Politics of evaluation

As program evaluation developed it became clear to many that the concept of neutral, objective social scientists carrying out impartial studies of the effects of programs was a myth. At least some program evaluators recognized quickly not only that the programs being evaluated were highly influenced by political considerations, but also that the evaluation itself could not be a neutral "objective" activity (Weiss 1991) for two reasons: evaluations were used by politicians to promote or destroy programs, and evaluations themselves reflected ideological views.

Program evaluation became embroiled in politics and every aspect of the evaluation enterprise was subject to criticism, not just about methodological orthodoxy or the quality of individual work, but about its function. An early issue of the journal *Evaluation* (Palumbo 1973) was devoted to this topic, and one paper by Carol Weiss (1973) "Where Politics and Evaluation Research Meet" became one of the most quoted papers in the field. Every part of the evaluation activity has its political component: which program to evaluate (and which to ignore), how to carry out the evaluation, who to choose to do it, what methods to use, what objectives to examine, how to ask the questions, how to analyze the data, how to present the results (and to whom!) – all have political implications.

Evaluation of museum exhibitions is usually not quite as explosive an enterprise as evaluation of major social programs with their potentially powerful influences on society, vocal supporters and opponents, and expenditures of billions of tax dollars. But even without considering controversial exhibitions, political factors may be significant within the museum's own sphere. Evaluation may have consequences for museum staff, may influence how budgets are developed and how money is spent, and may determine the policy direction of a museum. In cases involving controversial exhibitions – such as the Enola Gay exhibition at the Smithsonian Air and Space Museum, or the Making of the West exhibition at the National Portrait Gallery – the political issues involving the larger community may also come into play.

The controversy surrounding the Smithsonian exhibition on the Enola Gay and the dropping of the atomic bomb 50 years earlier illustrates how powerful the political influences on museum exhibitions may be. It was essentially a combination of front-end and formative evaluation (or the lack of it!) that brought out criticisms of the Enola Gay exhibition. No summative evaluation of the original exhibition was possible, since most of it was never installed. The exhibition touched so deeply on how a nation commemorates its past (Hein and Selden 1997) that it is difficult to imagine how results from any social science research could have resolved the controversy. A more careful reading of the reactions to the exhibition ideas might, however, have allowed the curators to consider a wider range of options. A simultaneous, parallel controversy surrounds a Japanese exhibition about the role of its military during the Second World War (Hammond 1995).

Can evaluators be neutral?

Closely related to political issues raised by evaluating programs and exhibitions are concerns about the status of the people who carry out these evaluations. Should they be employees of the organization (internal evaluators) or separated from it, on contract to the agency (external evaluators)? Some school districts established testing and evaluation departments responsible for carrying out mandated program evaluations, but some federal agencies required or strongly recommended that evaluations be carried out by independent evaluators who had no other connection with the program being evaluated.

Separating evaluation from the activity being evaluated has become an accepted practice and has supported the rise of large commercial organizations that specialize in evaluations of federally funded programs. As a result, program staff, who might benefit most from personal involvement in the evaluation process (especially formative evaluation), may only read a final report or a brief summary statement about the evaluation prepared by an external evaluator who shares little of the process with the staff.

In museum visitor studies, both approaches can be found. In some museums, visitor studies, including front-end, formative, and summative evaluations, have become part of regular staff activities. Talking to visitors or observing them, and then incorporating the results into their exhibition design activities, has become an integral component of the exhibition development process for staff members. In other museums, outside contractors may work independently or in close collaboration with staff but still separate from them, carrying out visitor studies in support of exhibition development.

Evaluators who work as independent contractors pride themselves on their independence and assert that they can be objective, since they are not employees of the museum and therefore escape pressures to support ideas that come from the staff. While their independence may make them feel able to be more objective, they may be so far removed from the organization and the day-to-day concerns of exhibit designers and production staff that their work may only tangentially influence the outcome of the exhibition design process. Evaluators who are staff members, or those who work closely with the staff and are in intimate contact with the day-to-day process of building an exhibition or designing a program, are more likely to carry out formative work that is of immediate value to the design process. However, external evaluators may bring to a new project a wealth of experience at similar or contrasting institutions, information that may be less familiar to internal evaluators, staff members who may have spent much of their recent professional working lives in the setting being evaluated.

In actual practice, the conflicting pressures of these various factors – the tensions between constituencies and realities of practical work – influence both internal and external evaluators, blurring the distinctions between them. Even external evaluators have to consider the political consequences of their findings; they are also subject to the pressures that staff members experience. For example, evaluators who consistently criticize their contractors may find few people who will hire them. In practice, agencies hire like-minded evaluators; those that have a predilection to view activities from the same ideological perspective as the program staff. Conversely, carrying out visitor studies internally does not guarantee that work will be done with due consideration for the immediate needs of those developing an exhibition. An internal visitor studies evaluator can build up his or her own constituency within an organization and may have considerable independence, even to the extent that work may be only marginally useful to the rest of the staff. Evaluation reports can be ignored regardless of their source.

In museums, as in other agencies, program and exhibition evaluation is now recognized as a practical, real world activity that requires careful balancing between irrelevance and intrusiveness, both technical skills and social awareness of the professional culture of the museum, and that has to be reviewed and monitored whether it is carried out by an external or internal evaluator.

Naturalistic research and evaluation

As program evaluation grew, other issues surfaced. Besides having to define types of evaluation, examine the roles of evaluators, and worry about the political consequences of their work, both evaluators and policy-makers recognized that the very nature of the work they carried out needed to be examined. Simultaneously, similar questions were raised about educational theory and research models in general.

The combination of dissatisfaction with traditional evaluation strategies, new conceptions of learning, and the application of ethnographic research methods to educational evaluation, resulted in an enormous debate between two major schools of evaluation. The two approaches to evaluation, often described as two paradigms, will be discussed below.

Traditional educational research

The dominant model for carrying out evaluation work in the 1960s was the model then prevalent in educational research, the experimental-design strategy of educational psychology. The classic description of how to carry out an evaluation of an educational activity was outlined in a brief but powerful monograph by Campbell and Stanley (1963), which is still used extensively in research courses in schools of education and psychology departments. The primary preoccupations of this methodological treatise concerned beginning and ending states – comparing subjects before and after treatment, with major concern that subjects be equal in all other parameters except "treatment" so that any changes observed could be attributed to the activity itself. In engineering terms, the activity to be evaluated was likened to an impenetrable "black box" and measurements were taken of antecedent and consequent conditions (the wires leading into and out of the box) to see if these differed.

This prevailing paradigm was based on the model of laboratory experimentation in the natural sciences. The discussion in Campbell and Stanley's monograph centers around the various "threats to validity" for the methods employed to isolate the experimental situation from outside influences. Campbell and Stanley did recognize that in much educational work, only "quasi-experimental" conditions would be possible.

> There are many natural social settings in which the research person can introduce something like experimental design into his scheduling or data collection procedures . . . even though he lacks the full control over the scheduling of experimental stimuli . . . which makes a true experiment impossible. Collectively, such situations can be regarded as quasi-experimental designs.
>
> (Campbell and Stanley 1963: 34)

As the newly professionalized program evaluators attempted to apply this approach to the evaluation of educational activities a number of issues emerged.

First, in many instances the necessary conditions for carrying out experimental design research could not be achieved. For example, some educational programs were aimed at the entire population of children who fell below a certain economic level. What equivalent control group could be found to which they could be compared? The evaluation of smaller programs in schools using rigorous treatment and control conditions required that some children receive the educational treatment and an equivalent group be assessed without receiving the treatment. But school districts moved children from one class to another for policy reasons beyond the bounds of any experiment and teachers, even when they were supposed to restrict their actions to those determined by the conditions of the experiment, were frequently influenced by activities of colleagues not enrolled in the experiment; and other circumstances would interfere with adherence to experimental design conditions.

In museum terms, a strict application of "experimental design" research would require that visitors be randomly assigned to experimental and control groups

– those who view an exhibit and those who do not. Allowing visitors to self-select whether they engage with an exhibit or not introduces a threat to validity.

Another concern was that, even if the formal conditions for experimental design were met, it was often difficult to determine the effects of treatment because the activity involved in an educational program is only one influence on the lives of the subjects. To what extent did children learn to read at school because a new children's television series premiered at about the same time that a new reading program was introduced? How did an unexpected teachers' strike or the appointment of a new superintendent in one of two districts influence the outcome of an evaluation that compared student outcomes for a curriculum innovation in one of the districts?

In addition, educational programs had a habit of changing as they were being carried out. In some instances, formative evaluations provided evidence that caused program staff to change what they were doing. In other instances, policy differences, replacement of key staff in the funding agency or the project, or budget constraints altered programs. So the quasi-experimental design developed for the program that required a stable program throughout the period of the evaluation became untenable.

In order to address the restrictions imposed by these real-world problems, many educational evaluators limited themselves to narrow measurements. They met the requirements of experimental design research but could only draw conclusions that were of little interest to practitioners. A parallel example from the museum visitor studies field is early studies that examined only single, adult visitors for purposes of research purity. Although the results are interesting and may be valid, they provide only limited guidance for exhibition development in family-oriented museums. Evaluation results were also frequently ignored by policy-makers, even if reasonable and experimentally sound.

A third problem involved questions about what results of evaluation studies to highlight. The experimental design approach stressed looking at the differences between two groups based on comparison of the difference in average results. Often these differences were quite small, as was the case in Melton's museum studies mentioned previously. The politically important Coleman study in the United States, which examined the consequences of integrating schools, illustrates the limitations of relying too heavily on averages as an outcome measure (United States Department of Health, Education and Welfare 1966). A major finding was that black children's test scores *on average* did not increase very much in integrated classes. Critics pointed out that in some instances integration produced enormous differences. Wouldn't it be more interesting to study these cases rather than concentrate on the average results from many communities?

The problems that may occur from an over reliance on measures of central tendency (medians and means) rather than looking at variance (the unusual, statistically unlikely cases) are discussed by Gould (1996) in a series of essays on topics ranging from his own response to a cancer diagnosis to the disappearance of .400 hitters in baseball.

In an early study of children's behavior in a science museum, Brooks and Vernon (1956: 180) noted that average visitor times concealed a wide variation in children's activities. (see Chapter 7). They went even further and commented that a fraction of the children they studied, mainly boys, were "*habitués*" who took enormous trouble to get to the museum. Some reported coming "20–40 times." This small group may have included the most interesting subjects of their study, but they did not fit into the model for research applied to the situation. Similar, unusual results are often mentioned in museum visitor study reports, but not considered major findings because they fall outside the scope of the analytic scheme applied to the data.

The difficulties faced by medical researchers attempting to determine the efficacy of a drug may provide a useful analogy for understanding the problems facing social scientists who attempt to evaluate the efficacy of a program, or visitor studies professionals attempting to determine the impact of a museum exhibit using experimental design procedures. Medical researchers have long recognized how difficult it is to carry out clinical trials. The best possible situation is when a drug is administered to two randomly selected samples of hospitalized patients who are enrolled in a double-blind experiment, an experiment in which neither the person administering the dose nor the recipient knows whether the active agent or a placebo is administered.

Three important conditions allow valid conclusions to be drawn from such a controlled clinical trial:

1 The subjects can have their entire input monitored; they are not free to ingest what they want, but receive only the food and medicine provided by the hospital staff.
2 A clear, well defined outcome for successful treatment can be specified.
3 The persons providing treatment do not know if they are administering medicine or a placebo, nor do the subjects know whether they are members of an experimental or control group.

Parallel conditions meeting all these requirements have never been met in the evaluation of educational programs or museum exhibits. Whatever the educational "treatment" might be, truly matched pairs of experimental and control groups are very difficult to establish; it is almost impossible to limit the activities of subjects to those experiences being studied; outcomes are usually less clearly definable than physical health outcomes; and evaluators are seldom in ignorance of which groups are receiving "treatment."

In summary, the application of traditional educational research strategies to program evaluation has raised three kinds of issues: it is difficult to achieve conditions necessary to properly apply methods based on the model of laboratory science; even if the model was followed, the number of variables that needed to be considered is overwhelming; and, perhaps, the emphasis of this model on average differences misses the most important consequences of the programs being evaluated.

New conceptions of learning

A second, parallel challenge to evaluation work based on traditional models was the emergence in the 1960s of a new conceptualization of teaching and learning. Piaget's developmental theory, and the research style he advocated (see Chapter 5) began to be acknowledged in the United States in the 1960s, although it had long been recognized in Britain. The "Cognitive Revolution" (Bruer 1993) changed researchers' approach to conceptualizing learning. Increasingly, the focus of study was the working of the "mind," a metaphysical concept banished from behaviorist approaches (Bruner 1960).

In the areas of practice, schools in both Britain and the United States began to rethink curriculum as well as classroom organization.[3] They moved away from strict adherence to linear curriculum, sharply delineated curriculum divisions, and sorting of children by ability towards more integrated approaches. Although these movements never affected a majority of children, they influenced policy and research.

What all these theoretical ideas and practical changes had in common was their acceptance of holistic conceptions of learning, the need to consider child development (that is, attributes of the learner), and a strong emphasis on learning by doing, on hands-on activities. Each of the components required a rethinking of how school programs should be evaluated and how children's learning should be assessed.

New models for evaluation

Finally, the 1960s also saw the beginning of a trend among field-based social scientists to examine their own societies, rather than distant ones. One of the first such studies, by Jules Henry (1963), examined specific institutions of modern society – schools, prisons, hospitals and old age homes – and concluded that each had a complex structure and rules of its own, which needed to be analyzed and dissected in order to understand what went on within them. In education, this approach included careful analyses of both classrooms and school culture, illustrated (in the United States) by Philip Jackson's *Life in Classrooms* (1968) and Seymour Sarason's influential *The Culture of the School and the Problem of Change* (1971).

Two aspects of this trend were particularly important for the development of evaluation activities. First, the methodology of this work provided an alternative model for research activities related to schools and museums. If the anthropologists' and ethnographers' models could be used profitably to examine our own institutions, perhaps they could also be used to carry out evaluation studies. Second, this work stressed the importance of context in any human activity. The experimental design model tried, as much as possible, to examine any intervention (any "treatment") in isolation, keeping it separate from other influences on the subject. The new research approach accepted the multifaceted complexity of real world educational settings and tried to interpret and understand how various environmental components contributed to the consequences of attempting to bring about some educational innovation. An ambitious program evaluation carried out by Robert Stake, Jack Easley, and collaborators (1978) examined the state of science education in the United States, using not only a survey instrument but also a dozen case studies of individual schools. Sociologists, anthropologists and other field researchers were sent to eleven school districts to experience the "feel" of science education and they wrote lengthy individual stories about each site. Their generally grim descriptions of the state of science education across the country influenced many readers. In museum visitor studies, Robert Wolf championed this naturalistic, anthropological work. During his tenure as evaluator at the Smithsonian Institution, he carried out ethnographic studies and gave workshops based on this model (Wolf and Tymitz 1978a, Wolf 1979).

Paradigms

Thomas Kuhn's (1962) analysis of the development of scientific thought has had a profound influence on social science thought and practice. Kuhn argues persuasively that the long established concept of "progress" in natural science, through which scientific work continually approaches nearer and nearer to a true explanation for the phenomena of the world and continually closer to ever broader generalizations (laws) that provide explanations of these phenomena, is not correct. Instead, he argues that scientific progress results from scientific revolutions during which one explanatory scheme replaces another, not because the new one explains more of the "facts" or because the new model is a closer approximation to some "truth," but because it provides a more satisfactory explanation for other, more complex reasons.

He argues against the traditional idea that once scientists note a phenomenon that cannot be explained by current theory, they discard the theory. No theory explains all the facts, and often in the history of science researchers have ignored inconvenient observations or experimental results that, if accepted, would require altering established theories. In some well documented instances, even what is observed – the "facts" of science – has changed after acceptance of a new theory. The facts also change as new equipment allows observations that were impossible previously.

Thus, the change from one theoretical stance to another – for example, from belief in a Ptolemaic universe to a Copernican one – is not simply a change in theory but a change in world view; it is a paradigm shift. Kuhn goes on to argue that similar paradigm shifts occur at all levels of science, including less dramatic and less historically significant theoretical disagreements. Although the paradigm concept has been challenged and revised by Kuhn himself, the fundamental idea that there are irreconcilable and qualitatively different ways of looking at the world is firmly embedded in current popular thought.

Appearing at a time of dramatic social change, Kuhn's concept of irreconcilable paradigms that are not more or less correct, but represent alternative ways of looking at the world, has been widely accepted and applied far beyond the classification of scientific theories. The word "paradigm" has entered our common vocabulary as a word to express any particular point of view.

Much of the heated rhetoric between proponents of differing research approaches results from the fact that the conversation crosses such paradigm boundaries. To traditional experimental-design researchers, the new approaches appear "soft," "subjective," incapable of leading to valid knowledge, and unlikely to contribute significantly to the growth of their science. To proponents of naturalistic study, the experimental-design traditionalists are not interested in understanding human nature, are limited to examining uninteresting and often trivial components of human behavior in an effort to find something they can measure, and fail to acknowledge the limitations of their methods.

Only when the two are recognized as distinct ways of viewing the world can the value of each be appreciated and accepted to gain more general information about the behavior of human beings and the meaning of that behavior. Only if the identifying terms are seen as descriptive of different paradigms can the somewhat pejorative connotations associated with terms such as "subjective" or "positivist" (depending on who uses them!) be interpreted.

What's in a name?

The terms "qualitative" and "quantitative" are frequently used to differentiate between paradigms. A recent major exposition of the former set of ideas is entitled *Handbook of Qualitative Research* (Denzin and Lincoln 1994), although several authors in that volume point out the limitations of this term. It is definitely not the case that "qualitative" research never relies on numbers, nor that all research in the "quantitative" model uses statistical correlations. The important distinctions between these two are not determined by a checklist of characteristics, all of which must be met to qualify as one paradigm or another, but by a family resemblance to one research style or the other. The various words used to describe them should be viewed as a collection of attributes, not all of which have to apply in any individual instance. A research or evaluation study is classified in one tradition or the other, depending on which set of terms describes the majority of its characteristics. Table 4.1 provides a list of parallel terms applied to the two research paradigms. I will use the term "experimental-design" to refer to the older, laboratory based research tradition, and the term "naturalistic" for the newer paradigm.

Some of the major characteristics of the experimental-design tradition are worth describing and contrasting with parallel positions in the naturalistic paradigm in order to discuss the applicability of naturalistic research and evaluation to the museum setting.

Table 4.1 Attributes of "experimental-design" and "naturalistic" paradigms

Experimental-design	Naturalistic
quantitative	qualitative
atomistic	holistic
objective	subjective
laboratory model	real-world based
experimental	naturalistic
hard	soft
confirmatory	exploratory
explanation	understanding
decontextualized	contextual
deterministic	responsive
analytic	synthetic

Objective vs. subjective: the researcher

Proponents of the laboratory model on which experimental-design social science is based make every effort to remove the researcher's personal involvement with the research from influencing methods or outcomes. The way problems are framed, the methods used, and the manner in which reports are written are all intended to render the work independent of the perspectives, idiosyncrasies, beliefs, or prejudices of the person carrying it out. The goal to strive for is research performed in such a manner that anyone with similar training, given the same situation, could repeat the research protocol, observe the same phenomena, and reach the same conclusions.

In order to do this, it is necessary to decontextualize the situation, to make the methods used as independent of the person using them as is possible, and to record data, analyze, and summarize results in a way that could be done equally by anyone. Thus, the emphasis on behaviors that require as little interpretation as possible and the impersonal style favored in most research reports.

That this model can lead to problems and prejudices has been amply illustrated by much recent criticism of science. From the problems chosen, instruments used, and questions asked, to the logical categories chosen for analysis – even the actual phenomena observed – all can be influenced by the researcher's perspectives and prior beliefs.

Proponents of the naturalistic model argue that not only is it impossible to remove the researcher from the research, but it is better to acknowledge the inevitable presence of the self and capitalize on the researcher's own perspectives and biases. Thus the methods used by naturalistic researchers – participant observation, clinical interviews, and document analysis – are precisely those that involve the researcher most directly and personally. The analytic methods favored – developing categories that emerge from the data, developing taxonomies and narrative summary descriptions – require intense cognitive input from the researcher; and the form of writing often used in reports – relying on quotations and excerpts from the original data – all emphasize the role of the researcher in the process.

From the experimental-design paradigm's perspective this is simply asking for trouble: choosing the least reliable methods, analyzing most subjectively, and reporting in a manner that defies duplication by other researchers. From the perspective of the naturalistic paradigm this is the most honest approach: respecting the subjects of the research and letting them "tell their own story"; recognizing the involvement of the researcher; and providing the readers with enough of a "feel" for the data so they can draw their own conclusions about the coherence of the study.

In the museum visitor literature this debate can be tracked both in the methods that have been used (see Chapter 6) and in papers arguing for the use of one approach or the other. Lawrence (1993), an advocate of naturalistic methods, argues

> What it means to be a 'good' museum visitor in a certain class or other social group may crucially affect responses to exhibits. To illuminate this question, some have turned to . . . survey work . . . but, in the light of the interpretive sociologists' criticisms of survey, we may ask how much closer to an answer we are likely to get by using further survey work. It is probably not possible to answer this question by asking individuals why they visit museums, or even why they do not – though this may be more promising.
>
> (Lawrence 1993: 119)

In turn, Miles, in a response to her criticisms of his work, complains that

> Lawrence would . . . damn empirical measures such as exhibit attraction and holding power, and empirical generalizations such as the exit gradient factor, for their behaviourist origins. My view is that origins are irrelevant.
>
> (Miles 1993: 28)

Feminist, cultural, and ethnic issues

One consequence of including the researcher back into the research process has been the emergence of a whole family of critiques of "traditional" science for its limited perspective on the human condition. It is precisely because feminists asked personal (subjective) questions about the science in which they were engaged that the growing bodies of critical studies reflecting "women's ways of knowing" (Belenky *et al.* 1986) have found a voice in the social and natural science literature. Discussions of feminist (Olesen 1994) or ethnic (Stanfield 1994) approaches usually stress the importance of considering the researcher's perspectives in any study.

> Where "We're doing science" was once the watchword, scholars are now experimenting with the boundaries of interpretation, linking research and social change, delving into characteristics of race, ethnicity, gender, age, and culture to understand more fully the relationship of the researcher to the research.
>
> (Denzin and Lincoln 1994: ix)

In the 1930s, Piaget was criticized because his approach was personal and resembled a novelist's story telling. Today, "personal experience methods" are advocated as a form of research. The narrative as a legitimate, alternative form of meaning making has been advocated by social scientists, and specifically applied as an explanatory scheme for meaning making in the museum (Roberts 1997).

Objective vs. subjective: data

Another distinction between the two paradigms is the rejection by experimental-design advocates of the "subjective" data characteristically collected during naturalistic research. Researchers' own field notes, narrative verbal responses from subjects, or information from individual informants is viewed as "subjective." There can be no doubt that the verbal response that a person gives to a question about his or her behavior is a different measure than the observation of that behavior. It is also clear that the kinds of factors that influence verbal responses are different from the factors that influence physiological behavior. It is also possible to call one a "subjective" response (that is, under the conscious control of the subject), and the other an "objective" response (not consciously controlled by the subject). But both are interesting phenomena for study. In fact, the finding that what people *tell* you they do and what they are *observed* to do (for example how much time they spent in a gallery or which objects they looked at) can provide insight into what messages an exhibition is communicating. *Both* of these measures provide useful, if different, information. If visitors think their visit was half an hour long when they only spent ten minutes in the exhibition, this finding is suggestive.

Our ability to talk and think about what we have done is one of the great advantages of any research or evaluation activity involving human beings. Using this information can provide insight into our understanding of the meaning behind people's behavior. It is "subjective," in the sense that it comes from a single subject, but not in the pejorative sense of being particularly unreliable or invalid.

Experimental-design research practitioners commonly make human speech part of the data by applying a laboratory-type restriction: both the prompt that generates a subject's response and the response itself are constrained. Subjects are asked to respond to specific questions, often in very limited ways. If the response is a check mark on a predetermined set of answers, then the constraints provide some of the controls of the laboratory situation and the responses can easily be converted into quantitative data. But the response is also limited by the assumptions, restrictions, and decisions that were made to develop the questions. Campbell (1978) recognized this when, in an important speech in honor of Kurt Lewin, he reflected critically on the limitations of quantitative methods.

> The qualitative underpinnings of quantitative data can be discovered by tracing back to its sources any punch on an IBM card or any numerical value on a computer print-out.
>
> (Campbell 1978: 192)

By allowing subjects more freedom to talk as they wish, using the entire responses in analyses, and reporting representative samples as part of research findings, naturalistic researchers employ an alternative approach that capitalizes on the unique quality of human experience. This approach is costly in time and energy in comparison to survey research. It requires skilled research assistants and much costly time in the field. Polling companies and large contract research firms prefer less personal, standardized methods.

Data analysis of qualitative data can vary enormously. In contrast to the methods discussed here, Miles and Huberman (1994) advocate a more rigorous methodology, much closer to the type of analytic schemes used by "quantitative" researchers. Their attempt to straddle the differences between the two approaches does not satisfy some naturalistic critics who believe it "remains basically unresponsive to the more post-structural, constructivist, cultural studies, feminist, and critical theory perspectives" (Denzin and Lincoln 1994: 357).

Laboratory vs. natural setting

Experimental-design researchers recognize that most human activity cannot be moved to the laboratory – it must be studied in natural settings. But within the experimental-design model this limitation is a necessary inconvenience, a limitation that needs to be overcome. Campbell and Stanley describe this inevitable situation as a limiting factor, which prevents the experimenter from fully controlling the situation, even as they urge social scientists to make the effort to study many situations.

> One purpose of this chapter is to encourage the utilization of such quasi-experiments . . . [The experimenter] should deliberately seek out those artificial and natural laboratories which provide the best opportunities for control. But beyond that he should go ahead with experiment and interpretation, fully aware of the points on which the results are equivocal.
>
> (Campbell and Stanley 1963: 34)

Naturalistic researchers take the natural setting as the appropriate place to carry out their research and, rather than trying to constrain the setting or the subjects to carve out a quasi-laboratory situation, they are more likely to exploit the unique characteristics of any setting. What do people do when free to pursue their own interests? What conversations do they carry out in museums? What do they think when they look at paintings? What significance do they give to these historical artifacts? These are the kinds of questions asked by naturalistic researchers who see the rich environment and unanticipated events as a component of what they are studying, rather than as a limitation on the reliability of their endeavor.

Correlating outcomes vs. making meaning

Another characteristic of the traditional research model is the attempt to define as accurately as possible a specific behavior which is then examined and correlated with the desired outcomes. In behavioral, experimental-design research, the only meaning that can be attributed to an act is the act itself. In Melton and Robinson's research, the rather grandiose strategy described at the beginning of the monograph – to examine learning in museum settings – is reduced to research on the holding and attracting power of exhibits.

Naturalistic researchers treat behavior as a tool to come to a deeper understanding of the meaning behind acts. The specific behaviors that are recorded, whether in narrative or more quantitative, abstracted form, are viewed as indicators of what lies behind them, as guides to enable the researcher to come to some understanding of the meaning of what has been observed. A characteristic pattern in much naturalistic research is a less than one-to-one correspondence between data and discussion. The researchers synthesize data, they don't correlate observed variables. Again, whether this process leads to understanding – whether, in fact, it is even considered science – depends to a large degree on the world view of any reader.

Causality vs. understanding

A major goal of experimental-design research is to build up a hierarchical structure of knowledge. The assumption is that every bit of research fits into a larger picture that will lead to increasingly general statements incorporating more and more of the data within a single framework. The goal is laws of behavior with broad applicability.

Naturalistic research has a different goal, to provide "rich" descriptions of specific situations that gain validity by being believable on their own terms, rather than as pieces of a larger hierarchical whole. The generalization comes from applications of these descriptions to an increasing number of instances. However, the instances cited usually remain descriptions (that is, a collection of individual cases), not a set of cases that are analyzed and generalized so that they can be combined statistically.

Data analysis: hypothesis testing vs. emergent meanings

When it comes to data analysis, the obvious, superficial distinction between experimental-design and naturalistic approaches is that the one uses primarily numerical, quantitative methods in data analysis, while the other uses narrative, qualitative methods. But as I have pointed out earlier, and as various critics have stressed, numerous "qualitative" studies use numbers, and some "quantitative" researchers, at least at times, engage in studies that are primarily narrative.

The important distinction between the two approaches has to do with the relationship between data and the working hypotheses, or conceptual frameworks, within which the data is collected. Experimental-design researchers collect data to support or refute a hypothesis. This kind of research requires a hypothesis amenable to empirical study as a precondition to starting data collection. The data then either support or refute the proposition. Thus, significant intellectual energy must be spent on defining the research question in such a way that relevant, valid, and reliable data that address the question can be collected. As a consequence, there is much concern that the research question be framed in behavioral terms, since only behavior can be observed. Within this system it is also difficult to discover anything that is outside the framework of the research questions that guided the inquiry. Unless the research is "exploratory" (and this often means naturalistic) it would be an indication of poor research design if any conclusions reached did not follow directly from the questions asked.

In contrast, naturalistic researchers, although their methods vary considerably, approach a human situation differently. They do ask questions, but these may be more general and may be framed in language that goes beyond behavior. "What does this custom mean?" or "What meaning will visitors make of this exhibit?" are reasonable questions in naturalistic research, and the data are not analyzed in terms of previously determined categories. Rather, the analytic categories grow out of the data; they are allowed to "emerge" from the narrative material collected, whether it is observations, interviews or other sources. Csikszentmihalyi and Robinson (1990) provide an example of such an analytic scheme.

> We did not begin with a coding system and then comb through the transcripts in search of supporting instances. Rather, separate groups of researchers read the transcripts with broad general questions in mind, such as, What are the most important elements in the aesthetic encounter? and What are the conditions under which an aesthetic experience can take place? From the initial readings, categories were derived using the terms of the respondents themselves. Then, the categories were refined as more transcripts were analyzed, until finally the entire body of material was recorded using the fully elaborated systems for each topic.
>
> (Csikszentmihalyi and Robinson 1990: 24)

McManus provides a parallel set of emergent categories (1989a) in her analysis of overheard conversations in a natural history museum.

This categorically different approach to data analysis also leads to different kinds of conclusions. Naturalistic research is more likely to provide insight into possible meanings or explanations; it does not confirm or refute since it describes. It is, of course, more likely to provide a means for noting unexpected outcomes, since both the preferred data collection methods *and* the analytic methods are intended to facilitate finding novelty.

Reliability and validity

Reliability and validity are concepts central to all research in social sciences. *Validity* refers to the extent to which information gathered is about the phenomena in question. Does the information gathered on a survey actually reflect respondents' views on the subject? Can student performance on a particular test be used to decide on student placement into an advanced class? *Reliability* refers to the repeatability of a measurement or data collection method. If I carry out the same activity will I get a comparable result?

Imagine, for example, applying these two concepts to shooting arrows at a bull's-eye target hidden behind a sheet. Reliability asks how close the arrows come to each other. It can be determined without removing the sheet, because it refers to a property of the data itself. Validity refers to how close the arrows came to hitting the bull's-eye hidden behind the sheet. It can be determined only by removing the sheet; only by reference to the phenomena being examined.

A simplistic description of experimental-design and naturalistic research is to say that the former is concerned primarily with reliability, sometimes at the expense of validity, while the reverse is true of the latter. Critics of standardized tests, for example, argue that the tests are not valid; a score on a multiple-choice test of writing ability does not provide valid information about the candidate's ability to write, although the test may be highly reliable – no matter how many times the candidate takes it the scores will be similar. Critics of naturalistic research argue that conclusions from it may be valid; perhaps no one doubts that the stories told by participants in a program are a valid description of their experiences. But the information is so embedded in the particular circumstances of subjective experiences that it is not reliable enough to constitute data for scientific inquiry – there is no way to provide statistical confirmation that another set of interviews at a different time would produce similar results.

Like many apparently simple concepts, reliability and validity have proven to be more complex than originally thought. As simplistic views of the external, objective verifiability of both observations and scientific laws have had to be abandoned for more complex and less certain categories, similar doubts have touched all ideas that relate to them. Within their own models, both experimental-design and naturalistic research traditions use concepts about "goodness" of the data collected and the match between the research findings and the phenomena that they describe. Experimental-design proponents continue to discuss reliability and validity, while naturalistic researchers increasingly choose a different vocabulary, such as "credibility" and "transferability" in place of validity and "dependability" in place of reliability.

In naturalistic research, reliability has no formal definition. In the absence of numerical, statistical results, there is no quantitative way to compare one set of results with another and come up with a reliability coefficient. Since most naturalistic research work does not attempt to make a one-to-one correlation with other research, and usually acknowledges the differences as well as the similarities between situations, reliability, in the statistical sense, is not a major concern.

In naturalistic research, the equivalent of validity is approached primarily through a complex process called "triangulation." The term invokes the analogy to the navigational process in which an exact location on the earth's surface is fixed by getting bearings from three different points. Similarly, naturalistic investigators rely on the overlap of information from three sources, three methods or three perspectives to convince themselves (and their readers) that the story they tell approximates a valid description of the phenomena observed. Again, since there is no quantitative aspect to the conclusions of naturalistic research, there can be no formal, mathematical discussion of validity.

Validity is also difficult to define in experimental-design research since, in many instances, there will be uncertainty about what the "real" phenomena are. Test results are often validated by their congruence with another test, which can lead to rather complex but circular arguments about validity. Traditional concepts of validity have been challenged in recent years (Messick 1989) as conceptions of learning have expanded and simplistic notions of intelligence have been overturned.

Naturalistic research does not make a sharp distinction between the more sociological, political concerns that determine whether a set of findings are accepted by critical readers and the methodological issues about the quality of the research. It acknowledges that the way in which conclusions are considered by readers is a part of the process itself.

Science and non-science

The debates between proponents of the two methodologies have ranged so far that some have accused proponents of naturalistic methods of abandoning science, of blurring the line between science and non-science. To these critics any methods that fall outside the canon of experimental-design approaches might as well be astrology; they should not be classified as science.

Naturalistic approaches stress the human, social component of science and supporters argue that constructing scientific theories is not teasing out of nature what is actually "out there" but is a human process of constructing meaning. Therefore, these approaches have been associated with an even more radical critique of science, which argues that the entire enterprise of science has no particular value compared to other forms of thinking, that science is only one of many belief systems, parallel to, but no better than, others. In this extreme view, science (empirical inquiry) is thus no different in standing from non-science, and, for example, astronomy and astrology are only two different ways of viewing the heavenly bodies, or creationism and evolution are only two equally plausible explanations of natural history, and various traditional religious views of medicine have the same ontological status as Western medicine.

It is important to distinguish this radical critique of any empirical approach to understanding human behavior from a more limited argument that there is more than one approach *within* the empirical tradition that explores nature. For example, it is now widely acknowledged, following the work of Popper (1962), that no number of experiments can ever confirm a theory, it is possible only to disconfirm theories. Further, Kuhn and others have argued that the replacement of one theory by another is not a simple act of weighing the experimental results on one side against the experimental data on another. However, criticism at that level does not mean that all speculations about how to explain nature are equal. Some have certainly been shown to have more predictive value than others, and a common conception of work in science is that it is at least *theoretically* capable of being refuted by empirical work. The differences between naturalistic and experimental-design methodologies discussed in this book are all disagreements within a shared framework. This common view acknowledges that empirical inquiry into both human behavior and natural phenomena provides different kinds of knowledge than do other forms of experience. They are both disciplined by nature; they are judged (in different ways, depending on the paradigm) in relation to their ability to conform with the experiences each of us has in the natural world.

Visitor studies evaluation and research

In museum visitor studies literature the same disputes can be found as in the broader evaluation and research literature. Alt (1977) and Shettel (1978) exchanged views on the appropriate approach to visitor studies, as did Lawrence (1991, 1993) and Miles (1993) more recently, and the topic is referred to frequently in conference proceedings. As indicated earlier, the two approaches have been used since the beginning of visitor studies, as illustrated by the work of Robinson and Melton (experimental-design) and Wittlin (naturalistic).

Most practitioners of visitor studies now recognize that the field needs both types of work in order to increase our meager knowledge about how visitors understand museum exhibitions. The actual situation in museums is that a vast preponderance of visitor studies are limited efforts to evaluate specific exhibitions or exhibit components and are governed more by immediate practical constraints than by the overarching concerns about research methodology.

Practical considerations often prevent evaluators from analyzing their own methodological style, and some evaluators seem to combine elements such as experimental design data collection with naturalistic analyses. If we apply the dictum that pragmatism rules in visitor studies evaluation, then any collection of methods may be appropriate to improve exhibits. If research is attempted, then some clarity about the methodologies used and the intentions of the project are useful.

The two approaches to research are based on fundamentally differing premises and lead to categorically different conclusions. Each has its own values and limitations and each provides evidence to support a different conception of learning. The contrasts between naturalistic and experimental-design research parallel the distinctions made earlier about theories of education. The relationship between these two domains – education and research – are discussed in the following chapter.

5

Ladder and network theories

Ideally . . . a world theory illuminates the world for us, and the world stands revealed to us not in imagination but in fact just as it is . . . But where pure fact ends and interpretation begins, no one in the absence of a completely adequate world theory, could possibly tell. And the better a world theory, the less are we able to tell fact from theory or pure fact from the interpretation.
                (Pepper 1942: 80–1, quoted in Davis 1985: 61–2)

I often think it's comical, fa la la, fa la la
How Nature does contrive, fa la la
That every boy or every girl, that's born into the world alive
Is either a little liberal, or else a little conservative, fal la la, fal la la.
                (Gilbert and Sullivan, *Iolanthe*)

Introduction

In Chapters 2 and 4, I have outlined, respectively, the possible range of educational theories that can guide the practice of museum education and the research traditions that have influenced visitor studies. In Chapter 2, educational theories were defined with reference to two dimensions, epistemology and learning theory, while in Chapter 4, approaches to research were described as experimental-design or naturalistic. These two analyses, although describing different domains, share many characteristics. In both instances, theories distribute themselves along continua that extend from the more formal, structured, and hierarchical to the less formal, more network-like, and more holistic. Each domain can be imagined as consisting either of a ladder-like hierarchy rising from the simplest level toward more complex levels or, alternatively, as a network, an integrated system of ideas without a single sequence or hierarchy.

In this chapter, I will discuss the relationship between these two domains and suggest that preferences for a certain educational theory and a particular research approach are not accidental, but represent similar overarching views of how the world works.

The positions discussed in the previous chapters are commonly described using contrasting terms that imply rigor – more "hard" or more "soft," more objective or more subjective. These descriptors carry with them both value and political connotations. Naturalistic methods are viewed by many as more liberal; experimental design methods as more conservative. This parallel use of terminology is also not accidental, but relates directly to the nature of the world views that support each of these theories.

Applying specific political labels makes connections to implications of the theories as well as referring to possible but not necessary associations. Those who consider the gathering of evidence and its interpretation as intellectual activities separate from any "subjective" considerations, may more readily accept theories and practices that others view as racist, elitist, or, worse yet, inhuman and immoral. Obviously, the attempt to divorce science from values can lead to science that offends someone's values. But this charge cannot be leveled at all who favor mechanistic descriptions of the world. Similarly, accepting as necessary a connection between science and values still leaves open which values are considered. Thus, parallels between particular theoretical positions about the nature of science and larger social questions are themselves both "soft" and "hard." Some are a necessary consequence of theory, others are only possible associations between pairs of systems of thought.

A further parallel between education and research theories concerns the ways that supporters of various traditions describe those who hold opposing views. Debates between experimental design proponents and naturalistic researchers are similar to those between didactic educators and those supporters of constructivist views. From each side, the rhetoric about the other is usually strong and often derogatory. For reasons discussed below, it is also often irrelevant.

The powerful and fundamental ways in which these positions differ from each other is exacerbated by the intensity of this debate. The discussions are qualitatively distinct from arguments that separate, for example, supporters of different views within the same larger perspective; they are not arguments about differences in facts. If people who share a set of concepts disagree – about the prowess of two sports teams, or the relative merits of two types of automobiles – their discussions may use heated language, but they remain within the bounds of a shared enterprise, the acceptance of the structure within which they disagree. Disputants might agree that the outcome of a match between the two teams would be a deciding event, or that the relative repair records of the two cars should be used as evidence.

But debates between supporters of didactic and constructivist education, or supporters of experimental-design and naturalistic evaluation, are of a different order. They are more like debates between people with differing political or social views. The two sides often have fundamentally contrasting views of the way the world is organized, including what constitutes evidence, and opposing positions on beliefs ranging far beyond the topic under discussion. As a consequence, their debates take on a harsher tone: the participants simply talk past each other. Disagreements tend to be carried out at a level where no evidence might be produced that could possibly influence the other opinion, no argument could be persuasive, and no common meeting ground could exist. I do not claim to be neutral in this discussion, but in the section that follows I will attempt to take a step towards broader understanding; to acknowledge that world views, which simultaneously encompass and limit our thoughts, do exist and that different conceptual schemes and forms of argument need to be considered if we wish to understand another's world view.

I will discuss these differences, not in an attempt to resolve them but to illustrate why they exist and to indicate why particular educational philosophies and different research styles are more or less compatible. In both education and research some theories make use of the ladder as their guiding metaphor, while others use the network as their model.

Paradigms and world views

In Chapter 4, I discussed research styles as examples of different *paradigms*, using the term that has been widely applied since Kuhn introduced it in 1962 to describe contrasting explanations in science. A previously obscure word, "paradigm" is now the common term used to acknowledge different approaches to many human enterprises. This broader use of the term follows a concept proposed two decades earlier by Stephen Pepper (1942). Pepper argued that there exist "world hypotheses," or "world theories," basic belief systems that are incompatible with each other, and that are so broad that humans cannot get outside their own world view to find a rational basis for choices between world theories. These theories represent different, fundamental ways of viewing the world. Pepper's ideas have been acknowledged as relevant to socio-cultural educational theory (Rogoff in press) and applied to adult education by Davis (1985).

> there are significantly different theoretical frameworks that have been used to construct answers to the question of how adults learn. These frameworks cannot be explained as transitory phenomena that will be resolved by more research and, eventually, a better theory. Instead, they reflect something fundamental about the learning process itself and about the persons who learn.
>
> (Davis 1985: 8)

In one sense, world hypotheses are like different developmental stages in a Piagetian scheme. The most important difference between a child at a pre-operational and operational stage, two crucial developmental stages for Piaget, is not the different answers each gives to the same questions, but that the individual at the later stage cannot even conceive of giving the previous answer. As an adult who has long ago internalized the concept of conservation of volume, not only do I think that the amount of orange juice stays the same when it is poured from the tall narrow glass into the short wide glass, I can't even imagine that there should be a difference in the volume. In carrying out conservation experiments with children, I have always been impressed most by the fact that once a child achieves the more advanced developmental stage, the question posed by the experimenter becomes trivial, and the responses often include the added comment, "Why would you ask me that?" As Piaget says in discussing the development of the concept of conservation of volume, once children have grasped it they "assume it as a physical and logical necessity" (Piaget 1941/1965: 13). Likewise, we hold our own world views so firmly that propositions that underlie them become logically and emotionally necessary for us and it is beyond our capability to question them.

But developmental schema also share another quality with world views. Although we may reach a particular stage and, in some instances, be blind to our previous mental constructs, in other situations we apply different developmental schemas. For example, I think I have reached the Piagetian hypothetical-deductive stage, I am able to reason abstractly; I don't require concrete objects in sight in order to carry out simple mathematical operations. But if you ask me how many days there are between March 29 and April 3, I still count on my fingers. That particular task just turns out to be easier (more efficient) for me if I do it in one mode rather than in another I am capable of using. Likewise, our world views are complete and encompassing in one sense, but particular, specific circumstances may reveal more fundamental beliefs.

From another perspective, world metaphors are strikingly different from stages. They are not developmental; they are complete and independent, each with its own virtues and limitations. According to Pepper, they are derived from acceptance of distinct "root metaphors" about how the world works. These metaphors are elaborations of "common-sense" conceptions of experiences which, once accepted, cause us to shape further experiences to fit within their overarching structures. Pepper considers four different root metaphors that can lead to viable world hypotheses – mechanism, formism, contextualism, and organicism. Whether his identification of a particular four is correct is less important than his argument that "each world hypothesis is autonomous," and "it is illegitimate to disparage the factual interpretations of one world hypothesis in terms of the categories of another – if both hypotheses are equally adequate" (Pepper 1942: 98).

Another way to consider the relationship between world hypotheses and research (and education) theories is to consider different analogies used to describe them. Traditional educational psychology uses as its model the (presumed) ideal physical science research laboratory; naturalistic research uses as models images such as investigative journalism and other professions that build up evidence from disparate sources. St. John (1991) recently outlined a range of models that have been used to describe research and suggested that these could be considered as metaphors for research in museums.

Each of these metaphors also entails a more or less appropriate educational theory. For example, Eisner (1991) uses criticism and the concept of connoisseurship, one of St. John's metaphors, as a basis for thinking about evaluation. The concept comes, of course, from the arts, where professional activity is usually pursued in naturalistic, qualitative ways, and where learning is often described in holistic terms. It is common for students in the arts to have their work subjected to this particular form of criticism as part of their education, thus why not apply this method to the educational process itself? Eisner makes a plausible case for this view. In contrast, a leading museum researcher describes it as "a second-class form of evaluation, due to its subjectivity," and states that the whole notion of suggesting such metaphors from other fields is not useful. "These metaphors will not recommend themselves to evaluators looking for something more substantial on which to base judgments" (Miles 1993: 27).

Ladders and networks

In a lovely essay on learning theory, David Hawkins (1974) uses as his central image the different behaviors of hungry and well-fed rats in a maze. Hungry rats will follow the behaviorists' expectations; they learn to manipulate the maze and get better at finding the food reward at the end. In short, they display the learning curves we associate with traditional psychological research. Well-fed rats, however, exhibit more complex behavior. They are more likely to wander around, to be more relaxed about their path. Their behavior cannot be easily summarized and described by the behavioral learning theory. The behaviorists' response to these two sets of phenomena was to stipulate that using hungry rats was a necessary condition for studying learning by rats in mazes.

Another version of this critique of traditional behaviorist experimental research as a model for learning theory is offered by Mary Catherine Bateson (1984) in an anecdote attributed to her father. He reports that a psychologist who used ferrets instead of rats and provided rabbit meat as the reward for successfully transversing the maze found that the ferret didn't behave as expected on a second trial and didn't retrace his steps down the passage where he had found the meat previously.

> Gregory [Bateson] had a collection of favorite antibehaviorist or anti-rat-runner stories that he used to tell, most of which emphasized the failure of experimental psychologists to look at context, indeed to look beyond learning at the very lowest logical level. [One story] tells of a rat-runner, more biologically sophisticated than most, who reflected that rats do not in nature live in mazes, and so maze-learning experiments are not testing genuinely adaptive tasks. Instead, the thoughtful rat-runner procured a ferret, for ferrets in nature hunt in rabbit warrens which are much like mazes. He put a fresh haunch of rabbit in the reward chamber and released the ferret. The ferret went through the maze systematically, exploring each blind alley until he reached the reward chamber and ate the haunch of rabbit. The next day, the experimenter started him off again to see how quickly he would learn his way. Again he went systematically down every alley until he came to the one that led to the reward chamber, but he didn't go down that one

– he'd eaten that rabbit. What he learned in the framework of the learning experiment was set in the context of his premises about how the world works.

(Bateson 1984: 170–1)

Ferrets have evolved as a species for whom learning means going to a different place once food has been found; ferret learning involves seeking new rabbit holes. Hungry rats have evolved to learn to retrace their steps once food has been found. Do we know what humans' evolutionary learning modes may include?

These stories illustrate that in order to achieve a simple, linear behavior it's necessary to restrict the subject's conditions for learning. The ladder-like hierarchies proposed by behaviorist educators are not just ideal – they are necessary for their experimental research. If you believe that the results of research can be combined step by step to build up a complete knowledge of the subject you are studying, and that in order to carry out a study you have to isolate one variable while holding all the others constant, then it is not only easier to do this if your model of the subject under investigation is built up of a hierarchy of independent components, it is, in fact, necessary that this be the case. Similarly in research, the study of isolated variables exclusively is worthwhile only if you have confidence that this will lead to a total understanding of the complete system being studied.

Conversely, the notion that all the factors in an environment are interconnected through a network of relationships that has no hierarchical order leaves little alternative for any research on that environment other than a naturalistic approach. If we cannot isolate components and study them separately (without destroying that environment), then it is necessary to study them as an integrated unit. That is exactly what naturalistic research sets out to do.

The best model for experimental-design research in the social sciences is often taken to be Fisher's work in agricultural research, intended to develop sound methods for determining the influence of individual variables, such as rainfall or properties of various fertilizers on growth. Kaplan (1964: 147) calls him "virtually the founder of the self-conscious and explicit design of experiments." Fisher himself, as Shettel (1991) has reminded us, recognized that not all situations are appropriate for the application of statistical tests. As Shettel puts it, "when there is a worm in your corn you do not need tests of statistical significance to prove it."

One challenge to directly applying Fisher's work on plants to educational research is that the method assumes that consideration of individual instances is not required, only a consideration of aggregated results. It doesn't matter, for Fisher's purposes, whether one particular plant in a field did surprisingly well or surprisingly poorly compared to all the other plants. Fisher was not deeply concerned about the health and safety of individual corn stalks, and certainly not about the moral status of over- or under-watering a field of corn.[1]

If Fisher's methods are applied to humans, problems arise not only concerning sample size and the greater variability found in individuals within the species, factors which in themselves can have powerful influences on results,[2] but also with the consequences of treating humans as "experimental" subjects. Intense debates about the use of human subjects in research are often about these fundamentally different conceptions of how to carry out science; strong disagreements arising from irreconcilably different world hypotheses.

The distinction between hierarchical and network conceptions of a subject appear repeatedly in discussions of both educational research and learning. Additional examples are considered in the sections that follow.

Focus on levels

Another way to view the relationship between the different approaches to both educational theory and research is to argue that they describe different levels of interest. There can be no doubt that within any field, whether biology or education, phenomena can be examined at different levels of complexity. But how are these "levels" organized and what is the relationship between them? Are some levels more complex in the sense that they are higher up a ladder in a linear arrangement, or do they represent a different perspective on an interconnected network of relationships?

As an analogy, we can consider biological research. There are different approaches to studying molecular biology and environmental conservation, although this does not necessarily suggest a contradiction between these research styles. If the intention is to elucidate fundamental relationships between molecules of biological interest, the appropriate methodology is likely to be the biochemical equivalent of experimental-design research. However, if complex interactions of a range of species (including human beings) within an environment is the subject, then naturalistic field-based methods may be more appropriate because the factors are simply too many to study separately; because many of the influential components have not been identified; and because the interaction among all the components is itself what is being studied.

Supporters of naturalistic research argue that the study of how visitors learn in museums is not a matter of examining individual variables and determining how each influences learning, but of viewing the entire visit as an interaction between the visitor(s) and the exhibitions that leads to learning. Several recent attempts to comprehend visitor experience in museums and develop theoretical descriptions use network models, not linear, hierarchical ones. McManus (1991) sees the communication system in a museum visit not as linear but as an interactive process where both the exhibition and the visitor contribute to the communication; Falk and Dierking (1992) conceptualize the museum experience as an interaction of personal, social, and physical contexts that need to be considered together. Others develop lists of factors (Hood 1983) that influence visitors' decisions to come to museums, identify several components (Perry 1992), or describe characteristics of successful visits (Roberts 1997), recognizing that these are not arranged in any hierarchy and do not occur sequentially. All contribute uniquely and simultaneously to the total experience.

But there is a more crucial reason for a shift in research methodology from studying single biological entities to examining complex systems. Proponents of holistic views argue that interrelationships between all species and actions that make up a complex system will be altered if broken down into their component parts. It is *necessary* to study the system as a whole to gain an understanding of its complex interactions. For example, when the topic is environmentally appropriate land use, it's not sufficient to understand the interrelationships among the non-human elements of an ecosystem, the human needs, desires, and values also have to be factored in.

The argument for the value of field-based methods and for more holistic approaches to research for certain topics in medicine was made elegantly by Tinbergen (1974) in his Nobel prize acceptance speech:

> a little more open-mindedness . . . a little more collaboration with other biological sciences, and a little more attention to the body as a whole and to the unity of body and mind could substantially enrich the field of medical research.
>
> (Tinbergen 1974: 26)

Application of these research methods – which Tinbergen (1974: 26) called "open-minded observation, 'watching and wondering'" – to museum settings by students of W. Laetsch, an ethologist (Laetsch *et al.* 1980), during the time that he directed the Lawrence Hall of Science, provided a new perspective on the behavior of visitors to museums. By focusing on the entire visit rather than examining visitor behavior primarily in a specific gallery, these studies not only added to our knowledge of visitors but also enlarged that knowledge in a way previous researchers had not considered. These research efforts may have been novel for visitor studies, but the doctoral students simply applied tried-and-true field methods in another research application.

Networks, not hierarchies

In addition to arguments based on complexity and the level of the domain of interest, a further argument can be made for the use of naturalistic approaches. Some people simply don't think that the content of a domain can be arranged linearly. For example, in discussing teaching of science, Hawkins describes the structure of scientific knowledge thus:

> But I should also like to make another claim, an a priori one in relation to the psychology of learning. This has to do with the inherent structural features of the adult world of science into which we propose to induct children. The order of this world is more complex than can be represented by the topology of linear orderings, or even branching trees. It is inherently a network, a network of experimental paths intersecting at knots or nodes of significant conceptualization. We map this network, or try to, into linear orderings when we go marching through the curriculum, the "little racecourse."

85

We ourselves do not know the multiplicity of paths – which is one of the reasons why teaching cannot be separated from the arts and heuristics of discovery. What we do know, from the theory and history of knowledge, is that in exploring and mapping such a domain the fundamental metric is not feet or miles but an informational measure in psychological space, such that a well-trodden path is in principle a short one, and the path always long to what is new. The economy of slowing down, even wandering, lies in the creation of highways.

(Hawkins 1966: 11–12)

Hawkins gives this description in discussing appropriate science teaching. He argues that curriculum needs to consider networks of relationships among topics rather than attempt to develop a hierarchy of material to be taught. The idea of curriculum as a "web" rather than a linear, progressive entity has been discussed repeatedly (Corwin *et al.* 1976).

A parallel use of the ladder–web analogy is provided by Stephen J. Gould in his critique of evolutionary theory. Gould (1996) following Darwin, suggests that the evolution of a group of animals is better represented by the image of a bush with many branches than by a linear chain. He argues that the empirical evidence only supports the view that organisms change through evolution so that they are better adapted to local conditions, not that they get "better" in any absolute sense. The most successful animal families existing today, widely distributed and abundant – bacteria and insects – are not necessarily the most complex, the largest, or the most "intelligent." Gould analyses the evolution of horses – a favourite natural history museum exhibition, "Does any major museum not have a linear series of cases against a long wall, or up the center of the main hall, one skeleton in each, and all illustrating the triumphant trend?" (Gould 1996: 57–8) – to demonstrate that there are many evolutionary paths, leading to a range of recent species, not one "upward" ladder to a single superior one.

We therefore arrive at my favorite subject of ladders versus bushes . . . Evolution rarely proceeds by the transformation of a single population from one stage to the next. Such an evolutionary style, technically called *anagenesis*, would permit a ladder, a chain, or some similar metaphor of linearity to serve as a proper icon of change. Instead, evolution proceeds by an elaborate and complex series of branching events, or episodes of speciation (technically called *cladogenesis*, or branchmaking) . . . The evolutionary bush of horses includes many terminal trips, and each leads back to *Hyracotherium* through a labyrinth of branching events.

(Gould 1996: 62–3)

The specific network metaphor has also been employed to describe learning.

Scientists who study the natural growth of vocabulary knowledge have demonstrated unequivocally that word meanings are never learned [by memorizing dictionary definitions] in normal circumstances. Word meanings are learned from repeated use and from context – from extensive conversations and reading. The meaning of a word is something like a location in a network – a pointer to a web of interconnected implications. Meaning is built; it must be constructed from other meanings that an individual already has. Vocabulary knowledge will not come into existence through memorizing dictionary definitions any more than nourished bodies will come into existence through memorizing recipes.

(Farnham-Diggory 1990: 147–8)

A wonderful example of network-like curriculum development in a museum activity is the description of a process used at the Museum Magnet School (St Paul Minnesota) for exhibit/curriculum development based on objects

> The first object we had to work with was a 3M safety product, the retroreflective tape. They were interested in nighttime visibility issues, but our staff had all sorts of ideas. We were trying to see how we could make connections with the interests that people already had and the interests the kids had . . . We started talking with the kids asking them what made them feel safe and what made them feel afraid . . . They were not very concerned with nighttime visibility. What they were worried about was stray gunfire. Some of them had seen people die . . . Everybody is taking a different aspect. Some people experimented with night vision, other people experimented with animal safety. Some used adaptations which tied in with other themes we were working on. Some people had money from Headsmart, another safety program, so they linked in with that. Violence prevention became a school focus as did bike safety. One of our teacher's friends was a bicyclist who treks all around Africa, so that brought in a whole geography component. It branches, and webs, and the connections become so rich.

(Science Museum of Minnesota 1996: 33)

Hawkins described a view of education theory, not educational research, but the consequence of this view for research is obvious; if there is no simple hierarchy of subject matter, then it does not make sense to study learning by finding out how many have mastered Stage 1, and then Stage 2, etc. If learning is a matter of making connections in a network, then research on this learning must be devised that can ascertain degrees of connections, not knowledge of isolated facts.

Educational programs are commonly analyzed in terms of a hierarchy of thinking skills that they strive to develop. When such a hierarchy is considered, it is also possible to plan the program to first teach lower-level skills, later moving on to higher-order thinking skills. If this conceptualization is accepted, the next step is to develop assessments that will determine the extent to which students have learned each of these skills.

But an alternative approach is to re-conceptualize the definition of thinking and consider it as much more holistic. Champagne (1990) examined the terms typically used to describe thinking skills and attempted to develop hierarchical taxonomies for these skills. Her first effort, Taxonomy A, to divide thinking skills into lower-order and higher-order skills, resulted in one category (lower-order) with no members, and another category with all the skills!

> Taxonomy A's primary division is between higher- and lower-order thinking skills. However, no lower-order skills are in the taxonomy. Candidates for lower-order skills do exist. For instance, concrete operational thinking is a possible candidate. However, the logical structures characteristic of concrete operational thinking are quite complex. Even the performance of relatively simple academic tasks (subtraction with borrowing, for instance) requires complex mental processing . . . As more is learned about the complexity of the so-called lower-order thinking skills, the usefulness of the distinction between higher- and lower-order thinking skills comes into question.
>
> (Champagne 1990: 75)

Other classification schemes proposed in her article provide taxonomies that distinguish between thinking skills that develop naturally and those that develop as a result of formal education and a taxonomy that categorizes thinking skills in terms of how they are used to solve problems and how they might be used in assessment exercises. But all such taxonomies are efforts by a researcher to understand thinking. They are *not* taxonomies that attempt to describe how the skills are hierarchically developed in the learner.

In a similar vein, constructivists argue repeatedly that the process that occurs in education is not hierarchical but is best represented by a dynamic network of interactive components. Consider the following description of constructivist learning that incorporates both the personal and social interactions necessary for the construction of meaning:

> From this perspective, learning is a constructive process of meaning-making that results in reflective abstractions, producing symbols within a medium.
>
> . . . The process can perhaps be represented by a dialectical tripartite [model] . . . The cognizing individual generates possibilities and contradictions when [mental] structures are perturbed. In attempting to represent these reflective abstractions in a medium, to make them conscious and to communicate them to others, further tugs occur. But the process is not linear. Indeed, language is almost too linear a medium to use to describe the transactional nature of the interplay. For "others" are other cognizing individuals, therefore a composite of constantly shifting and evolving ideas – not a static entity but a dynamic one. Further, the cognizing individual is operating with symbols that are derived from past negotiated "taken-as-shared" meanings. Nor is the medium static. While each medium has limits and features that affect the symbols, as humans create within media they push against the limits and formulate new features.
>
> (Fosnot 1996a: 27–8)

Researchers who consider learning a socio-cultural process, rather than a combination of individual factors that each contribute to learning, reach similar conclusions. Rogoff (1998) describes socio-cultural theories regarding cognition as "a collaborative process."

> In socio-cultural theories, individuals' cognitive development is regarded as inherently involved with the socio-cultural activities in which they engage with others in cultural practices and institutions, in a mutually constituting relationship.
>
> (Rogoff 1998)

Rogoff (1995) also argues that the distinction between learning and teaching as separate sides of an equation, or domains that can be separated, is incorrect. Learning and teaching need to be considered as parts of a whole; the entire concept of a boundary between the individual who learns and the material to be learned, whether the source is from the external world or from some internal transformation, is too narrow. The process needs to be considered as a holistic enterprise, involving the community of learners and their shared meanings.

Analysis and synthesis

The assertion that learning involves access to a network, rather than a hierarchical building up of knowledge, not only has implications for research on how people learn but also raises questions about any analytic scheme that intends to describe a subject. Even if learning is a complex, social activity, it is still possible to develop structures of *subjects*; the world is full of textbooks that describe various fields of knowledge, both practical and theoretical, using some form of rational organization. It is impossible to talk about physics or gardening, about learning to read or teaching voice, without organizing the essential components into some order. Even naturalistic research often leads to taxonomies, to ordering of the subject studied into categories. Claims about the holistic nature of a learning experience don't preclude such analytic schemes; they only challenge the ontological status of these schemes. The issue is defining the relationship between any scheme that provides an outline of a subject and the subject itself. Is the taxonomy a convenient way of dividing the subject, so it can be described and compartmentalized for discussion, or is it a description of a property of the *subject itself*? In terms of the diagram presented in Figure 2.4, is the structure of the subject something that is inherent in the subject, does it exist in the domain represented in the top half of the diagram (realism) or is it a construction made in the minds of humans – a convenience for discussion and comprehension?

When a physics text divides the subject matter of physics into mechanics, light, heat, etc., does the text reflect a natural division of the subject based on its fundamental properties in the world, or does it reflect a human structure imposed on the world with the intention of making it intelligible to students? A newspaper article informs us that

> Today, Al-Serai Palace in Baghdad, once the seat of the Ottoman
> Turkish governor, now contains a museum devoted to the country's

reconstruction effort. Models of every major industrial complex bombed by the allies show the damage inflicted and how it has been repaired.

(*New York Times* 1993: 1)

Does the exhibition of how the Iraqi forces valiantly rebuilt their country after air raids represent what actually exists, or is it a particular interpretation constructed by the curators?

The distinction is important because it influences pedagogy and then research on what students have learned. If the structure of a subject reflects its component parts, then there is good reason to teach the subject according to that structure; if that structure is only a convenience of organization, it may or may not represent the easiest source of access for a learner. An analytic scheme that may have great utility for professional practitioners of a subject may not be the most appropriate basis for teaching a novice about the subject.

An analogy from chemistry is relevant. Chemists use three different types of experimental structuring schemes to understand the structure of organic compounds. First, there are *analytic* schemes, both intellectual and practical methods for understanding the composition of matter. If I want to analyze a chemical compound, there are standard ways of breaking it down into its component parts and determining unequivocally the nature and amount of all the components. Such analytic schemes stress the necessity of accounting for all the components and being able to distinguish between possible different structural elements.

A second set of schemes are *synthetic* methods, ways of creating compounds in the laboratory. Synthetic and analytic methods gain validity from their complementarity. Confidence in an analytic scheme is reinforced if the component parts can be demonstrated to make up the synthesized compound in the amounts predicted. But methods used for synthesis are qualitatively different from those used for analysis. For instance, in analytic work, it's important to have a precise measure of the amount you start with; in synthetic work, the important measure is the amount of product produced, and that sometimes can be accomplished by using large amounts of some starting material.

Classic chemical synthesis, although dramatically different from analysis, uses test-tube methods more energetic than could be tolerated by living organisms. It was of limited applicability in creating complex biochemical molecules. In the 1920s a new approach was developed to build up biologically important molecules under conditions that could exist in nature. Chemists found to their amazement that by combining the appropriate ingredients under ambient conditions in aqueous solutions that resembled biological situations, they could build up more complex molecules from simpler ones! The field of *biosynthesis*, the construction of biologically active molecules under biological survival conditions, has allowed the ingenious synthesis of complex molecules and is now a major activity in research laboratories and at drug companies.

The point of this story is that even a complete analytic description of a chemical compound may have little relationship to how it could be synthesized, and even synthetic schemes, although successful in the laboratory, may differ from how compounds are constructed in nature. Similarly, our analysis of a subject may indeed yield a complete description of all its components, but it does not necessarily follow that this analytic scheme bears any resemblance to a reasonable way of reconstructing, that is teaching (or learning), that subject. Gagné's analytic schemes for complex concepts (see Figures 2.5 and 2.6) may describe all the components but may not relate to how these concepts are learned.

In pedagogy, it is important to distinguish what is in a teacher's mind (what structure of the subject the teacher uses as a guide for her actions), how the subject is presented to the students, and what is in the minds of the students. The constant balance between the students' perceptions of a field and the (hopefully) more organized understanding in the mind of a teacher is what makes teaching both difficult and exciting. I can hold in my head a whole set of phenomena that I think are pedagogically useful, a variety of conceptual maps that I have found provide opportunities for students to expand their own understanding, or a handy checklist of explanatory schemes that have helped students progress in the past, without attributing to any of these an existence in the external world. It is thrilling when one of these models helps a student; it is frustrating when I find that the approach I have taken doesn't help. The danger for education occurs when I try to force the student to accept my model, example, or organizational scheme as the only possible one.

A parallel error in developing pedagogy is to assume that an appropriate way to analyze a subject for instructional purposes is to look to the history of the development of a discipline as a guide. Science education, for example, is full of pedagogic schemes that seem to have little to recommend them except their historic significance. Children are expected to swing pendulums in order to "discover" the relationship between the length of the string and the period, and for decades it was common in elementary classrooms to urge teachers to burn mercuric oxide in an open test tube as a way to demonstrate production of oxygen and mercury vapor because Lavoisier discovered oxygen with this experiment.

The application of analytic schemes to instruction

Gagné developed hierarchical subject schemes to provide a basis for instruction. His efforts represent a noble attempt to apply the concept that subject matter is composed of hierarchical arrays of components and that a theory of teaching requires that subject matter be broken down into its component parts. His schemes illustrate the enormous task required to carry this out. Few educators have endeavored to duplicate this effort, not, I suspect, because they fundamentally disagree with the concept, but because it is so difficult to do.

For proponents of Gagné's learning hierarchies, there can be no question about the appropriate research or evaluation strategy for studying learning. Education is successful if the students learn the material, and, since learning is defined as hierarchical and structured, that is the way to organize the evaluation of it.

Many educational goals in museum exhibits and programs focus on simple concrete "outcomes" for visitors. These are chosen from a much larger domain because they appear to be attainable in a short time with a limited exposure, follow directly from the exhibits and their objects, or, simply, because they can be framed in the language of educational objectives. By choosing such specific goals, staff implicitly accept the structured conception of curriculum and learning and simultaneously dictate the range of research methods that might be applicable for evaluating the exhibition or program.

In many instances the analytic approach to subject matter may have become so commonly accepted that its behaviorist origins may no longer be evident. Such is the case for the common distinction between "affective" and "cognitive" factors. As McManus (1993a) has pointed out, the distinction arises from efforts to describe all learning using hierarchies. In developing these taxonomies Bloom and his committee accepted behaviorist views of learning. They describe the hierarchical nature of their taxonomy as follows:

> Our attempt to arrange educational behaviors from simple to complex was based on the idea that a particular simple behavior may become integrated with other equally simple behaviors to form a more complex behavior. Thus, our classifications may be said to be in the form where behaviors of type A form one class, behaviors of type AB form another class, while behaviors of type ABC form still another class.
>
> (Bloom 1956: 18)

The legacy of behaviorist thinking in education is deeply rooted in both schools and museum education. Fifty years of dominance in schools of education has left its mark. Discussing the influence of Edward Thorndike (1874–1949), a leading proponent of behaviorism (he is the author of the often quoted phrase, "Whatever exists, exists in some amount. To measure it is simply to know its varying amounts"), Sylvia Farnham-Diggory (1990), states

> By 1940, when Thorndike retired, nearly one teacher in ten in the United States had attended Teachers College. More than two out of every ten big city superintendents had been trained there, as had nearly three out of every ten deans of colleges of education. Instructional practice as we know it today preserves, in more sophisticated and elaborate forms, the fundamental principles that Edward Thorndike invented some seventy years ago . . . Thus, the schoolchild of the late twentieth century is but a very small cog in an enormously complex educational machine that continues to justify itself primarily in terms of early twentieth-century theoretical concepts. What can a child do other than learn to fit in, to become a proper bureaucrat?
>
> (Farnham-Diggory 1990: 27–8)

The distinction between analytic and holistic research is illustrated by a recent report of a novel method used to elicit descriptions of suspects from eye witnesses in criminal cases. Traditionally, witnesses have been asked to look at hundreds of drawings of individual parts of faces, eyes, ears, noses, lips, etc.

An artist then draws a face that is a composite of all the witness-identified details. An alternative approach, apparently used with remarkable success by Jeanne Boylan, an American psychologist, is more indirect. According to a news report

> She sits down with witnesses, without distractions, for as long as it takes to win their trust. Instead of talking about the crime or the suspect she talks about anything but – "anything that elicits positive responses" – from hobbies to the weather. Eventually, often in the last hour of the interview, she asks abstract questions about texture and shape.
>
> (Whittel 1996: 13)

Framing behavioral objectives for an educational goal of an exhibition is to accept a particular definition of education, based on an assimilation model of learning and on acceptance of specific outcomes for learners. Within the context of school curriculum, there is some justification for accepting such outcomes, even if the psychological analysis of how people learn is questioned. "I don't care how they learn it, but in order to pass this course they need to know the dates of the Civil War, or they need to know Newton's first law." Such assertions from school educators can be defended as appropriate outcomes for a system that provides credentials asserting that students have mastered certain facts as well as certain concepts. But when museum staffs adopt behavioral objectives they are accepting restrictions that are not necessarily the most appropriate for developing museum educational programs. The conclusion that visitors learn very little of the "content" of exhibitions, a frequent outcome from assessments of museum educational programs using behavioral objectives as guides for both instruction and assessment, should serve as a warning to museum staff. If learning of this type is so difficult to accomplish, maybe it's the wrong outcome to expect from a museum visit.

As the authors of the *Museum Impact and Evaluation Study* report state:

> Visitors often reported not learning anything new at exhibits they particularly enjoyed. Upon further probing and analysis, however, it appears that visitors did in fact come away with new information. Often this information was not central to the main idea or theme of the exhibit, but still contributed to a basic understanding of the scientific concept.
>
> (Anderson and Roe 1993 vol. 2: 27)

The Piagetian perspective

When Piaget first began working with children, he served as an assistant to Simon, one of the developers of the first modern intelligence tests, in standardizing these tests. Piaget soon realized the following:

> Now from the very first questionings I noticed that though Burt's [reasoning] tests certainly had their diagnostic merits, based on the number of successes and failures, it was much more interesting to try

to find the reasons for the failures. Thus I engaged my subjects in conversations patterned after psychiatric questioning, with the aim of discovering something about the reasoning process underlying their right, but especially their wrong answers.

(Evans 1973: 118–19)

The methods he developed to study this interesting problem were, of necessity, naturalistic ones. He adopted the clinical interview of the psychotherapist, later adding the manipulation of materials to this approach, and then analyzed these individual records in order to reach conclusions.

Perhaps the most lasting legacy of his work is that the more than sixty book-length research publications Piaget and his collaborators wrote always retained the naturalistic style that he developed and that dominated his work. Piaget's books are often described as hard to read. One reason may be that the general summary and broad generalizations we expect from research publications are hard to pull out of the texts. The pages are dominated by countless quotations from original data. The reader is required to absorb page after page of quotations on each point, illustrating how children of various ages respond to interview questions or probes with materials. Only after reading confident, simple but non-canonical answers of younger children; confused, self-contradictory and awkward responses of children in some transition stage; and familiar "adult" common-sense responses of the oldest children, does the reader understand what is meant by a stage transformation and the process of "equilibration" as the child "accommodates" to a new "schema." The technical terms gain their meaning directly from the qualitative data. It is impossible to imagine the Piagetian approach described in any other way.

Roschelle (1995) recently stated that

Piaget influenced educators not only by his theory but also by his method. He spent long hours coming to know children's modes of thinking (using the clinical interview) . . . After Piaget we must assume that children will make sense of experience using their own schemata. Yet we also must carefully interview children, seeking an understanding of their form of coherence. Most followers of Piaget are constructivists who cultivate a deep appreciation of children's sense-making, and they design interactive experiences accordingly.

(Roschelle 1995: 44)

Piaget describes the development of the concept of volume in a chapter that, typical for his reports, consists of transcripts of clinical interviews with children for approximately one-third of its 21 pages. The argument that stages of development exist and that these lead to the concept of conservation of volume is not supported by tables, statistical analyses, or numerical evidence but by individual interviews reprinted at length. The excerpts below are only two partial quotations, from 23 transcript extracts provided in the chapter. The first describes Blas, age 4;0 (four years and no months,) comparing amounts (volumes) when "juice is poured from large glasses of equal volume (A_1 and A_2)

into smaller, similar glasses, (B_1, B_2, B_3 and B_4). The second describes Edi age 6;4 (six years and four months) trying to pour equal amounts of liquid into two containers one tall and thin, the other wider.

> Blas (4;0). 'Have you a friend? – *Yes, Odette.* – Well look, we're giving you, Clairette, a glass of orangeade (A_1, 3/4 full), and we're giving Odette a glass of lemonade (A_2, also 3/4 full). Has one of you more to drink than the other? – *The same.* – This is what Clairette does: she pours her drink into two other glasses (B_1 and B_2, which are thus half filled). Has Clairette the same amount as Odette? – *Odette has more.* – Why? – *Because we've put less in* (She points to the levels in B_1 and B_2, without taking into account the fact that there were two glasses). – (Odette's drink was then poured into B_3 and B_4). *It's the same* – And now (pouring Clairette's drink from B_1 + B_2 into L, a long thin tube, which is then almost full)? – *I've got more* – Why? – *We've poured it into that glass* (pointing to the level in L) *and here* (B_3 *and* B_4) *we haven't* – But were they the same before? – *Yes* – And now? – *I've got more.*'
>
> (Piaget 1941/1965: 6)

> Edi (6;4). Glass A was 1/5 filled. 'Pour as much orangeade into this one (L) as there is there (A). – (He filled L to the same level as that in A). – Is there the same amount to drink? – *Yes.* – Exactly the same? – *No.* – Why not? – *This one* (A) *is bigger.* – What must you do to have the same amount? – *Put some more in* (filling L). – Is that right? – *No?* – Who has more? – *Me* (pouring some back). – No, the other one has more (A). – (He continues to add more and then pour some back, without reaching a satisfactory conclusion).'
>
> (Piaget 1941/1965: 15–16)

But this very method is not acceptable in traditional experimental-design research. Hence, the kind of criticisms that were leveled at Piaget by behaviorists. Even a sympathetic critic wrote:

> It is evident that Piaget's latest work will not silence his critics altogether. He still does not pay much attention to questions of sampling. Some projects, e.g., Inhelder's on adolescents, seem to have used a large part of the school population of Geneva. The data on the sensori-motor period, on the other hand, came mainly from observation of Piaget's own three children, hardly the children of the Average Man! ... Except for some means and mean deviations in his reports of perceptual experiments, he provides few statistics. There are generally no measures of variance, which one suspects must be considerable, no tests of significance, just a categorical statement that at such and such an age children do such and such, with a few specific illustrations. He is not much affected by the growing vogue for rigorous theories, with precise statement of assumptions, derivation of predictions and operational definition of concepts.
>
> (Berlyne 1957: 11)

Berlyne points out that 25 years before, a more severe critic (Pratt 1933) had described Piaget's work as "subjective approaches to the analysis of child behavior . . . little removed from ordinary literary speculation."[3]

Piaget did not conclude that qualitative differences in developmental levels existed from statistically significant correlations. He did not code each response and then compare the instances of particular responses with the ages of the children interviewed. Instead, his conclusions represent his understanding of the *qualitative* differences in the answers. The method used and the results arrived at are inseparable, and both represent a particular world view – both about the nature of learning and about the way to do research.

Reading followers of Piaget usually involves immersion in a similar style of writing. Duckworth (1987), who studied with Piaget and served as his translator on some of his visits to the United States, uses the same density of quotations from her students' work or her notes to build up her arguments.

In contrast, consider again the alternative explanation of the development of the concept of conservation of volume proposed by Gagné, illustrated in Figure 2.5. Gagné's educational model postulates a series of concepts, each layered above the one below, which are (which *must be*) learned in sequence in order to achieve the concept of the conservation of volume. The various rectangles in Figure 2.5 do not differ from each other qualitatively; they represent the sum of the concepts that build up to them.

Practical inquiry

In previous chapters we have discussed the distinction between research and evaluation, between the formal activities carried out principally by academics that are intended to increase our fundamental understanding of human behavior, and the practical work, primarily carried out by museum staff, intended to improve exhibits. Although there is no requirement that the former be primarily experimental design research and the latter follow naturalistic inquiry approaches, such often turns out to be the case.

Visitor studies in museums is carried out in every conceivable way from very informal, casual observations of visitors by staff to structured, elaborate research projects involving multiple institutions devoting significant sums to multi-year projects. Some writers (see Cochran-Smith and Lytle 1990, 1993) have argued that naturalistic methods are particularly useful, and indeed, are more appropriate for "practical inquiry" – action research carried out by practitioners – than are experimental design methods.

In discussing practical inquiry as an activity that is appropriate for teachers who desire to improve their own practice, a situation comparable to that of museum staff making an effort to improve the educational value of their own exhibits, Richardson (1994) states

> There is no formal research methodology associated with practical
> inquiry, although recent acceptance of qualitative research has

accompanied an increased interest in and advocacy of practical inquiry. The telling of narrative and story, dialogical conversations about practice, and writing of journals have been advocated for this type of inquiry . . . Another example of practical inquiry is the maintenance of extensive records on observations of student progress by teachers . . . Practical inquiry, then, is not conducted for purposes of developing general laws related to educational practice, and is not meant to provide *the* answer to a problem. Instead, the results are suggestive of new ways of looking at the context and problem and/or possibilities for changes in practice.

(Richardson 1994: 7)

Most of the research carried out by teachers on their own activities with the intention of improving practice is, in fact, naturalistic and the conditions under which it is carried out, the types of research questions addressed, and the uses to which it is put, usually make naturalistic approaches more appropriate. Practical inquiry usually occurs under conditions in which random selection of subjects and strict control of experimental conditions are not only impossible but also not desirable, and the outcome is intended to help the practitioner in that particular situation. Whether the results can be generalized to all class-rooms or all exhibits is irrelevant. Hooper-Greenhill and collaborators in the Museum Education Evaluation Project at the Department of Museum Studies, University of Leicester have recently carried out such a practical inquiry in visitor studies using primarily naturalistic methods (Hooper-Greenhill 1996).

If we believe that knowledge is context dependent, and if we desire that an inquiry be useful to inform day-to-day practice, then our notion of what kinds of inferences should be drawn from observations and experiments of any kind may shift towards those resulting from practical inquiry rather than those resulting from experimental design research. House *et al.* (1989) consider the kinds of conclusions that can be drawn from evaluation studies and argue that we need more studies where

the practitioner draws inferences based on his or her own experience and applies it in context. [This] is more important than [other kinds of inferences] as far as the conduct and improvement of professional practice are concerned . . . The differences between causal inferences in formal research studies and practitioner inferences may be deep ones. Researchers usually express their findings as propositions we test . . . By contrast much of the knowledge of practitioners is tacit rather than propositional in form, elicited only when practitioners face a particular problem. In fact, practitioners often cannot state what they know in propositional form. Nevertheless, it is the validity of their causal knowledge that is critical for professional practices like teaching.

(House *et al.* 1989: 15)

The authors go on to argue for the need to understand practitioners' inferences better and to develop better methods of describing the kinds of inferences that come from practice as we develop better formal research models. The practitioner inferences are going to arise from various forms of naturalistic inquiry.

Eclecticism in practice

In the preceding discussion I have tried to develop some conceptual clarity about theoretical positions. It is important to know the origins of our ideas, and the consequences of what they imply. But theoretical purity does not necessarily translate into coherent practice. As Pepper (1942: 330) advocates, we need "rational clarity in theory and reasonable eclecticism in practice."

A common practice in schools and museums is a half-hearted acceptance of the idea that teaching consists of taking an analytic scheme and reversing it for learning. Educators and museum staff develop "educational objectives," specific outcomes for lessons, and then assess whether these have been met at the end of the session or program. But in the course of their day-to-day teaching, they may stray far from the direct instruction methods intended to impart the specific objectives to students. Teachers may pause to comfort a child, listen to a personal story, or skip an idea to capitalize on a child's immediate interest. Museum educators may delicately avoid a potentially controversial question, stray from the topic to deal with a specially troublesome student, or modify their plan after realizing that the some background knowledge had been erroneously assumed.

Nor can we expect any of us to consistently follow one world view or another. I believe quite fervently in using constructivism as the basis for all my educational work, and make a great effort to develop teaching opportunities that allow me to do this. I also know that this approach was not how I taught my children to cross the busy street in front of our house. I used quite basic transmission–absorption, behaviorist methods, with adverse conditioning and rewards to train them to learn the behavior I had decided was most beneficial for them!

The use of behavioral objectives may also be appropriate for other reasons, including that they may be required by administrators. More likely our intention may be to teach very specific content, or, in research, to obtain clearly defined answers to questions about behavior. The analytic mode allows us to perform certain kinds of research efficiently. Tracking studies are used by almost all researchers in museums. What is important to remember is that any form of practice is limited in its application and its possible outcomes.

Research and politics

The previous discussion suggested that positions on intellectual issues also reflect social political views. There are certainly political *implications* associated with intellectual positions. Arguments about appropriate educational theories and legitimate research methods necessarily imply views about social issues. A belief that all children can learn is more compatible with a constructivist view of learning than it is with a didactic one that assumes knowledge has an existence independent of the learner and learners are passive recipients of that knowledge. The traditional view, with its focus on possible deficiencies of the learner, easily accommodates notions of the hereditary properties of intelligence, the need to restrict access to complex curriculum for some learners, and a focus on "lower-level" skill acquisition by specific students. Conversely, the acceptance of the idea that all learners construct meaning and that all knowledge builds on the conceptions already in the minds of learners (if it is coupled with a belief that all humans do acquire such experiences) will focus more on universal educability and the value of what people already know.

The connection between qualitative research and political issues is not always greeted with enthusiasm. For example Cizek (1995) complains

> it seems to me that qualitative research has become inextricably linked with sociopolitical causes: feminist pedagogy, multiculturalism, ecosensitivity, human rights, lab-animal welfare, gay/lesbian advocacy, socialist politics, organic gardening, liberation theology, low cholesterol high fiber crunchy granola diets, and so on.
>
> (Cizek 1995: 27)

Intemperate remarks are not confined to one side of the issue, and experimental-design researchers and, especially, behaviorists, have been accused of racism, sexism and xenophobia. Unfortunately, the attempts to "measure" human qualities have been associated with horrendous views. The high minded effort to recognize the abilities of children classified as mentally deficient through IQ testing were converted into restrictive, social-Darwinist views by leading psychologists (see Gould 1981) and, as discussed above, the behaviorist museum studies of the 1920s and 1930s incorporated the then prevalent views about inherited intelligence. In the museum world, Louis Agassiz, the founder of the Harvard Museum of Comparative Zoology, was also a vocal and outspoken racist.

Association between preferences for educational theory and research approaches and political views is inevitable if we accept the concept of world hypotheses, the idea that our entire approach to viewing the world is influenced by the root metaphors that guide our construction of reality. We can only strive to recognize our own limitations and recognize the possibility that others may see the world differently.

6

Studying visitors

But the crucial question [about any logic of research] concerns, not the intrinsic virtues of the reconstructed logic taken in itself, but rather its usefulness in illuminating logic-in-use. There is a story of a drunkard searching under a lamp for his house key, which he dropped some distance away. Asked why he didn't look where he dropped it, he replied, "It's lighter here!" Much effort, not only in the logic of behavioral science, but in behavioral science itself, is vitiated, in my opinion, by the principle of the drunkard's search.

(Kaplan 1964: 11)

The drunkard's search is relevant here; the pattern of search, we feel, should be closely related to the probability of the thing sought being in the place where the seeker is looking. But the joke may be on us. It may be sensible to look first in an unlikely place just because "it's light there" . . . The optimal pattern of search does not simply mirror the pattern of probability density of what we seek.

(Kaplan 1964: 17–18)

Introduction

Kaplan's imaginative interpretation of the familiar story of the drunkard looking for his keys reminds us that what is considered appropriate methodology depends on our perspective. What method is most likely to give valid and reliable data? This is not a simple technical question but a profound one and, like all profound questions, the answer is not simple, it depends on other components of our belief system – it depends on our world view.

In this chapter, I will examine the broad spectrum of methods that have been used for visitor studies, describe examples of each, illustrate the kind of information we can obtain about museum visitors from them, and indicate how they match with different approaches to research and evaluation.

Visitor studies are carried out because we are interested in finding out what visitors think and how they feel about their visits. The actual empirical work of visitor studies has to be limited to a study of human *behavior* (including speech). No matter how much we wish to ascribe meaning to this behavior, and no matter how much we may believe that the significant action takes place in the mind, we must still begin with what people actually *do* and *say*. Whether more quantitatively or qualitatively inclined, all researchers and evaluators are limited by what they can actually "see" (or "hear" or "feel") about others, and the only attributes that are directly available to us are people's behavior, or changes in that behavior.

Differences in the attitude toward that observable behavior distinguish the various research paradigms. On the whole, quantitative researchers are more likely to analyze and classify the behavior itself. They use concepts and language that remain closely related to observed behavior and generalize about levels of behavior. Thus, they are likely to focus on those properties that can be quantified, carefully defined, and used to generalize.

Advocates of behaviorism avoid terms that cannot be directly translated into behavioral characteristics. Thus, the research uses action verbs, with the implicit assumption that each term corresponds to observable behavior. Educators have tried to follow guidelines such as those developed by Mager (1975) in planning educational objectives. Unfortunately, as generations of proponents and critics alike have noted, meaning is complex and one person's observable, objective behavior turns out to be another person's assumption about an unobservable state of mind.

Naturalistic researchers, in contrast, are interested in the meaning behind a behavior and in explanations that provide a description of the behavior within a theoretical scheme. They do not limit themselves to schemes where all the components can be linked to the same causal chain. Consequently, qualitative researchers are more likely to cast a wide net in looking at behavior, to examine activities that may not be easily quantified or totally specified, but which they believe can provide some insight into the meaning a subject makes of his or her experience.

Considered as a whole, the range of methods available to look at human activity is as wide as human ingenuity will allow; that is, it encompasses a broad range of tools, probes, and indicators for recording what people do.

All methods fall into three broad categories:

- observing what people do;
- taking advantage of the amazing human property of speech – either talking with people about their activity or asking them to write about it;
- examining some product of human activity. For example, an early review of visitor studies is called "Noseprints on the Glass" (Anderson 1968, quoting Webb *et al.* 1966).

Each of these broad categories will be described and illustrated in turn.

Observation methods

Tracking and timing

Robinson and Melton's work, discussed previously (see pp. 47–9), provides the pioneering studies of how to observe visitors in museums. They began the tradition of *spatial tracking*, recording the movement of visitors on a rough floor plan of a gallery. This procedure has been carried out thousands of times since. Figure 6.1 is an example of a visitor route through a gallery from Melton's work. A more recent visitor tracking data sheet from an evaluation of an exhibition at Boston's Museum of Science, Figure 6.2, shows the selective way a family group viewed an exhibition.

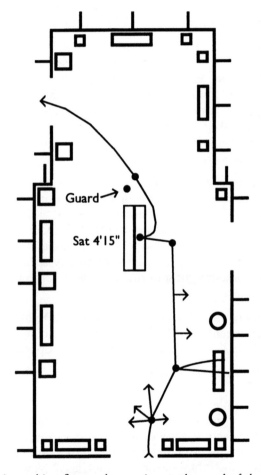

Figure 6.1 Melton's tracking figure: the routing card record of the behavior of a visitor in the French Gallery. *Source:* After Melton 1935/1988. Reprinted with permission from *Problems of Installation in Museums of Art* by Arthur W. Melton. Copyright 1935, 1988, 1996 by the American Association of Museums. All rights reserved.

Observer: Maureen   Date: 11 / 29 / 91   Time In: ___3_ : _17_
                                             Time Out: _3_ : _25_
Exhibit : Two of Every Kind   Total Time: ___8___ min.

Sex: M F (Mix)   Age: < 6 (7-10) (11-14) 15-18 19-24 (25-32) (33-45) > 45

Group Size: ___5___   Group Type: (Kids) (Adults) Mixed   Ages: _____

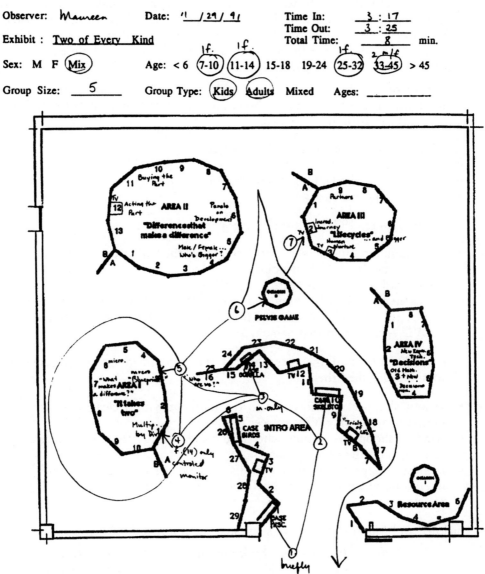

⑤ youngest f. (7) wanted to view micro, so all stopped

6 m. touched pelvic bones; while f. (33-45) lked. at same display but watched "lacred. Journ
    fr. same spot. (2 min.) (♯7)

Figure 6.2 Museum of Science tracking, *Two of Every Sort*

Traditional tracking Tracking studies, the backbone of many museum visitor studies for decades, established that visitors follow individual paths, that most visitors spend very little time in front of individual objects, that almost all visitors stop at only a fraction of objects on display, and that after about 15–20 minutes of viewing, all but the most dedicated visitors become fatigued and stop less frequently or terminate their visits.

A variety of metaphors have been used to describe visitors' paths through exhibitions. The earliest known observation of visitors in a museum (Higgins 1884: 186) categorized visitors as:

- students (i.e. serious visitors) 1–2 per cent;
- observers, about 78 percent;
- loungers, including children, about 20 per cent;
- emigrants (no number given).

Wolf and Tymitz (1978b: 10–11) categorize visitors as:

- the commuter – the person who merely uses the hall as a vehicle to get from the entry point to the exit point;
- the nomad – the casual visitor;
- the cafeteria type – the interested visitor who treats the entire museum like a cafeteria as he or she searches for objects or exhibitions of interest;
- the VIP – very interested person.

Falk (1982: 12) used the metaphor of the department store to categorize visitors. He classified them as

- serious shoppers – who come to the museum with a clear, predetermined notion of what they want to see;
- window shoppers – people who have come "to do" the museum, and who can turn into the next group;
- impulse shoppers – visitors who discover one or more exhibits sufficiently interesting to them and become more engaged with exhibits than they had planned.

Bicknell and Mann (1993) have suggested the following four categories

> The "buffs" – the experts who know the location of every rivet on the Spitfire. They are often male, usually adult, often solitary visitors . . .
>
> "It's for the children" – usually families with children of ages four to fourteen, who implicitly or explicitly are a "learning unit." . . .
>
> "I'm museuming" – often couples, often tourists, often older. Culture-vultures who know the international museum code, they tend to systematically work their way through the museum.
>
> School visits – in the UK these group visits are usually related to the national curriculum and range in age from five to seventeen.
>
> (Bicknell and Mann 1993: 94)

A French tracking study in a natural history museum (Veron and Lavasseur 1989) classified visitors into the following categories:

- ants, who moved methodically from object to object;
- butterflies, who moved back and forth among the exhibits, alighting on some displays;
- grasshoppers, who chose specific objects and "hopped" from one to another;
- fish, who glided in and out of the exhibition with few stops.

The common characteristic of all these attempts to categorize visitors by observing their paths through exhibitions is that exhibition visitation is a highly individual activity.

Some visitors arrive at a gallery, take one quick look around and then leave. Evaluators sometimes leave out these groups and only track or time those visitors who stay longer than 30 seconds. The extent to which this in-and-out behavior is characteristic of all museum visits is open to debate. It is frequent in large museums with many galleries from which to chose. Large museums also are the venues for almost all published visitor studies. Small museums, which constitute the bulk of the world's museums – although not the majority of museum visits – may have different visitor tracking patterns. When there is only one gallery or one setting and the museum or historic site is removed from a city center, in-and-out visitors are less likely.

Some observers restrict observations to single visitors, obviously the easiest to track, but unfortunately only a small minority of visitors. Others track visiting groups as one unit, or track one member of a visiting group. On the whole, "family" groups, i.e. groups of approximately 2–5 people who come to a museum as a unit and not part of a larger group such as a school class or an organized tour, tend to stay together and move through galleries roughly as a unit.

Classifying visitors into categories is characteristic of methods that focus on generalizing and providing quantitative, comparable data. If the focus is on providing access to each visitor, such classifications may be less useful than detailed descriptions of individual paths, or the behavior of small groups. The Higgins (1884) study mentioned previously (p. 42) provided a powerful example of a category of visitor which did not otherwise fit the general pattern. Individuals who follow idiosyncratic paths for personal meaning making are observed frequently. In our small sample of visitors who were asked to "think aloud" at Boston's Museum of Science, we found one who toured an exhibit labeled "Cells" was focused on finding information about AIDS. An art teacher guiding a group of college-age, art education majors to the Museum of Fine Arts noted one who refused to enter a gallery of nineteenth-century portraits; she was overwhelmed by memories of a frightening childhood experience when she was required to sleep in a room full of such faces. My own visits to museums often include limited paths that lead to a favorite painting or object, and ignore most of the museum's content.

Visitor time in galleries Besides providing evidence for visitors' actual paths through a museum and through individual galleries, tracking studies also provide information on the time visitors spend in a museum. One early distinction derived from this work, and still used, is the definition of the *attracting power* and *holding power* of an individual exhibit item, a set of exhibits, or an entire museum.

Figure 6.3 from Melton's early work, shows a typical plot of visitor time in a gallery. As indicated earlier, the time scale is not long. Tracking studies give quantitative data and lend themselves to statistical analysis of various sorts. A common characteristic, recorded in many studies, is *average* visitor time in a gallery. This information is useful to compare the results of a change in a gallery – for example, whether people, on average, stay longer if labels are altered, exhibits are rearranged, or other modifications are made. But the valid statistical manipulations possible from this data are limited because, as most researchers recognize, the distribution of visitors over time is not symmetrical; it does not follow a normal distribution. Some have argued that visitor time in a gallery can be described by a bimodal distribution, with a set of short-time visitors and another set of long-time visitors, corresponding to the "uninterested" and the more "interested" visitors, to use Melton's terminology (Melton 1935/1988: 16). Although some data does appear to approximate this pattern, the fit to a bimodal distribution usually is only approximate at best. More commonly, visitor time drops off quite rapidly, and a small, decreasing percentage of visitors remain for longer periods. This can be neatly represented by "visitor survival" curves which plot the fraction of visitors remaining after a given time. Menninger (1990) was among the first to present data in this form and they have

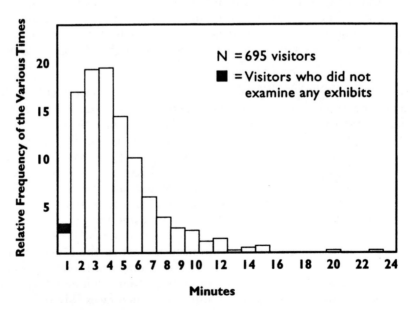

Figure 6.3 Time spent in the gallery
Source: After Melton 1935/1988.

been used extensively by Bicknell (Bicknell and Mann 1993, Bicknell 1995). Some typical visitor survival curves are illustrated in Figure 6.4. Visitor survival curves can be used to calculate a visitor "half-life": the time when half the visitors have left the gallery. Half-lives ranging from a few minutes to almost forty minutes are illustrated in Figure 6.4.

Serrell (1993) has summarized a large number of tracking and timing studies in support of her proposal that a "successful" exhibition be defined as one in which:

- Visitors move through the exhibition at a rate of less than 3,000 sq. ft. per minute.
- 51 per cent of the visitors stop to attend at least 51 per cent of the exhibits.
- Visitors can correctly quote or recall specific facts, attitudes or concepts related to the exhibition elements or the exhibition's objectives.

More recently Serrell (1995) has further quantified the first element to specify that 51 per cent of visitors move at or below this rate and has modified the third element to read

> Can 51% of a random sample of cued visitors, immediately after viewing the exhibition, express general and specific attitudes or concepts that are related to the exhibition's objectives?

(Serrell 1995: 8)

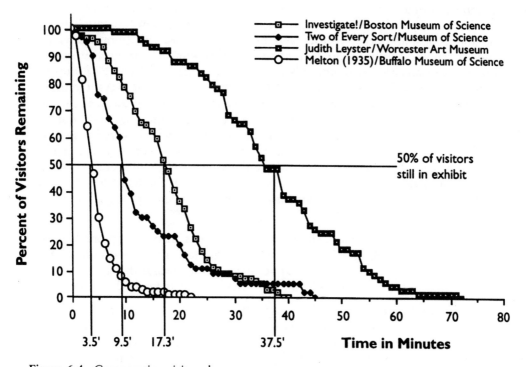

Figure 6.4 Comparative visitor decay curves

Unlike the first two elements of "success" this third one requires interviews; it cannot be determined from tracking data alone.

Tracking studies show that these apparently rather modest goals, are, in fact, seldom met. Summarizing data from 48 studies in 30 different museums – including science, natural history, cultural history and art museums – Serrell finds that the "per cent of use" (average number of exhibition components at which visitors stop for longer than 2 seconds) ranges from 2 to 79 per cent, with only five of the 48 studies reflecting her 51 per cent criterion. Whether her criteria are appropriate for all exhibitions has been challenged (Shettel 1995).

Time in a gallery can, of course, be recorded much more simply by noting beginning and ending time; it does not require tracking. The time visitors spend in an exhibition provides the single most useful, most widely recorded, easily obtained visitor behavior. But a note of caution is also required. While time is a necessary condition for learning, time in a gallery does not correspond directly to time spent attending to exhibitions. People may spend more time in a room with sofas, as compared to another gallery without that amenity, but not spend more time interacting with exhibits.

Naturalistic observations Observing visitors and noting their behavior as a primary means of visitor studies received additional impetus from a series of studies carried out by Laetsch and his students (Laetsch *et al.* 1980) when he served as director of the Lawrence Hall of Science in Berkeley, California. This group instituted a series of "naturalistic" observational studies of visitors based on ethnographic observations from Laetsch's background in biology. Families, school groups, and other visitors were observed in zoos, science museums, and similar venues. An important characteristic of this work is that the visitors were observed for an entire visit, not only in an individual gallery. Laetsch's group and others since (see Dierking and Falk 1994) concluded that an average museum visit is approximately two hours long, is very much a family social event, and that only approximately one-quarter to one-half of the time – about 30 minutes to one hour – is spent at the exhibits. The rest of the time is devoted to orientation and activities such as shopping at the museum store, eating, and using the toilets. As Falk and Dierking (1992) also emphasize, a museum visit is more than time spent in viewing exhibitions; it is an experience that can be understood only by considering the entire environment – personal, social and physical – in which it takes place.

The more qualitative approach to observation was also championed by the work of Robert Wolf and Barbara Tymitz in the late 1970s and early 1980s. They carried out a series of qualitative, naturalistic studies in which the data were summarized in narrative form. They describe their method as follows:

> This study was conducted by employing what we have referred to as
> naturalistic/responsive methodology . . . We have taken the exhibit
> as a complex set of stimuli. The complexity of the exhibit relates not
> only to the artifacts and concepts implicit in its design, but also the
> assumptions, expectations and philosophical differences that exist among

curators, the design persons, and the administrators . . . We have treated this study as anthropologists would treat early visits to a new culture.

(Wolf and Tymitz 1978b: 2)

Structured observations Some studies use forms coded for predetermined behaviors to assist in recording data on visitor behavior. An observational study conducted at National Museums and Galleries at Merseyside provides an example of such a form (Sudbury and Russell 1995). The expected behaviors of interest to the evaluators are listed down the left-hand column and then, when noted, are recorded at various time intervals in the boxes provided (see Figure 6.5).

Event-based observation Traditional, experimental-design tracking studies, as well as many ethnographic observations of visitors, are usually designed to consider the visitor action spatially and temporally. They start with a delineation of space, usually with a floor plan as a guide for the field worker, and record the visitors' movements through this space. Both naturalistic and traditional studies,

Date	Time	Target Visitor Number	Male or Female	Age	Or over				Collector's Name			
					30	40	50	60				
TIME TAKEN												
EXHIBIT NUMBER NAME												
Observed Actions	Tick Appropriate Column											
Helper present in view												
Interacts after help												
Engages with label												
Touches apparatus												
Moves part of apparatus												
Works alone												
Works with others												
Talks with others												
Watches others												
Questions helper												
Questions others												
Repeats action												
Has to queue or wait												

Figure 6.5 Liverpool observation form
Source: After the Observational Checklist in Sudbury and Russell 1995.

whether or not they use a floor plan, often use time as the anchor. A field worker records what the visitor is doing after set time intervals or otherwise links the observed behavior with the passage of time.

Another way to carry out observational studies of visitors in museums is to focus on *events*. Visitors are observed as they move through an exhibition, with a change in activity triggering a new observational mark, independent of time. A good example of such an observational study is work carried out by Hilke (1989) at the National Museum of Natural History at the Smithsonian Institution. She developed a set of categories to describe family visitor behavior. Her scheme called for coding a family visit by "actions undertaken by the family." It listed these by the following categories:

- the agent, the family member primarily engaged in the action;
- a description of the event using a set of predetermined codes;
- the topic/content of the action, whether it involved the exhibit or another group member; and
- the social content of the event, whether it was performed alone or with another visitor group member.

A sample "transcript" of the coded observation form is provided in Figure 6.6 (Hilke 1988). "Action Events," including 45 different possibilities, are listed in Figure 6.7 (Hilke 1989). Hilke's formal approach to observations permits detailed correlation of observed activities and specified visitor attributes. Such elaborate forms usually sacrifice the ability to note unexpected behaviors.

Experience sampling

To assist his effort to "measure the quality of subjective experience" that eventually evolved into a description of the "flow" experience, Csikszentmihalyi (1990) developed the Experience Sampling Method and later applied it to museum visitors.

> This technique . . . involves asking people to wear an electronic paging device for a week and to write down how they feel and what they are thinking about whenever the pager signals.
>
> (Csikszentmihalyi 1990: 4)

Visual tools for observation

A range of photographic methods can be used to assist observation. As indicated in a previous chapter, one of the first visitor studies (Gilman 1916) used photographs to illustrate how difficult it was for a visitor to examine objects in a museum that used floor-to-ceiling cases and very wide table top cases to display objects.

Time lapse photography provides a method for presenting striking evidence to museum staff of visitor behavior in a gallery. By mounting a camera in a strategic corner and taking individual frames at set times and then playing back

**Sample transcript: A young girl enters
an exhibit hall with her family**

Line	Agent	Action-Event	Topic/Content	Social Context
1	girl	go to	static exhibit	alone
2	girl	look intently	static exhibit	family
3	girl	look text	static exhibit	mother
4	girl	ask name of	static exhibit	mother
5	mother	respond w/name	static exhibit	girl
6	mother	ask to show	static exhibit	girl
7	girl	respond/show	static exhibit	mother
8	girl	leave	static exhibit	alone
9	girl	go to	static exhibit	alone
10	girl	look intently	static exhibit	alone
11	girl	ask to come	static exhibit	boy
12	girl	does not respond	static exhibit	girl
13	girl	go to	mother	alone
14	girl	state neg. evaluation	boy	mother
15	mother	does not respond	boy	girl
16	girl	go to	static exhibit	mother

Figure 6.6 Hilke transcript
Source: After Hilke 1988.
Note: During observation of a family visitor every action undertaken was recorded on a separate line as a sequence of four two-digit numbers reflecting who (agent) did what (action–event) about what (topic/content) to or with whom (social context). A new behavioral line was recorded any time one or more of its component numbers changed, or after 15 seconds, whichever came first. This table provides an English translation for a sample of the behaviors recorded.

the film as a movie, a powerful sense of how a space is used can be produced. The first use of this technique appears to have been Nielsen's (1942) study of visitors at the Chicago Museum of Science and Industry. He mounted a camera unobtrusively in a corner, had it set to take a picture once every 5–15 seconds, and analyzed the resulting film. He concluded that "the analyses . . . corroborated subjective impressions that visitors were not seeing the exhibit [on magnetism] in proper sequence" (Nielsen 1942: 109).[1]

Van der Stoep (1989) discusses the use of time lapse photography to monitor the way visitors interact with outdoor monuments.

Film and video can also be used to facilitate observation. The advantage over direct observation is that researchers can analyze film at their leisure and solicit different observers' insights. They can also examine the same behavior repeatedly in an effort to understand it. Falk (1983) used film to record visitor times of children at a science exhibition and correlated time spent with the results from a multiple choice test given the children after their visit. Students who

Action-Events Making up the Observational Code
(A) Action-Events Which Are Considered
Learning-Related

————————————— **Pure Info** —————————————

	Learn first hand or fact-oriented	*Learn second-hand or interpretive*
COOPERATIVE	Ask to verify 11,0 Verify 4,0 Verify resp 162,25 Ask to deny 1,0 Deny 0,0 Deny response 39,6 Ask inform 189,23 Inform 231,29 Inform resp 138,18 Ask name of 105,0 Name 77,0 Name response 72,2 Ask to show 19,9 Show 215,5 Show response 140,3 Ask minimum 3,0 Say minimum 8,0 Min response 50,1 Say don't know 21,0 Repeat 41,1 Correct 28,2	Ask to describe 2,0 Describe 54,0 Describe resp 39,0 Read aloud 64,1 Ask what someone thinks 7,0 Ask interpret 1,0 Interpret 75,0 Interpret resp 39,0 Ask explain 35,2 Explain 39,2 Explain resp 42,1 Ask for analogy 2,0 Make analogy 18,0 Analogy resp 3,0 Verbal cooperation 59,15 Show how 20,0
PERSONAL	Touch 94,6 Move-on-look 159,35 Gaze at 495,172 Look intently 49,2 Manipulate 42,12	Look graphics 241,9 Listen 17,1 Listen intently 0,0

Figure 6.7 Hilke categories
Source: After Hilke 1989.
Note: The number pair adjacent to each entry reflects the absolute frequency with which the action-event was observed for exhibit and non-exhibit contexts, respectively. The total number of action-events observed (N) was equal to 5996.

spent significantly longer times appeared to learn more about the exhibition. Loomis (1987: 221) and Morrissey (1991) describe other examples of the use of film and video.

An interesting application of video to observe visitors is the use of security film to capture visitor reactions to an exhibit. In the course of a study of what visitors learned from exhibition objects, staff at Herbert Art Gallery and Museum, Coventry, noted that a security video camera trained on a precious object also recorded visitors at an exhibit in front of the "Build a Clock" exhibit in the "Godiva City Gallery" (Buckley 1995). They began to look at the film and observed that people usually worked on the construction in groups, were sometimes frustrated if the model clock had been put together by previous visitors, and sometimes left the exhibit and came back to view it or work on it.

Lachapelle (1994) provided visitors with simple video cameras and, for research purposes, asked them to visually record their visit and, simultaneously, orally record their comments. He suggests that informant-made videos provide a basis for multiple methods of data analysis – tracking, discourse analysis, study of gestures and physical relationships – using one single primary source of information.

> Contrary to other means of data collection, informant-made videos provide visual documentation of the work of art to which the informant is responding. This makes the informant-made video recording a complete and coherent body of data. With the exception of biographical information about the informant, no other source of data is required to make sense of the recording. The investigator is not dependent on her or his memory of the session in question in order to interpret the informants' comments about specific aspects of the works of art.
>
> (Lachapelle 1994: 241)

Other observation methods

Methods for observing the interaction of visitors and museums are limited only by the ingenuity of the observer. The influential book *Unobtrusive Measures* (Webb *et al.* 1966) cites as its first example the observation at the Chicago Museum of Science and Industry that the floor tiles surrounding the chick hatching exhibit became worn out and had to be replaced every few weeks, while floor tiles in other areas of the museum lasted for years.

The rate at which interactive exhibits break down, the use or non-use of explanatory pamphlets, the amount of litter in some areas, questions asked of guards, all can become significant data for evaluation studies. In order to use such unobtrusive measures it's important to:

- make policy decisions about why data are being collected;
- collect data systematically;
- develop an accurate and consistent recording system;
- decide on an analytic scheme for handling the data.

The application of a systematic structure for recording and analyzing data converts anecdotal, informal, and subjective information into acceptable social science methodology. There is no secret recipe for developing observation protocols or for deciding what result of visitor interaction with an exhibition "should" be observed and noted. Good social science practice consists of providing systematic structure to the observation and recording of human behavior, whether this is done within the framework of experimental-design models or naturalistic ones. Using methods previously employed by others has the benefit that some problems, especially technical ones, may have been addressed. But every evaluation study has its unique limitations as well as opportunities. Valid and reliable data comes in many forms, but it must always be collected and analyzed using some systematic, rigorous framework.

Observing visitors is a stimulating and remarkably informative method museum education staff can employ to improve their own practice and to understand their visitors better. Tracking is relatively easy to learn and even less formal observations of few visitors can be enlightening. It can be shocking to find that visitors routinely ignore your favorite object, repeatedly miss a special label, or expend enormous energy using an interactive exhibit in a way that, to you, does not appear to be particularly fruitful!

Language-based methods

Concerns about the "subjectivity" of respondents, inability to develop reproducible data, or doubts about their capability to be reflective have prompted some researchers to reject the most human of all qualities, our ability to speak and to reflect on our activities, as a research tool. I discussed Melton's comments about interviews previously. Higgins also doubted that many visitors could reflect on their experience:

> it became obvious that the visitors conversationally approachable were but as the scattered taller flowers amidst the innumerable culms of grass in a meadow.
>
> (Higgins 1884: 185)

And Murray, another early observer of museum visitors (Murray 1932), noted that visitors could not tell him anything about what they had learned and only commented that the exhibits were "interesting." He, too, opted for observational data exclusively.

Others have either used the standardizing methods of modern sociology and psychology to develop questionnaires and interview forms that provide "objective" data or have adapted the more in-depth interview methods of clinical psychology and field work to try to gain insight into visitors' responses to the museum and its exhibitions.

Questionnaires or surveys

The most common response from museum personnel when faced with the need to carry out a visitor study is to generate a "survey." Often what they mean is a type of interview; staff develop a set of written questions, but visitors are approached and asked to respond orally. When the total visitor population sampled is in the range of fifty or less, this method is probably the most efficient means of finding out what people have to say on any subject. If in-depth responses are expected, interviews are also much preferable to questionnaires.

On the other hand, if larger samples are to be surveyed or if quite specific answers (checking a box, making one choice out of several, or answering true or false) are expected, then written answers from respondents are more likely to be appropriate and are certainly more cost effective. In this chapter I will call anything that requires a verbal response from a visitor an interview, and any instrument that requires a written response from the visitor a questionnaire.

Questionnaire advantages and disadvantages The most direct, simple way to obtain reproducible data from subjects is to develop, test, and administer a survey or questionnaire. Among the many advantages of a questionnaire are:

- Once questions have been developed and field tested they don't change. Answers obtained at different times or under different circumstances are still responses to the same prompt and can be combined for analysis.
- A direct person-to-person encounter for the length of time it takes to fill out a questionnaire is not required with a subject. Questionnaires can be mailed back, mailed out (or both), or otherwise distributed in a variety of settings. Even if questionnaires are distributed to be filled out and returned on the spot, it is possible for a staff member to engage more than one visitor at a time.

These advantages present certain disadvantages:

- It is difficult to develop good questions, and particularly difficult to write questions that cannot be reinterpreted by the respondent. The more subtle the question and the more complex the information desired, the greater the problem.
- The flexibility provided by the ease of distribution of questionnaires is offset by the problem in getting them back. Survey response rates of 40–60 per cent for questionnaires sent out in the mail are usually considered quite good, even with telephone or mail reminders sent after an appropriate interval. This rate always raises questions about whether the respondents are representative of the whole sample polled.

On the whole, questionnaires are particularly suited for large samples (for example, demographic profiles of museum audiences), for front-end testing of general ideas among a general population, or determining preferences visitors would have for certain leisure activities.

In the United States, Marilyn Hood is known for her careful work using written surveys.[2] Her publications provide useful advice on how to use surveys, as well as discussing results of her own research. She recently summarized this work, as well as a multitude of other surveys over the past 90 years (Hood 1993):

> We know from hundreds of museum visitor surveys that the typical frequent museum visitor . . . is in the upper education, upper occupation and upper income groups . . . This social class factor applies across the spectrum of museums – from zoos, science-technology centers and children's museums to historical sites, botanical gardens and art

museums. Our frequent visitor base and our volunteers and members normally come largely from this group of people because they are attracted to the kinds of experiences museums offer and they find those offerings and activities satisfying.

These folk emphasize three factors in their leisure life: opportunities to learn, the challenge of new experiences, and doing something worthwhile for themselves. The occasional visitor, on the other hand, is drawn more to leisure activities that emphasize opportunities for social interaction, participating actively, and feeling comfortable and at ease in his or her surroundings.

(Hood 1993: 17)

Referring to the interests of visitors and non-visitors alike, she stresses that

six "attributes" of leisure participation are basic to adults' decisions to participate or not participate in a variety of leisure activities and places, such as going to arboretums and botanical gardens, to zoos and aquariums, to museums and historical sites. The six leisure attributes are, in alphabetical order, being with people (social interaction), doing something worthwhile for oneself or others, feeling comfortable and at ease in one's surroundings, having a challenge of new experiences, having an opportunity to learn, and participating actively.

(Hood 1988: 85, summarizing Hood 1983)

Types of questionnaires Evaluators frequently use simple, short questionnaires in conjunction with observations of visitors. Many published evaluation reports provide the questionnaire that was used to obtain the results. It's tempting to use a questionnaire developed previously, on the assumption that this will provide a valid instrument that has had all the problems removed through use and refinement. The best advice for anyone proposing to use a questionnaire in conjunction with a visitor study is to look at others' questionnaires for examples and suggestions but to make up every questionnaire fresh for its particular purpose. There are several reasons for this:

- Just because a questionnaire has been published does not mean it has been extensively field tested or that it worked well in a previous setting.
- Times and conditions change. A question that was clear in one context may be confusing to visitors in another setting. Factors such as the geography of the building may change the meaning of a question, even if it refers to a specific exhibit.
- The ability of visitors to apply their own interpretation to a question should never be underestimated.
- The task of thinking through the questions to be asked is worth the effort, if for no other reason than that it will help clarify the objectives of the current investigation.

In short, all questionnaires have to be field tested in the setting in which they will be used and with the people who will be expected to respond to them.

Trying out questions with colleagues, family members, or friends is useful and a simple way to spot some problems, but it is *not* a substitute for piloting – that is, field-testing questions in the exact setting where they will be used.

People can be asked factual questions or questions about opinions or feelings as illustrated in Figure 6.8. They can also be questioned about their views on these topics now, what they were in the past, or what they might be in the future. For each of these domains, the validity of the answers diminishes as we move along that dimension, as illustrated in Figure 6.8. Visitors' responses are less likely to match what is in their minds as we move from facts to beliefs to feelings, and increasingly less likely to be accurate as the events discussed are something that happened in the past, or have not yet occurred.

Webb *et al.* (1966), in their book on the use of unobtrusive behavioral measures, deplored the over-reliance on interviews and surveys. Their comments are applicable to visitor studies.

> Today, the dominant mass of social science research is based upon interviews and questionnaires. We lament this over dependence upon a single, fallible method. Interviews and questionnaires intrude as a foreign element into the social setting they would describe, they create as well as measure attitudes, they elicit atypical roles and responses, they are limited to those who are accessible and will cooperate, and the responses obtained are produced in part by dimensions of individual differences irrelevant to the topic at hand.
>
> *But the principal objection is that they are used alone.*
>
> (Webb *et al.* 1966: 1)

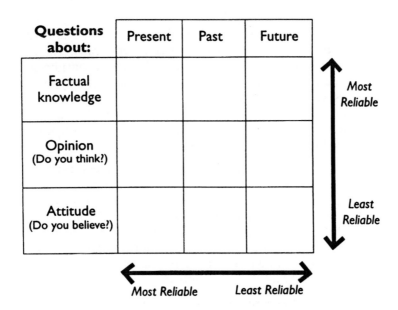

Figure 6.8 Types of questions for questionnaires and interviews

117

Although researchers today routinely use a broader range of methods, including many in-depth approaches to studying human behavior, a great deal of work in museums (and formal educational programs) still relies on *"the* evaluation" which means, for the practitioner, a survey.

Webb *et al.* did not deplore the overuse of human *language* as a source of data, but the particular application of formal questionnaires and interviews as the only source of data. They suggested that social scientists pay more attention to the methodologies used by detectives in mystery stories, by journalists and others in investigative fields. They also acknowledged that all methods have weaknesses, but, by varying methods, at the minimum, a range of weaknesses (and a range of strengths) are brought to bear on any situation studied.

Other written responses   Other types of writing that have been used in visitor studies include the following.

Comment cards   Many museums collect comment cards from visitors, but some never use them. They can provide a rich source of ideas about visitor concerns, and used comparatively they can provide excellent information about visitor response to exhibitions and programs.

It is usually impossible to determine how representative visitor comments are of the total visitor population. But so long as the cards are not intended to substitute for a formal visitor study, that represents no problem. There are many situations where representativeness is irrelevant. If the museum staff want to know if some exhibit is offensive to any individuals or groups, want to solicit new ideas, no matter what the source, or are eager for selective responses from visitors for illustrative purposes, then it doesn't matter who filled out the card, as long as it was a genuine visitor.

Second, if visitor comment cards are analyzed systematically and regularly, then changes in the nature, volume, or quality of comments can certainly be taken as legitimate data for decision-making. Again, the key to turning information on comment cards into evaluation data lies in developing a systematic collection and analysis scheme. The design of the cards, with possible prompts on them, may also enhance their value. If museum staff have a specific question concerning their visitors, then the most direct way to obtain information is specifically to ask for answers to that question.

Third, for some kinds of evaluation questions, comment cards – generally filled out by the most vocal opinionated visitors – may be the best source of information. For example, in a study we conducted for Boston's Museum of Science, the staff was interested to know whether anyone objected to the content of an exhibition about sexual reproduction. We read hundreds of comment cards, including dozens by teenagers that illustrated their embarrassment or their newly acquired knowledge about reproduction, but found none that were critical of the exhibition's major content.

Ironically, we found a few cards from animal rights activists who objected to the use of animal materials in the exhibit. For example, the exhibit included a small fish tank that some visitors felt was not an adequate environment for the specimens it contained. These cards confirmed that anonymous comment cards were an appropriate method for finding ideological critiques of the exhibit.

Participant journals If the subjects of an evaluation study have some long-term involvement with a museum, such as teachers who spend several days at a workshop or visitors to a multi-visit program, then participant journals can be an immensely rich source of information about a program. If such journals are to be used as data for an evaluation, it's important to negotiate early who will read the journals and whose property they will ultimately become. Participants may be willing to write candid, personal journals and leave them behind for the museum staff, but only if that is agreed upon at the start of a program. It takes considerable effort to keep journals. Providing good quality blank notebooks can help, and providing time during the scheduled activities for participants to write in the journals is essential.

Other written responses Bicknell and Mazda (1993: 45) employed an ingenious form of written response in evaluating theater performances at the London Science Museum. She gave visitors cartoon drawings of stick figures with bubbles and asked them to fill them out. A sample is provided in Figure 6.9.

Beside providing feedback to museum staff, variations on the typical comment cards can enhance exhibits. In some situations, used most often in children's museums and discovery rooms, visitors are asked to contribute their own ideas to exhibitions. An exhibition on families may ask visitors to add comments on their own families; one on measuring devices may ask visitors to add their own measurements to a list; or an activity room at a pop art exhibition may provide visitors with the opportunity to make their own cartoon. The extent to which visitors engage in the activity, the disappearance of the materials, and the nature of the responses can all be used to find out something about the visitors' response to an exhibition.

As with all evaluation means, some systematization is needed to turn a written response into a component of an evaluation study. This usually includes:

- careful documentation of the *initial state*;
- systematic recording of the *changes over time*;
- a system for *analyzing* the changes; and
- a *theory* for relating the changes to something significant about the visitors and *ruling out alternative explanations*.

For example, if comment cards are used to decide on the popularity of an exhibition, it's important to know what the typical numbers and kinds of comments are before analyzing the responses to a specific exhibition. It's important to monitor the cards regularly, making sure there are always blank ones (and writing utensils) available, and to develop a systematic way of analyzing the responses. Finally, if the responses change it's necessary to make sure that the reason is the change in the exhibition and not some change in visitors. If an

Figure 6.9 Stick figure "bubble charts"
Source: Bicknell and Mazda 1993.

overnight, teenage, camp-in group has been to a gallery, its members may fill out hundreds of cards in a single visit and skew the results when compared to a week's worth of visitor responses not including such a group.

Part of the evaluation of the Birmingham Museum and Art Gallery included visitors' memories of their visit (McManus 1993b). These were solicited months after a visit by writing to people who had given their addresses when they filled out comment cards and asking them to respond by "writing about your memories of your visit to *Gallery 33* on the attached sheet." (McManus 1993b: 371). The study, not surprisingly, had a low response rate (21 per cent) but produced rich data indicating that, even without prompting of any kind, visitors retained intense and specific memories of objects and experiences and were willing to write about them.

Pre- and post-tests   Pre- and post-tests are a specialized form of questionnaire, appropriate for some circumstances. In school situations, tests are the most common way of assessing learning. The term "test" can be applied to performances (driving tests, musical auditions, and practical exams) and oral and drawing tasks as well as to written examinations, but written ones are most common. When given both before and after a potential learning exposure, they become pre- and post-tests.

Museum researchers generally acknowledge that significant learning in a museum setting usually cannot be assessed by matched pre- and post-tests just before and after a typical short visit. Most visits are for such a brief time, so unfocused, and overshadowed by so many important other contributors to each individual's overall knowledge (e.g., background, experiences, prior learning, and personal interests) that such tests don't inform us a great deal about what visitors gain from a visit. However, pre- and post-tests can and are still used. If a museum visit has a specific objective, often the case for school groups, it is legitimate to ask whether that objective has been achieved. For a good example of such a use of Piagetian tasks as pre- and post-tests, see Linn (1980).

Since short-term knowledge gains can be deceptive, or people may show a change in their responses immediately after an experience and not retain much later on, it is desirable to extend the test period and either give the post-test weeks or months after the visit or repeat the post-test after some time to see what is retained. Long-term gains are much more impressive than short-term ones and have been noted in some studies of visitors in museums.

Written pre- and post-tests can be developed for both quantitative and more qualitative research approaches. Drawings, reflections, and written journals can be used instead of questionnaires to compare visitors' reactions before and after a visit of any length or following a collection of exposures to a museum.

A great advantage of matched pre- and post-assessments of any kind is that behavior can be compared rather than measured absolutely. This tactic is desirable in almost any study, since comparison of two situations is simpler and more accurate than efforts to measure or describe behavior and compare it to some standard. Ratios in the same metric are easier to determine than absolute values. For example, an accurate timing device and an accurate measure of a distance are needed to determine how fast a runner can go. However, to compare two runners, all you need is identical starting points, and a way of determining who finished first.

What is required for using pre- and post-tests is a systematic collection of data, good recording of information and to make sure that the *same* questions are asked under the same conditions before and after the activity to be assessed.

Visual means

Visitors can be asked to use symbolic language, as well as, or instead of, words. Several published reports illustrate the use of drawings and other visual means to find out what visitors have gathered from a museum visit.

Maps and floor plans Visitor studies practitioners have used both physical and conceptual maps of museums as evaluation tools. Novak and Gowin (1984) proposed concept maps as appropriate means for assessing students' knowledge of school subject matter. Asking students to draw visual descriptions of the relationships between concepts forces them to think beyond the isolated facts to find connections. Teachers can gain an understanding of how their students have thought about a subject by looking at these concept maps. VanLuven and Miller (1993) employed concept mapping in exhibit development. They asked visitors to draw such maps, to arrange cards with words on them related to the exhibit content ("rocks," "molecules," "cells," and "atoms") for a chemistry exhibition into any order that made sense to them, or to link cards with connectors that included phrases such as "are made of" or "are the same as." The exhibition developers used the visitors' ideas about the conceptual connections to reflect on how best to organize the exhibition.

Karen Wizevich (1994) provided visitors with floor plans of an exhibition and asked them to annotate these. Her model for this approach was the way in which architects use scale drawings to help them think about the space they are developing. Anderson and Roe (1993, vol. 2: 13) reported that children were asked to draw maps of places they visited at a children's museum.

By asking visitors to respond in ways that allow them freedom to express themselves as they wish, and that may be unusual to them, it is possible to get insights into visitors' thinking that might not be available through more conventional questioning.

Drawings Both children and adults have been asked to draw to gauge their response to exhibitions. As part of a front-end analysis of what children know about skeletons, Jack Guichard (1995) asked children 6–8 years old to draw a skeleton into an outline of a human body. He found that most children filled the drawing with a "bag of bones" not connected in any way. Others drew long bone sections, such as a single bone for the entire leg, or what he called "fish knuckle-bones" skeletons, in which the bones were connected to a central support, but not in the form that a human skeleton is articulated. Only a very small fraction drew skeletons that resembled human figures. When children were given a school lesson on the structure of the human skeleton with a skeleton as an illustration, they produced drawings that resembled the proper human anatomy shortly after the lesson but reverted to their original drawings six months later. However, a significant number of children of the same age who had experience with a museum exhibit that allowed them to make a skeleton move as they moved (they rode a stationary bicycle and saw a skeleton before them perform parallel motions) drew human-type skeletons not only immediately after the experience but also six months later.

Other researchers (Coe 1988, Crosthwait and Mask 1994) have asked children to draw zoo animals to gauge what children had learned from a visit to a zoo.

Adults can also be asked to draw to reveal aspects of the museum experience. Wittlin (1949: 239–51) refers to drawings in her early experimental work in visitor studies, and Worts (1993) has used drawings on comment forms as one evaluation tool in his studies of visitor responses to newly developed galleries in an art museum. Over nine months, about 12,000 cards were used and 5,000 left in drop off bins. He describes the results thus

> the bulk of comments are personal and reflective. Many provide insight into how visitors are interacting with particular objects or groups of artworks. Often there is great sensitivity and intensity in the responses. A large number of visitors who use the cards choose to draw imagery of one kind or another. Some people copy pictures on display. Others adapt images on display to their own creative ends. Still others will create wholly new images, presumably inspired by their time in the gallery, which reflects what is on their mind at the moment. Often, people seem to want to see themselves reflected, either literally or symbolically, in their imagery – and in their writing for that matter. This has been an important psychological phenomenon for Gallery staff to become aware of – people want to see themselves reflected in their visits to museums. This has the potential to affect dramatically the way in which art displays are conceived and installed.
>
> (Worts 1993: 48)

Interviews

Museum professionals have asked visitors what they think about an exhibit for as long as visitor studies have been carried out. Interviews represent an almost irresistible technique for any museum professional interested in making the museum responsive to its clients. Nothing is easier than to go to the public areas of a museum and talk to visitors. But few visitor study activities are harder to carry out so that useful information results. I have already commented on both Higgins's and Murray's frustration on finding that most visitors could not articulate what they had learned.

Interviewing is a skill that can be learned but also *must* be learned. Interviewers need to ask the right questions and not lead their interviewees. They must also learn to listen rather than talk. In general, people respond to interviews honestly; that is, they try to answer the questions asked to the best of their ability. Thousands of interviewers have learned from experience that very few people deliberately lie when questioned by an interviewer. It does not follow, however, that what people say therefore matches what they do, believe, or feel. As in the case of questionnaires, responses about factual matters are more likely to be reliable than those about opinions or beliefs, and responses about the present (or very recent past) are more likely to correspond to what happened than are responses about the distant past. Projections about the future are necessarily subject to modification.

Many observers have noted that museum visitors, like other respondents, are eager to please, and tend to give what they consider an "acceptable" response or what they think the interviewer wants to hear. For example, one reason election exit polls sometimes differ from actual voting results is that voters may not admit racial prejudice or that they voted for an unpopular candidate. Thus, interviewers need to frame their questions neutrally, consider how the question will sound to the person hearing it, and consider how the interviewer's *perceived* characteristics and affiliation may influence the respondent.

When visitors are asked about exhibitions, they often don't remember what they have seen or have done. It is unfair to people from whom you want information to ask them to remember a great deal, especially when they had no notion that anyone would ask them about it. If visitors are simply asked which exhibit they liked best, they may not remember. In their effort to please, they may make up an answer (including reference to nonexistent exhibits!) or simply name what they do remember. Post-visit interviews should provide visitors with a chance to recall what they might have seen. Evaluators have used a variety of ways to help visitors remember an exhibition. They may provide a list of exhibits, a floor plan, or show visitors photographs of an exhibition to remind them of where they might have stopped. Two museums that collaborated in a multi-site study (Anderson and Roe 1993) found that providing visitors with instant cameras and asking them to take pictures as they toured the museum was a useful adjunct to interviews.

Using photographs not only focused visitors' attention, but stimulated memory and verbalization.

> In the researchers' experience, a person – not wanting to be perceived as giving a wrong answer – will often try to tell the interviewer what the person thinks the interviewer wants to hear. But by taking their own pictures, visitors seemed to gain a sense of ownership and take control of the process. Even when looking at photographs taken by other visitors, subjects responded in greater detail and depth than would be expected in interview situations *sans* photographs.
>
> (Anderson and Roe 1993, vol. 2: 41)

Types of interviews Interviews, like questionnaires, can be carefully prepared and standardized, or they can be more naturalistic. Each has its advantages and problems. Very brief informal interviews may provide sufficient information to reveal the shortcomings of a prototype exhibit; a single interview with a knowledgeable respondent is better than nothing if you need to find out in a hurry whether a label may be offensive to a specific audience segment. Preparing interview formats is easier than preparing questionnaires because it is possible to change the wording if a question is not interpreted as expected. But awkward and ambiguous questions still make an interview difficult to interpret, and in most real life situations interviewers have only a short time with respondents. If you have to spend time explaining questions, not only does it make the answers less reliable, it also uses precious time before a respondent will lose patience with you.

Research studies tend to use longer and more detailed interviews than many evaluation studies. Some special types of interviews are discussed below.

Clinical interviews Naturalistic evaluators have adapted the methodology of developmental psychologists and use clinical interviews to try to understand what is going on in the minds of their respondents. Feher and Rice (Rice and Feher 1987, Feher and Rice 1988) pioneered Piagetian interviews (Piaget 1929) to determine visitors' science conceptions and to guide development of appropriate exhibits. They asked children who were examining physical objects under study to describe what they saw and predict what would happen as they manipulated the objects.

> Our methodology for this work is a field version of the Piagetian task-based clinical interview. The interviewer, much like an anthropologist in the field, stations herself at the chosen exhibit. When a child approaches and starts investigating the exhibit, the interviewer engages the child in dialogue using questions from a protocol. The protocol is developed from a large number of preliminary test interviews, to ensure that the wording, content and sequencing of the questions yield the best possible information.
>
> (Feher 1990: 37)

Another example of such interviews comes from a comprehensive study in an art museum to "develop a conceptual framework for interpretive materials for novice, or lay, visitors" (McDermott-Lewis 1990: 1) and to create some experimental labels and gallery guides. The author and her colleagues used tracking, question boxes for comments, and a 1,000-plus visitor survey.

> But, ultimately, what was most useful and thought-provoking were the in-depth interviews we conducted, trying to understand our visitors' experiences with art. What went through their heads as they looked at individual pieces? What were their most memorable experiences with objects? And what expectations did they bring that shaped their encounters with art?

125

> Our in-depth interviews and evaluations were not pristine, academic
> studies. Instead they were vehicles for us to gain insights that could help
> us make better decisions.
>
> (McDermott-Lewis 1990: 5)

The author concludes that the following factors are important in creating
explanatory materials for lay visitors.

> First, visitors want their learning experiences to be directly related to the
> objects they see . . .
>
> Second, visitors tend to learn in short bursts. They want to commit, at
> least initially, to things that will only take a little time . . .
>
> Third, every interpretive device won't work for every visitor, so we need
> to accommodate the range and variety of our audience . . . We ended up
> with a buffet analogy, of having a variety of options available. Every
> offering may not be meatless, but there should be at least one vegetarian
> item . . .
>
> Fourth, we need to send a clear hospitable message to our visitors.
> Many novices have a fragile, though positive, attitude about art and
> museums, and they need to see that we care about their experiences . . .
> Finally, successful interpretation for novices means accepting where they
> are – keeping their backgrounds, preconceptions, and values in mind
> and, most importantly, taking the position that we're not there to
> downplay their experiences, but to build on and broaden them.
>
> (McDermott-Lewis 1990: 137–8)

Focus groups Focus groups were first used by market researchers to explore
consumer responses to new products and have found a use in museum research.
Some authors have called any group interview a focus group. Focus group
methodology consists of gathering a selected group of interviewees, usually up
to a dozen, who discuss a topic with a trained interviewer in a room that
is equipped with a one-way mirror, behind which the people who desire to learn
from the focus group listen in on and observe the interview. The primary
audience gets the benefit not only of the respondents' words, but also of their
gestures and body language as they discuss whether they prefer one exhibition
theme to another, how they might react to an exhibition of a particular kind,
what they know about a potential exhibition topic, or how they feel about
museums. As these examples suggest, focus groups are most commonly used
for front-end studies.

The most extensive published use of the focus group method in a museum
visitor study was a research effort sponsored by the Getty Center for Education
in the Arts and the J. Paul Getty Museum (1991) that involved eleven major
United States art museums in an attempt to better understand their visitors
and non-visitors. Each institution held focus groups with both visitors and
non-visitors. Here is how their report describes the method as used in this
project:

The method consists of round-table discussions among eight to twelve prescreened participants selected from a targeted population. The group is led by a trained moderator who follows a discussion outline prepared in consultation with the client. Focus groups are held in special facilities with a conference room for the group discussion and an observation room behind a one-way mirror. Facilities are equipped with audio and videotape recording equipment for record keeping.

As a qualitative research technique, focus groups serve two important objectives. First, they provide insight into visitor attitudes, perceptions, and behavior. Second, they provide a catalyst for communication among the observers of the group (i.e. those people behind the one-way mirror). Often the interaction among observers is as powerful a product of the research as the findings themselves.

(Getty Center 1991: 4–5)

The project involved conducting five to six focus groups for each museum. First, the team held a focus group for museum staff, then two pairs of focus group discussions were held for both visitors and non-visitors. In each instance a visit to the museum was scheduled between the times of the pair of group discussions. The authors list a number of conclusions from the focus groups, generalizations from analyzing the tapes of all the discussions. They found that museum staff expectations for their visitors do not necessarily match the reasons why people come to museums nor what the visitors say they get out of their visits. Non-visitors stressed that they found art museums intimidating, that they were unaware of them, had insufficient free time to visit, were not interested, or found the locations of the museums not to their liking. Among the findings for visitors and non-visitors alike ("non-visitors" had at least one visit to a museum between the two focus groups) are that they found museum visits "meaningful and rewarding" but also made individual meaning of their experience. They want and need introductory information, "on how to organize the visit, what to see and how the museum is arranged." The more people know about specific objects the more they can connect with them, but the informational material in art museums is often inadequate, and the environment of the museum – the physical surroundings and presentation – influences the response to the visit.

The project created not only a written report but a videocassette with excerpts from some of the focus group meetings that provides an informative glimpse into the United States public's response to art museums in the late 1980s.

Types of respondents The most obvious respondents for visitor study interviews are the visitors themselves, but powerful information can be gathered from other groups. Museum staff of all kinds have been used successfully to find out about visitors. These include interpretive staff (Hein 1995a) as well as security staff (Davidson 1989). We once interviewed highly knowledgeable 13 to 14-year-old boy scouts who volunteered at the National Museum of the Boy Scouts in Murray, Kentucky. They were extremely helpful in informing us about the likes and dislikes of visitors and the problems they encountered with some exhibits.

Another special type of person to be interviewed is experts used to assess museum exhibitions or museum environments. Information from interviews with various kinds of experts – those knowledgeable about the subject of an exhibition, about museum visitors, or about other aspects of museumology – should not be confused with information from visitors, but their response can nevertheless provide useful information to improve exhibits and make places better able to communicate with visitors. The special qualities of this source of data have been discussed (Frisch and Pitcaithley 1987, Shettel 1994).

Interview time-scale Interviews can be carried out immediately following an experience or after some time has elapsed. Increasingly, museum evaluators are using delayed interviews to find out what people remember from a museum experience one to six months after the immediate impact (and distractions) have receded. It is also possible to interview people about their long-term memories of museum experiences. What do they remember from childhood (Falk and Dierking 1994)? What were the most memorable museum experiences?

At a recent conference of museum professionals (Falk and Dierking 1995, although the following material is not included in the publication) participants were asked to reflect on their most memorable museum experience. Not only could most participants recall highly memorable experiences, they often described them in religious terms, as "epiphanies."

> This session profoundly influenced the rest of the meeting. The experiences participants articulated were profound, often representing important intellectual, as well as emotional experiences. What was striking, though, was the breadth and uniquely individual nature of the recollections.
>
> (Hein 1994b)

The kinds of experiences most frequently mentioned were:

1 The value of being able to go behind the scenes, or to see a rough work in progress. Several of these referred to the powerful effect of such an opportunity as a child.

2 The nature of the family museum experience. Many of the examples shared by participants included descriptions of exhibits that led to family discussions, physical accessibility/inaccessibility of the museum when visiting with multigenerational groups, parents who are museum phobic, parents who took children and/or provided their own interpretation. For example, there was a description of a family visit to MoMA that did not lead to any discussion for this family, but a visit by the same group to the exhibition about Japanese internment at the National Museum of American History that did stimulate family discussion because of the relevance of the topic to the family.

3 The power of museums to provide contexts for connections and "getting it." One person commented "[I finally understood] why my one-eyed son has trouble catching a ball" after interacting with an exhibit at a science center. Many of the epiphanies (described in those terms) were about experiencing art or had occurred in art museums. At least nine comments were of this kind. Not all were described as an epiphany, but they all share the idea that museums can generate a "Eureka" response.

4 The value that light, air, and connection with the outside, real world can contribute to the museum experience.

5 The importance that personal connection plays in the value of museum experience: what one knows about, can appreciate, can understand (or is frustrated by because one's needs are not met) is memorable.

6 Museum fatigue does seem to play a role in the museum experience and for some visitors, visiting alone is the primary way to have a pleasurable experience and avoid the stress brought on by matching a personal pace to a companion's needs. It's impressive that museum professionals admit that, for them, periods of time *less than 30 minutes* are the limit of tolerance for an exhibition. Also, we need to consider the frequent references to the pleasures of visiting alone that occurred when museum professionals often stress the value of group visits.

7 Early museum experiences seem to be an important part of many people's childhood memories.

(Hein 1994b)

Probing visitors' memories of their museum experiences has become a particularly attractive activity among museum visitor researchers. If the traditional methods of experimental-design research do not reveal much impact from immediate pre- and post-tests of visitors, perhaps memories of visits will reveal the long-term impact. In addition, memory may be a better indicator of cognitive change than short-term recall of what must necessarily be rather superficial information. Stevenson (1991) carried out a careful study of family visits to Launch Pad, an interactive exhibition at the London Science Museum. His work included visits to the families' homes six months after their visit. He found that families were delighted to discuss their visit and could generate uncued, spontaneous memories about their visit. Even more memories were brought forth when prompted with photographs. Specific details of the exhibits and family interactions with them were conspicuous in his results. Falk and Dierking (1992) have reported parallel results.

Memory research, as it is currently used in visitor studies, is itself a product of the cognitive revolution and the re-emergence of mind as an acceptable component of psychology. Visitor studies research emphasizes "episodic memory," a memory of personal experiences, as distinct from "semantic" memory (knowledge) and procedural memory (how to do things). Ironically, one of the standard criticisms of Piaget's work by experimental psychologists was that he did not study traditional components of learning theory, such as "memory." His critics defined and restricted memory to semantic memory, usually assessed by having subjects memorize random series of numbers or nonsense syllables in a sterile, laboratory environment.

All the research to date on visitors' museum memories reinforces the conclusion that visits are memorable, that visitors combine personal agendas with an opportunity to enlarge their understanding of the world, and that visitors incorporate novel elements into reformulating their conception of the world.

Interviewing for staff development   Finally, visitor interviews, besides providing information about visitors, can play an important role in staff development. Staff who have the experience of interviewing (formally or informally but systematically) visitors often significantly change the way they carry out their roles as interpreters. At Colonial Williamsburg, for example, interviewing visitors has become a major part of staff development activities (Graft 1989), and Springuel (1996) used it "as a framework for developing docent training." Some years ago, for a similar aim, Hayward and Jensen (1981) carried out parallel interviews of staff and visitors to contrast their views on exhibitions and the interpretation process.

Other methods

Visitors' conversations

In an attempt to overcome the limits of interviews, Lucas *et al.* (1986) describe mounting a microphone on selected exhibit cases in a natural history museum and recorded visitor conversations. They analyzed the conversations using a carefully constructed coding scheme developed from a pilot study. A similar approach was devised by Tunnicliffe (1995) who studied family visits to zoos and natural history exhibitions.

Museum objects as prompts

In a variant of the method above, Dierking and Holland (1994) noted the questions that visitors asked when they interacted with manipulative materials. As part of the evaluation of an exhibition at a natural history museum the researchers positioned themselves along with an interpreter who had a cart that contained objects similar to those in the displays. They then noted the conversations between visitors and the interpreter.

Protocol analysis

A technique some cognitive psychologists have favored to explore what goes on in people's minds as they solve problems consists of asking a subject to "think aloud" while carrying on some task (Ericsson and Simon 1993) – solving a mathematical problem or classifying a set of objects, for example. By listening to and recording the verbalization of what the subject thinks he or she is doing, researchers can gain clues about mental processes. Dufresne-Tassé and Lefèbre (n.d.) have used this technique to build up an understanding of how visitors approach objects. They carried out a series of experimental studies with adults who visited selected galleries in a range of museums and experimental settings, and who thought aloud as they viewed the objects.

> we found that if an adult is asked to describe what he sees, thinks, feels or imagines as he walks through a museum gallery, one can construe his psychological functioning from what he says . . . A topical analysis shows how this functioning is structured, while a sequential analysis reveals its organization in time and, to a certain extent, provides an explanation of the particular form that this organization takes.
>
> (Dufresne-Tassé and Lefèbre n.d.: 4)

The analysis of the transcribed tapes of the visitors' comments is based on the following categories, developed from preliminary work:

> The MENTAL OPERATIONS, performed by the visitor to process his experience . . . [such as] expressing, taking note of, comparing-distinguishing and verifying . . .
>
> The particular ORIENTATION of the visitor's psychic activity at the moment the operation is performed . . .
>
> The DIRECTION OF ATTENTION during the operation, to the object observed . . . the creator of the object, other objects, other contexts . . .
>
> The particular FORM the operation may take . . . question, a hypothesis, exclamation . . .
>
> (Dufresne-Tassé and Lefèbre n.d.: 5–6)

They conclude that:

> Contrary to the expectations of museum educators . . . visitors are not passive when they look at natural science objects, even when these objects are displayed as they might be at a jeweler's . . . visitors' mental operations, when looking at objects, do not vary according to their level of education and that this functioning, even if it is cognitively and effectively intense, constitutes the major benefit of a visit by virtue of the multiple pleasures it brings about.
>
> (Dufresne-Tassé and Lefèbre n.d.: 12)

Others have also used this method (Ohta 1996, Korenic 1996). Korn (1992) gave visitors a tape recorder to carry with them during a visit to an art gallery and instructed them:

> I would like for you to spend as much time with [this painting] as you like. Here is a tape recorder. I would like for you to speak into it and say what you are thinking about when you look at this painting. You can talk about anything that comes into your mind. There are no right or wrong things to say – we just want to know what our visitors think about when they look at it.
>
> (Korn 1992: 182)

Visitors as teachers

As part of a detailed study of children's activities at a science center, Gottfried (1981) asked older elementary school children to go to classes of younger children two weeks after their visit and tell the first and second graders about their experience. The children were able to teach others in detail about their visit although they had taken no notes and were not observed to be particularly attentive to, or reflective about, their experience.

Combinations

Meta-analysis

In the formal educational literature, one effort to overcome the limitations of individual studies involves the use of "meta-analysis" of research (Glass 1977), the attempt to sum the knowledge gained from different studies by analyzing results across studies, even if the individual situations and experimental conditions varied. Such results, often illustrated in review articles, usually require qualitative judgments about the overall conclusions, and frequently lead to controversial discussions about the "strength" of the findings. There have been few attempts to reach similar conclusions in the museum literature that combine studies, although recent publications in research journals are increasingly referencing this growing body of literature.

Walberg, the author of many meta-analyses, and colleagues (Ramey-Gassert *et al.* 1994) reviewed studies on learning in informal science settings. These authors find from their perspective that there is little research literature they can use to build a systematic description.

> Museums provide opportunities for students to be active participants in learning by manipulating real objects in a stimulating setting thus enhancing conceptual learning in the classroom. Both components of learning are important for understanding of complex science concepts. Much of the literature pertaining to learning in museums is anecdotal and craft wisdom, indicating that more collaborative research efforts are needed in the area of science education in museum settings
>
> (Ramey-Gassert *et al.* 1994: 345)

Multiple methods

The examples provided above were all chosen because they exemplify particular methods that have been used in visitor studies. Many of the studies, as indicated or at least hinted at in the examples, used more than one method in the research or evaluation. Interviews were supplemented by observations, and vice versa. Small-scale visitor studies, carried out with limited resources and time, often use only one method. Thorough studies, especially those that hope to gain some insight into visitors' understanding beyond the immediate technical problem presented by a particular exhibit or display, usually use more than one way of obtaining information.

Studying human activity is neither simple nor easy – either the effort involves interfering with the activity, which inevitably distorts the natural situation, or the observer tries to examine what goes on "unobtrusively," with all the limitations which keeping a distance (and making assumptions about the meanings of what is observed) imposes. Also, human activity always involves the past experiences people bring with them and the future of their intentions, whereas our methods usually examine only the present, provide only snapshots of what happens now. Thus, all methods have limitations. The key to deeper understanding of how and what visitors learn in museums is not to try to achieve a single, perfect method of study, but to recognize the limitations of all individual means for doing so and make an effort to gain information and insight about what visitors learn using multiple methods.

Doctors' diagnoses result from the combination of evidence arrived at from laboratory tests, personal examination, and conversation with the patient (or so we all hope is the case); journalists are troubled if they have only one source for a story; lawyers and detectives "build a case," putting together the clues and the evidence. Similarly visitor studies researchers and evaluators need to examine multiple sources in their attempts to understand how visitors make meaning in museums.

In a detailed study of a multiple-visit education program for schoolchildren at the Valentine Museum, an urban history museum in Richmond, Virginia, Luetjen and Holmes (1994) employed the following means:

- pre- and post-visit surveys;
- pre- and post-program questionnaires;
- pre- and post-program drawing tasks;
- student journals;
- ethnographic data collection (a descriptive narrative prepared by an observer who records speech, actions, and the body language of students and the teacher).

In a summative evaluation of an exhibition at Boston's Museum of Science, Hein and Mello (1993) used:

- observations of general visitors;
- interviews with general visitors (prompted by pictures of the exhibition);
- observations of school groups;
- interviews with the school groups' teachers;
- observations of camp-in groups in the exhibition after hours;
- staff interviews;
- a small number of "thinking-aloud" interviews with single, adult visitors.

And in a thorough evaluation of a new gallery at the Birmingham Museums and Art Gallery (Jones 1993), evaluators employed nine different methods:

- exit questionnaire;

- tracking study;
- visit memories, obtained from a postal survey of visitors;
- questionnaire concerning an interactive video program;
- data on numbers of "hits" on two touch screens;
- study of school use of specific components, involving observations, interviews, tape recordings of visits;
- visitors' written comments.

Multiple methods are desirable in any research study; they are essential in qualitative work, which relies on triangulation, on the congruence of different sources of data, for validity.

Discussion

The amazingly wide range of methods employed in museum evaluations and research attests both to the complexity of the task and to the recognition by visitor studies practitioners that they need to use all the methods available from the wide world of social science research.

Although much exhibition and program evaluation may still consist of simple (often poorly) designed surveys and interviews, all professionals in the field recognize the need for using multiple methods, and, especially, for using the appropriate method for the research questions of interest. In our own work (Engel and Hein 1981, Hein 1982, Hein 1995a), we have consistently used an evaluation matrix on which we match issues to be evaluated with means for doing so. This graphic display of the evaluation concerns and the methods we plan to use to find out about them allows us to make sure that all issues are addressed (usually by more than one means, and, if feasible, by three different means) and also provides a guide for developing the actual instrument that we use for each evaluation.

In comparison with other educational settings, long-term, sustained efforts to examine learning in the museum are missing from the visitor studies literature. There have been longitudinal studies of children's growth in school, observational studies that span an entire school year as well as other developmental approaches to examine learning that span many years. The voluntary, fleeting nature of most visitors' involvement with museums has made such an effort difficult. To date, no one has carried out such a study. Studies of visitors' memories, usually interviews about past experiences, are a step in the direction of attempting to understand both the long-term and the cumulative impact of museum visits.

Another area of study, examination of the exhibit development process itself, has recently received some attention (Macdonald and Silverstone 1990, Roberts 1997). This work does not involve new methods, but will be discussed for its relevance to the Constructivist Museum in Chapter 8.

7

Evidence for learning in the museum

The most casual observer of educational methods could not fail to notice that the receptive mind of a child or a youth learns from an infinite variety of sources. We all know that we begin at one end of education, but there is no period in life of the most aged where the other end is reached . . . Whatever becomes suggestive to the mind is of educational value. That Museums have from their very nature the very essence of suggestiveness is patent.

(Greenwood 1893: 246)

Introduction

As a venue for understanding learning, museums present unique difficulties. Learning does occur in museums; but unlike formal schooling, work, or recreational pursuits (chess, weaving, etc.), visiting museums is not only voluntary, it usually occurs in family groups who spend only a brief time (for research purposes) on a complex set of activities. In every other activity used as a source of research on learning, the learners engage in the tasks repeatedly and the purpose is usually clear – they wish to become better at what they do, they want to accomplish the activity most efficiently or with least cost, they want to pass an exam, or the activity is a vocation or avocation, something on which they spend considerable time and effort. Little of this applies to museums; even the purpose of the museum visit can be challenged.

Studying learning in museums is limited not only by the short duration of typical visits but also by infrequency of visits. Even dedicated museum-goers, "expert practitioners" (who can be contrasted to "novices"), may visit museums only a few times a year. This is in marked contrast not only to school attendance, but even to the time spent by street vendors, ski instructors, or industrial workers (all subjects of learning research) at their pursuits (Rogoff and Lave 1984). Consequently, our knowledge about learning in museums seems remarkably incomplete. We have many documented instances, but little coherent theory. There is considerable evidence about what visitors do in museums, yet what the results of these experiences are for the visitor is ill-defined.

135

One of the marvels of museums is that the brief encounters visitors have with exhibitions do appear to lead to learning, do result in some change in the visitor that is often remembered with pleasure and can influence future behavior. Research on museum memories discussed in the previous chapter confirms this.

In this chapter I will review what is known about learning in museums by discussing results to date in relationship to broader research on learning. As indicated in previous chapters, what we "know" about visitors' learning is determined by our choices among possible definitions of learning and differing research paradigms.

Results from different research traditions are combined in the following sections to describe factors that influence learning in museums. Unfortunately, even the appropriate terminology is theory dependent, since in the constructivist view, visitors do not learn but make their own meaning from their experiences. I will use the vocabulary of learning for consistency, recognizing that learning needs to be defined in the broadest terms possible.

Setting the stage for learning

By any definition, there can be no learning (or meaning making) if there's been no interaction. In order for learning to occur in the museum, the visitor has to attend to something. The wealth of recent studies has greatly expanded our knowledge of factors that increase opportunities for learning. Chapter 8 covers broader environmental factors that influence learning. This chapter concentrates on visitors' understanding of exhibition components.

Exhibitions that attract

The physical factors that support or limit visitors' comfort and attention to exhibit components (Evans 1995) as well as the more specialized field of human factors research (Hedge 1995), called ergonomics in Europe, have been recognized as crucial for learning in museums.

There is a large literature now available on the human factor components of exhibition design, including such aspects as various options for illumination, appropriate heights of exhibits for different audiences, human responses to different uses of space and design features. Miles *et al.* (1988) and, to some extent, McLean (1993) discuss these components from an educational perspective.

Conclusions about visitor interactions with exhibitions, first published by Weiss and Bourtourline (1963) more than thirty years ago and still advocated as useful (Bitgood *et al.* 1994), include:

- Large vivid exhibit elements become "landmarks" in exhibitions
- Visitors' paths tend to be prominent between landmarks
- The most direct route from the exhibit entrance to the exit is most used

- Visitors rarely zig-zag between exhibits that face each other, and therefore, facing exhibits compete with each other.

(Bitgood *et al.* 1994: 76)

Attention to ergonomic factors and more sophisticated interpretive devices (Serrell 1996) can make a difference in visitors' attention and engagement with exhibits, as well as in their learning, regardless of the definition for learning. In many instances visitors' interaction with individual exhibitions has been improved by changing the physical conditions, providing more opportunities for visitors to engage, feel rewarded, or be motivated.

Visitor comfort is an important prerequisite for visitor learning in museums. Comfort covers a wide range of factors from simple physical comfort (Are there places to rest, convenient facilities, and soft floors on which to walk?), to psychological conditions, such as the discomfort humans experience when they face away from open spaces, as they often do in museums (Olds 1990). The concept of comfort also encompasses the comfort level of different groups in particular social or physical settings (What does the imposing museum building represent to this ethnic group?) and the discomfort felt by anyone in novel and unfamiliar settings. For example, Balling and Falk (1980) found that children on school visits needed an initial exposure to acclimatize themselves to a nature center setting before they could attend to the learning activities their teachers had designed. Comfort is a necessary, although not sufficient, element for learning in the museum.

In general, orientation and other environmental psychological factors play an important role in museums, as they do in all perceptions of spaces (Lynch 1960, Hiss 1990). Light levels, wall colors, placement of exits and entrances, noise, crowds, visitor traffic flow, all influence visitor perceptions and, therefore, visitor comfort. There is a growing literature on the influences of each of these factors in specific museum situations that has been reviewed twice in the past eight years in a single journal (Conroy 1987, Lankford *et al.* 1995). However, the implications of conclusions from these studies for new museum settings are often difficult to predict. Environmental factors compete with other variables, and all are mediated by the specific issues generated by a new museum situation, a new installation, and the preferences visitors bring with them as they enter the museum. For example, the extent to which visitors' predispositions match the spatial organization of an exhibit will influence their comfort level and their ability to learn in a given setting. Visitors who go in a planful way may prefer an organized exhibit; spontaneous visitors may prefer free-choice environments (Griggs 1983). Of course, the same individuals can fall into either category, depending on their reasons for visiting, the company they are in, or the mood generated by the situation that they find as they enter the museum. The unplanned, short stop at the museum may turn into a longer, thoughtful visit (or vice versa) if the weather changes, the group turns out to be of different composition than was expected, or a museum interpreter is encountered in the gallery.

Getting visitors' attention

Empirical data supports the view that visitors spend little time at individual exhibit components (often a matter of a few seconds and seldom as much as one minute); seldom read labels; usually stop at less than half the components at an exhibit; are more likely to use trial-and-error methods at interactive exhibits than to read instructions; that children are more likely to engage with interactive exhibits than adults, and that attention to exhibits declines sharply after about half an hour.

Studies also demonstrate repeatedly that the time visitors spend attending to individual exhibitions or exhibit components can be dramatically increased. Doubling (or more!) of visitor time, both in the per cent of visitors that stop at an exhibit and in the average time spent by visitors viewing or interacting with an exhibit, has repeatedly been achieved. Perhaps least surprising is the finding that explanatory labels, as distinct from no labels at all, make an enormous difference in visitors' attention. Borun and Miller (1980: 15) reported that the per cent of visitors who made a comparison of the perceived temperature of two metal plates by actually touching them went from 6 to 78 per cent when a label was added to the exhibit. Increasing accessibility to the physical and intellectual content of an exhibition (Davidson *et al.* 1991) doubled average visitor time in the gallery; by adding labels, pictures and sound to animal exhibits, Peart (1984) essentially doubled visitor time, as well as knowledge gain, for first-time visitors measured with a questionnaire; Bitgood *et al.* (1987) showed even more dramatic increases by varying placement, content, style, and length of labels.

Advanced organizers

An important pedagogic concept that has found much application in museum exhibitions is the concept of advanced organizers (Ausubel 1968). Ausubel's formulation is difficult to comprehend, his language is quite dense, but the idea of telling visitors what they might learn or that the principles contained in the exhibits that follow is sound, has been advocated by Screven (1986) and others, and has been demonstrated to increase learning in exhibits.

> Advanced organizers can be useful aids to the informal leisure learning that takes place within exhibition environments . . . They provide a framework for deciding ahead of time where you are, what to see, how to get there, what is most important to focus on, and why something may be important, as well as for helping unguided visitors to pre-organize information. They are of several types: conceptual pre-organizers, overviews (what can be seen, what can be done, what may be learned) and topographic organizers (simplified maps).
>
> (Screven 1986: 123–4)

Conceptual organizers assume that there are concepts presented, that there is an intellectual structure to an exhibition. Overviews and topographic organizers apply to every museum; some form of organization of activities and galleries is unavoidable and visitors respond positively if informed about what to expect. A common outcome from formative evaluations is that visitors report that they are confused, both about their physical surroundings and the conceptual content of exhibitions. Informing them explicitly in advance what they are going to see, what they might find, or what the intention of the exhibition is, makes visitors more comfortable, more able to engage with the exhibitions and, therefore, better able to learn.

Koran and Koran (1996: 6) reported an unpublished doctoral dissertation (Ellis 1993) that "explored the extent to which visitors could be influenced by perspective-taking instructions prior to visiting an exhibit." Providing visitors with instructions such as "think of yourself as a geologist" produced positive effects on learning, as did visitors' prior knowledge. Koran and Koran (1996: 6) speculate that "providing visitors with lists of key concepts or unifying generalizations may prompt prior knowledge and increase interest and learning from an exhibit."

Museums as a restorative

Prolonged mental effort leads to mental fatigue. This can be viewed as a matter of discomfort that interferes with learning, or the opportunity to overcome fatigue and be restored can be seen as a form of learning itself. A variety of situations can play a restorative role, not only such obvious restorative processes as sleep, but also more active pursuits, including exposure to nature, such as gardening and wilderness trips (Kaplan and Kaplan 1989). Museum visits can also play such a role, since museums combine four factors considered important for a restorative experience:

> Being Away . . . an environment different from the usual . . .

> Extent . . . a pattern of stimulation that is extended in time and space, that is perceived as an environment that one can enter and spend time in . . .

> Fascination, the qualities of an environment that one finds inherently interesting and engaging . . .

> Compatibility, the degree to which the environment supports what one intends to do, or in other words, one's purposes.
> (Kaplan *et al.* 1993: 727)

Kaplan *et al.* (1993) analyzed focus group transcripts from the 1991 Getty *Insight* study, as well as results from visitor questionnaires they distributed in art museums, and concluded that visitors' comments about their experience in museums supported the view that visits do provide restorative experiences.

Interpretive materials

The assessment of the value of interpretive materials added to objects and interactive exhibitions in museums illustrates both the strength and limitations of traditional research methods. Traditional experimental design research –

139

rmal with control groups and careful planning, as well as less formal
ind-dirty methods – can help museum staff learn about visitors' use
els. "I used to think evaluation is optional. It's not. It's mandatory,"
ierrell (1996: x) in her definitive work on this subject. It is a measure
e still infrequent use of visitor studies of any sort, as well as ignoring
gnorance?) of research from other fields about legibility, that one can still
routinely find museum labels that are difficult to read, longer than most people
will attend to, placed so that their referent is not obvious, or containing text
that is misleading, trivial, or just plain silly.

Such problems can be addressed by studying visitors' reactions as labels are
prepared. But the final assessment of the interpretive power of labels cannot
be divorced from the entire experience of the museum visit, and, if studied in
isolation, provides only a partial view of the visitor experience. The visitor's
interaction with labels is part of a larger whole to which a visitor both
responds and contributes. In concluding her advice for developing labels,
Serrell notes:

> No matter how hard you try or how experienced you are, there is no
> way to know how the whole exhibition will look and work until you
> have the whole thing up and running.
>
> (Serrell 1996: 219)

Others have noted that although a majority of visitors appear to ignore labels
as they walk through an exhibition, or do not pause long enough to "read" the
text, based on knowledge of common reading speeds, some still capture the
content of the interpretive materials. McManus (1989b) reported 70 per cent
"text echo" – that is, use of text language by visitors – when she analyzed
transcripts of their conversations, although they didn't appear to read the text.
Davidson *et al.* (1991) noted that when asked about what they had read on the
labels, some visitors reported what they had heard on audiotapes.

Museum learning as a developmental process

Understanding learning as a developmental process has given rise to two
different kinds of approaches to studying visitor learning. On the one hand,
researchers have focused on categorizing visitors by their previous experience
with museums and their familiarity with the subjects on display. On the other
hand, visitors have been studied in terms of their general stages of development,
with younger and older children and adults considered unique categories of
visitors.

Novice and expert visitors

Learning in art, history, and science museums has been analyzed in terms of
developmental stages of visitors. Much of this data comes from clinical interviews around objects, thinking aloud protocols, and other forms of open-ended
"qualitative" methods described in Chapter 5.

In art museums, two major efforts are Housen's ongoing work on aesthetic development, which she describes in terms similar to Piaget's stages of intellectual development, and the Denver Art Museum Interpretive Project (McDermott-Lewis 1990). Housen carried out extensive interviews with hundreds of museum visitors, children and adults, and arrived at a five stage developmental model[1] to describe increased aesthetic development, based on experience with art. A brief summary of the stages is provided in Table 7.1.

Table 7.1 Housen's stages of aesthetic development

  I **Accountive Stage.** Viewers are storytellers, using concrete observations, personal associations, and sense to create a narrative. Their evaluations of the art are based on what they like and what they may know or think they know about the art. Comments are colored by emotional terminology as viewers seem to enter the work of art, becoming part of an unfolding drama.

 II **Constructive Stage.** Viewers build a framework for looking at works of art, using their own perceptions, knowledge of the natural world and social, moral values, and conventional world views. If the work does not look the way it is "supposed to" (for example, a tree may be orange instead of brown or themes of motherhood may be transposed into wars on sexuality), then the viewer judges the work "weird," lacking, or of no value. The craft, skill, technique, hard work, utility, or function are not evident. Emotional responses disappear as viewers distance themselves from the work of art, focusing on the artist's intentions.

III **Classifying Stage.** Viewers describe the work in analytical and critical terminology similar to art historians. They identify the work as to place, school, style, time, and provenance. They decode the surface of the canvas for clues, using their library of facts and figures. Once categorized, the viewer explains or rationalizes the work's meaning and message.

IV **Interpretive Stage.** Viewers attempt to create some kind of personal encounter with a work of art. They explore the canvas, letting possible interpretations of the work slowly unfold; they point out subtleties of line, shape, and color. Feelings and intuitions take precedence over critical skills, as these viewers allow the meaning and symbols of the work to emerge. Each new encounter with a work of art elicits new comparisons, insights, and experiences. Viewers accept the idea that the art's identity and value are subject to reinterpretation, and see a given interpretation as subject to change.

 V **Re-Creative Stage.** Viewers, having established a long history of viewing and reflecting about works of art, now "willingly suspend disbelief." A familiar painting is like an old friend – known intimately, yet full of surprise, needing attention on the daily level as well as on an elevated plane. In all important friendships, time is a key ingredient. Knowing the ecology of the work – its time, its history, its questions, its travels, its intricacies – and drawing on their own history with the work, in particular, and with viewing in general, allows this viewer to combine a more personal contemplation with one which more broadly encompasses universal concerns. Here memory infuses the landscape of the painting, intricately combining the personal and the universal.

Source: From Housen 1992.

McDermott-Lewis arrived at complementary conclusions from interviews with museum visitors self-described as art "novices" or "advanced amateurs." Novices expected a pleasant social and learning experience from their visit. Among their common characteristics when looking at works of art were a reactive stance toward the art ("I just let [the art] hit me") (McDermott-Lewis 1990: 11), allowing themselves to have an emotional response to the art; making value judgments, "searching for humanity"; and making connections between the art and human contexts. Advanced amateurs also expected an enjoyable experience and saw their visits as learning experiences, but they more deliberately planned what they were going to view. Their looking was also characterized by making human connections and included emotional reactions, but they were more likely to recognize that preferences will vary among viewers and were more likely to spend time with works of art they don't particularly like, to "give things they don't like a chance" (McDermott-Lewis 1990: 34).

Children

A relatively early visitor study (Brooks and Vernon 1956), a basically traditional one, examined children in a science museum. The authors concluded:

> It may be seen less than half of the exhibits are looked at by 50% or more of the children, and that less than half are studied for more than 1 min. by the average child who looks at them at all. This is much what one would expect from any museum visiting. However, these average figures conceal a wide range of variation. A proportion of children do spend 5–10 min. or more at particular exhibits that arouse their interest. Almost always these are the working model rather than the static diorama type. But a larger proportion tend to flit from one thing to another, stopping to press buttons and turn handles, and treat the Gallery more as an amusement arcade than as a source of scientific information.
>
> (Brooks and Vernon 1956: 178–9)

The wide range of children's activities has been documented repeatedly since then; children, like adults, can spend long periods at exhibit components. Bailey *et al.* (1996) recently noted a child who spent 35 minutes building a solar car and getting it to function. Children need time, usually more than one visit, to become oriented to a museum. The random activity that is noted frequently in tracking studies, resolves itself into much more purposeful behavior when examined more closely (Hein 1991). Children orient themselves, engage in fantasy play, carry out investigations, and generally interact with objects. They may not do what exhibit designers intended, but indulge interests of their own ranging from casual interactions to pursuing personal and social agendas. Their activities usually are at least triggered by the exhibition and often involve the objects and concepts displayed. Children seldom record information unless required by teachers, but can recall what they have done and explain it to others after strikingly long intervals – they have demonstrated this weeks or months after their visits through drawings, memories reported in interviews, or by teaching younger children. The social setting of a visit is important. Children act differently on school visits than they do during overnight camp-ins or when visiting museums as part of family groups.

To classify all young visitors simply as "children," means glossing over vast developmental differences. Piaget's major stages of development all occur within the population usually labeled as "children." Obviously, the youngest visitors still unable to read are developmentally different than older, elementary school visitors. But these latter, in turn, are quite different from teenagers. Vukelich (1984) presented a developmental analysis of how children may be able to understand the concept of time to guide educators in history museums. His sensible suggestions illustrate the adaptations required to reach different groups.

A model for children's behavior in museums may best be found in comparing it to children's play rather than to school work. The acknowledgment of play as a significant learning activity is itself theory-dependent. Piaget has called play "the work of the child," but this view is not universally shared:

> people who mistrust play have an implicit theory of learning that argues against play. They believe . . . that learning results only from direct instruction: you learn when someone teaches you. There's always a hierarchy, with one person, the teacher, knowing more than another person, the student. With this kind of theory about learning it's not surprising that play is viewed with suspicion.
>
> (Sykes 1996, quoting Chance 1979)

For Piaget children's play illustrated their intellectual development, and play provided the means for children to confirm their understanding of the world. More recently, Nicolopolou (1993) has argued, following Vygotsky, that play "contributes significantly to cognitive development – rather than simply reflecting it" (Nicolopolou 1993: 9) and should be studied for its own sake, "as one expression of imaginative activity that draws and reflects back upon the interrelated domains of emotional, intellectual, and social life" (Nicolopolou 1993: 13).

It may well be, for both children and adults, that museum-going involves a parallel, unique interaction in the world that provides its own intellectual benefits and should be examined not in terms of what is known about learning in other settings but by what can be learned about learning from studying it.

Experience, "hands-on" The value of experience for learning, which comes from a long educational tradition dating back to Comenius (see Piaget 1967), is strongly advocated by progressive educators (Cremin 1961) and is supported by research in developmental psychology. The value of allowing visitors to interact with exhibits in museums was first documented by Melton (1936), who demonstrated that average time at an exhibit went from 13.8 to 23.8 seconds if visitors manually manipulated components at an electricity exhibition. Since then the importance of interactive elements in exhibitions, as well as younger visitors' preference for them, has been demonstrated numerous times (for example, see White and Barry 1984: 62).

The formal education literature has suggested for decades that students would learn more if they were able to be involved in *meaningful* physical activity. Some museums interpreted the value of activity as including any form of physical action, such as buttons to push, flaps to raise to find answers, or any activity that involved the hands, without necessarily involving the mind. More recently, formal education literature has stressed the need for "minds-on" as well as "hands-on" (Duckworth *et al.* 1990) and museums, likewise, are increasingly including exhibition components or activity rooms where visitors engage in problem solving, complete craft activities, pursue inquiries at length, and participate in other activities that require attention, time, and engagement, not simply physical action. At the Minnesota Museum of Science (Sauber 1994), for example, exhibit developers have constructed physical settings that allow visitors some privacy, to permit them to engage for longer periods of time with exhibit components. Among the principles used to develop these exhibitions are the following:

5 *The experiment labs are designed for one to three users at a time*. They are designed to provoke and to facilitate conversations – between the visitor and the phenomenon and among the visitors themselves . . .

6 *The experiment labs provide visitors ownership for the duration of the experiment time*. Each experiment lab is contained by a fence or knee wall. The enclosure points out to visitors that there is something special about what they are about to engage in doing. It provides a threshold that asks for a commitment of interest and time.

(Sauber 1994: 7)

A social history museum for children in Barbados is set in an old workshop:

it honours the artisans who practiced these disappearing skills. The youngest children sweep enthusiastically with the yard broom, rock the little rocking chair, whirl the potters wheel round and round. Older juniors want to know how and why. They use traditional planes on the workbench, tighten the staveholder, check the labels to identify tools . . .

(Donawa 1996: 161)

Adults

The growing field of adult development was brought to the attention of the museum community with the publication of Collins's (1981) monograph that included an article by Malcolm Knowles, pioneer in the study of "andragogy" (Knowles 1970). Knowles stressed that adults were different from children in three ways:

One is that they have had more experience in taking responsibility for their own lives than most children . . . the second . . . is that adults have a broader and deeper accumulation of experience . . . The third

difference is that adults typically (although not exclusively) are
motivated to undertake education in the hope or expectation of learning
something that will enable them to cope more effectively with life or
enjoy life more.

(Knowles 1981: 56–7)

This approach to adult education is based on qualitative studies of adults as
learners carried out in the 1950s and 1960s and incorporates psychological
principles about actualization and satisfaction, postulated by Erikson (1959),
Maslow (1968), and others. Knowles coined the term "andragogy" to distinguish adult education from children's education, ("pedagogy" is derived from
a Greek root for "child," while "andragogy" incorporates a Greek root for
"adult"), but broadened the definition so that andragogy referred to self-
directed learning, while pedagogy was restricted to what I have called didactic
traditional education.

One method of acknowledging the particular needs of adults is to develop
programs for adults that utilize museum resources. At King's Lynn museums,
for example, adult education institutions, including the local workers' educational association as well as higher education institutions, were encouraged
to use the museum collections in their teaching (Kalloniatis 1995), while at
the Geffrye Museum in London, museum visits were incorporated into English
language instruction for adults (Hemming 1995). At the Fort Worth Museum
of Science and History a collaboration with the local university has resulted in
a learning laboratory that is used both by children and families visiting the
museum and for inservice education of teachers (Martin and Reynolds 1996).

The rich experiences adults bring with them to the museum influence learning
just as these experiences are acknowledged to facilitate learning in formal
settings (Baldwin *et al.* 1990). Thus, including adult reminiscences in videos in
history museums, stressing the connections between objects and experiences or
events that may be familiar to adults, or providing connections to particularly
adult themes – aging, career choices, caring for parents, dieting – can enrich
exhibitions for adult visitors.

Other aspects of adult learning theory that have been applied to museums are
Csikszentmihalyi's concept of intrinsic motivation, leading to "flow" experiences, periods of intense involvement that can lead to learning.

> Studies conducted in a great variety of settings by different investigators
> have shown that a common experiential state characterizes situations in
> which people are willing to invest psychic energy in tasks for which
> extrinsic rewards are absent. Chess players, rock climbers, dancers,
> painters, and musicians describe the attraction of the activities they do
> in very similar terms, stressing the fact that what keeps them involved in
> these demanding activities is the quality of the experience that ensues.
> Many activities that are also well rewarded with money and prestige,
> such as surgery and computer programming, also seem to offer intrinsic
> rewards in addition to extrinsic ones; and these are similar to the ones

that artists and athletes mention. We have called this common experiential state the flow experience, because it is generally described as a state of mind that is spontaneous, almost automatic, like the flow of a strong current . . . If a museum visit can produce this experience, it is likely that the initial curiosity and interest will grow into a more extensive learning interaction.

(Csikszentmihalyi 1995: 69–70)

Recognition of the importance of motivation dates back to an older behavioral tradition. Loomis (1996), stressing that three factors are important in considering learning in museums (motivation, control and meaningfulness), points out that Melton wrote on motivation. Many current writers emphasize motivation when discussing adult learning in museums.

Museum learning as a social process

An alternative to concentrating on individual development as a starting point to understand visitors is to focus on a variety of social factors that influence learning. Three different approaches are possible. Researchers can study visiting social groups (since family groups make up a majority of visitors), they can consider learning in the larger social context in which it occurs, or they can examine learning itself as a socio-cultural process.

Families

Several authors have recently reviewed the research literature on family groups in museums (Borun *et al.* 1995, Dierking and Falk 1994, McManus 1994). "Family" groups are usually defined as any multi-generational social group of up to 5–6 people that comes as a unit to the museum. Families follow purposeful, but personal, agendas during visits and engage productively with museum exhibitions and programs. Families and adult visitor groups come to museums for entertainment and social reasons, but also to learn. They do attend to the exhibit components, often transforming the formal agenda of the educational objectives into personal activities based on their family background, mode of interaction, or the adults' parenting and teaching styles.

In describing family museum visits, McManus (1994) uses the image of a

coordinated hunter-gatherer team actively foraging in the museum to satisfy their curiosity about the topics and objects that interest them, and to satisfy their curiosity about the topics and objects which museum professionals collect and study. Their behavior is practical and economical since the exploration and information gathering is shared out between the family members.

(McManus 1994: 91)

Falk and Dierking (1991: 94), summarizing data from family recollections of museum visits, concluded that the visit had become personalized for each family member. "Early museum experiences are recalled within a larger social, physical and temporal context [and] are bound into an individual's memory in often idiosyncratic ways."

Borun *et al.* (1996) take a different approach to studying family learning; they adhere closer to an experimental-design research method. They have developed a hierarchical system for classifying visitors' behavior at exhibitions at four cooperating museums to identify "learning." Based on museum staffs' analysis of learning goals they developed a rank order of learning levels, defined as "identifying," "describing" and "interpreting and applying," in increasing order of complexity and richness. They then recorded all statements for family visits at selected exhibitions and demonstrated that some performance indicators are more frequently associated with particular learning levels. Families classified at a higher learning level more frequently "ask, answer, comment/explain, read aloud, and read silently" than families at lower levels. They also state, generalizing beyond the data reported,

> Another important aspect of this study is the notion of family learning. While learning happens in individual brains and is perhaps best thought of as a change in the person's neural set, there is also a group effect. The individual's learning experience is enhanced and shaped by input from other family members. Families have a culture of shared knowledge, values, and experiences. A family group that visits a museum can enrich its culture, storing knowledge for later sharing among family members. We can think of this as "potential learning" in analogy to potential energy. If information and associations are acquired by a member of the group, they are available for exchange with other family members, not just at the moment of acquisition but at any time in the future.
>
> (Borun *et al.* 1996: 135–6)

Once again, we see a combination of meaning making based on the interests and background the visitors bring with them and visitor reaction to the topics and objects provided by the museum. These two themes constantly interact, visitors respond to the objects and the intended messages of the museum, while at the same time developing their own understanding, based on their background, prior knowledge, culture, and the qualities of the particular social occasion – there would be no camel to see in the cloud if there were no cloud present in the sky, but, of course, there would also be no camel, weasel or whale to imagine without the contents of Hamlet's mind.

Cultural groups

Generations of anthropologists have demonstrated that culture influences learning despite the fact that the very concept of "culture" is ill-defined. In reviewing experimental work on the relationship between culture and cognition, Cole and Scribner (1974) pointed out that in trying to understand this relationship one of the many problems was the lack of agreement on the meaning of the term "culture." Over twenty years later, Ogbu (1995: 79) reiterates that even "within cultural anthropology there is no agreement as to what culture means."

Culture also affects the outcomes of any research on learning (or meaning making) both in the way in which the research questions are interpreted and the process by which we come to any conclusions. If an attempt is made to compare members of different cultural groups, the criteria for comparison are themselves subject to cultural interpretations. For example, Ogbu (1992) has demonstrated that the relationship between a dominant culture and a minority culture (i.e., whether the members of the minority culture are voluntary or involuntary immigrants) can lead to very different results for members of the same culture in schooling and other social situations in various parts of the world. Finnish immigrants to Sweden, as a group, don't do nearly as well in school as Finnish immigrants to Australia. The same is true for Korean immigrants to Japan, as compared to Koreans who emigrate to the United States. The qualities that we often attribute to "cultural differences" may not be inherent attributes of one group, but arise from the interaction of that culture with a new situation. Our whole language and formulation of learning (we speak of formal and informal learning) are themselves concepts rooted in our own culture, and not phenomena of nature. This realization makes any attempt to explain cultural differences in learning in museums difficult.

We can only be certain that the powerful cultural heritage each visitor group brings to the museum affects who attends museums and what they learn from their encounters. For example, a civil rights exhibition in Birmingham, Alabama attracts many more African-American visitors than groups of other visitors (Bitgood *et al.* 1996) although, in general, African-Americans are under-represented among museum visitors. African-American attitudes towards museums are different from majority attitudes (DiMaggio and Ostrower 1993, Falk 1993).

In her ongoing survey work on visitors and non-visitors to museums, Hood (1996) has discussed the relationship between socio-economic status and interest in an art museum relative to a living history museum that intended to add a farm to its site:

> the higher the rank that respondents gave a local art museum, the lower their likelihood of being very interested in interaction with farm interpreters and in participating in farm activities, such as making apple butter or feeding animals . . .

> Whereas upper education/occupation/income groups are usually the people most interested in museums and historic sites, they were not the most enthusiastic about a potential farm. Individuals who were not in the top two education categories not only favored the farm, but were more willing than other segments to pay for a visit and to purchase food and handicrafts on site.

> (Hood 1996: 85)

Increasingly, museum staff are aware of the cultural diversity of their audience and make efforts to include exhibitions and programs that appeal to specific audience segments. They anticipate that such efforts will broaden their total attendance, not limit it. A recent publication on the educational value of museum exhibitions (Durbin 1996) provides case studies from the museum literature of exhibitions that were designed to appeal to specific cultural or ethnic groups.

> Most of the case studies involved careful identification of the primary intended audience for the exhibition, and generally this was specifically targeted . . . [such as] a community group (the Chinese community in London). This does not exclude other groups, but enables detailed attention to be paid to the needs of the target group. Experience has shown that this is rarely a problem for other visiting groups.
>
> (Durbin 1996: 155)

To summarize, generalizations about the museum visiting habits of different cultural groups may be as informative about (and dependent on) the content of museums as they are about the characteristics of various groups.

Socio-cultural learning

Socio-cultural theories (Vygotsky 1962/1978) suggest that the origins of intelligence should be sought in people's social interaction rather than by examining the interaction of individuals with the environment. These theories hold that all complex forms of thinking (including self-regulation, metacognition, reasoning, and problem solving) appear first between individuals and only gradually over the course of development become adopted and adapted by the individual.

Socio-cultural theories emphasize that meaning emerges in the interplay between individuals acting in social contexts and the mediators – including tools, talk, signs, and symbol systems – that are afforded by culture, environment, and history. Individuals shape the environment that contains these mediators, as they are simultaneously shaped and changed by them. These general emphases (albeit with considerable variability in the precise accounts and issues studied) are reflected in the work of both classical theorists and contemporary researchers in human learning.

Much of this perspective is incorporated into what is now called constructivism (Steffe and Gale 1995, Fosnot 1996b; see also Lave and Wegner 1991, Wertsch 1991). Although Vygotsky carried out his pioneering work in the 1920s and 1930s (Vygotsky 1962) the significance of his research did not become clear to researchers and practitioners in the United States until brought to our attention by Jerome Bruner and others (see Bruner 1986b). Since then, the social components of learning have been widely studied. The application of these ideas to research on how people learn in museums is only recently bearing fruit.

Interpretations of museum learning

Learning as complex interplay

As I indicated at the beginning of this chapter, and illustrated by means of brief synopses of some research studies, a definition of learning in museums is dependent on theories of education, as these are embedded in other, larger concepts. At the Annapolis Conference gathered to consider learning in museums (Falk and Dierking 1995), participants came up with a list of attributes of "what people learn as a consequence of museum experiences":

1 Museums make content and ideas accessible, facilitating intellectual "connections" and bringing together disparate facts, ideas and feelings.
2 Museums affect values and attitudes, for example facilitating comfort with cultural differences or developing environmental ethics.
3 Museums promote cultural, community and family identity.
4 Museums foster visitor interest and curiosity, inspiring self-confidence and motivation to pursue future learning and life choices.
5 Museums affect how visitors think and approach their worlds, in contrast to what they think.

(Falk and Dierking 1995: 20–1)

In addition, institutional learning outcomes were identified – the messages conveyed by the museums themselves, the institutional messages, different for various groups of visitors – and related to the role museums play as part of the total educational infrastructure of their communities. The learning outcomes listed above must be seen, of course, as possibilities, not necessary consequences of visits to the museum. These are what we can hope to accomplish, not what we actually accomplish. The domains are present for every visit, the interaction with the museum necessarily addresses the visitor's sense of comfort, culture, community, curiosity, etc., but just what this impact will be will vary with the visitor, the occasion and what is encountered at the museum.

The socio-cultural perspective, suggesting that the museum experience must be viewed as a complex whole, makes research difficult. Conclusions about learning in museums based on experimental design research are not much different. In summarizing what is known about learning in museums from such studies (besides the ergonomic factors listed previously), Bitgood *et al.* (1994) include the following from Boutourline and Weiss's conclusions, suggesting that unraveling the complex interplay of factors that make up visitors' experiences will be difficult no matter what research orientation is applied. The last point is quoted directly from the original article (Weiss and Boutourline 1963: 26):

- Complex, difficult concept exhibits get visitors' awe and respect but not comprehension
- Different styles of exhibits elicit different ways of responding, and adults and children respond in different ways
- Exhibits function best when they relate to visitors' prior interests
- "Effective communication of knowledge, as distinct from creating of an experience, is a very difficult task within the museum situation."

(Bitgood *et al.* 1994: 76)

150

Museum narratives

Acknowledging that the museum is not the repository of the "truth," but that its contents are arranged by fallible and culturally influenced humans, leads to the suggestion that the messages emanating from museums are themselves stories, narratives to be read and understood by visitors. The image of the story and its possible multiple meanings as a model for teaching and learning – in fact, as a model for constructing our understanding of the world – has a long tradition – it surfaces in the clash of the Apollonian and Dionysian views in *The Bacchai*, for example. An articulation of this view and its application to the study of how the mind works, how education takes place, are discussed by Bruner (1986a). He argues that literary "truths" have their own standing in contrast to linear, scientific truths, and match the way we construct the world. He contrasts his views of the way the content of education is constructed – by teachers and pupils through their negotiated meanings using language – with an older system that sees education "as a *transmission* of knowledge and values *by* those who knew more *to* those who knew less and knew it less expertly" (Bruner 1986b: 123, emphasis in original).

Roberts (1997) has taken the concept of narrative as her central theme in describing the current state of museum education. In her analysis of the process involved in developing an exhibit at a botanical garden, and connecting this activity with the historical development of museum education, she concludes:

> [museums] comprise . . . not a synopsis of wisdom, but a multitude of voices. Theirs is an enterprise that is concerned less with knowledge than it is with narrative. Indeed, in museums, it has become fashionable to speak of the making of meaning by staff, by visitors, or by anyone who holds a relationship to museum collections. Objects, it follows, hold multiple stories and meanings, and, depending on the context, all of these stories and meanings are potentially valid . . . Now, the task of education is about not just interpreting objects, but also deciphering interpretations.
>
> (Roberts 1997: 3)

Models

When researchers' attention shifted from measurement of learning – the degree to which the museums' messages are understood by visitors – to examination of the meaning that visitors make of exhibits, models developed to describe learning changed. McManus (1991) and Bicknell (1995) have suggested that museum communication should not be depicted as a linear process but as an interactive one where both the exhibition and the visitor contribute to the communication. Falk and Dierking (1992) proposed that the "interactive museum experience" consists of an overlapping of personal, social, and physical context to produce the highly varied actual experiences visitors have in museums. Perry (1992) has argued that a successful museum experience that leads to learning includes six factors:

Curiosity – The visitor is surprised and intrigued.
Confidence – The visitor has a sense of competence.
Challenge – The visitor perceives that there is something to work towards.
Control – The visitor has a sense of self-determination and control.
Play – The visitor experiences sensory enjoyment and playfulness.
Communication – The visitor engages in meaningful social interaction.

(Perry 1992: 9)

Viewed from these perspectives it becomes clear that visitors do "make meaning" in museums; they construct an understanding from what they see, touch, and manipulate. Often this understanding differs from the intended "learning" at the exhibition, but it is related to it and comes from attending to the exhibitions. Although visitors seldom read labels, components of label copy appear in their conversations, and the topics of the exhibition form some aspect of their expressed thoughts; although visitors may take paths through exhibitions different from those intended, they purposefully view objects and make associations among what they see; visitors' conversations are about the exhibits and families engage in extensive "learning" activities; although visits are only marginally intended to educate, memories of the visit are full of detail concerning the exhibits viewed and affect visitors' future actions.

In addition, through exposure to objects and designed exhibits, visitors can make new connections, expand their thinking to reach different levels of awareness, and change conceptions, despite the evidence that conceptual change is rare and difficult.

Museums are particularly effective in providing novel, interactive settings where children and adults can encounter striking, unusual and surprising objects and settings, thus capitalizing on the learning potential of "cognitive dissonance" (Festinger 1957/1962). The unique qualities of museums that can lead to disorientation and inattention can also be exploited to support novel, surprising, and disconfirming experiences, now recognized as crucial for conceptual understanding. In order to facilitate learning, not only do the distracting characteristics of unfamiliar settings need to be overcome (both by making the environment friendly and inviting and by recognizing that visitors need time to orient themselves and need as much assistance as possible in doing so), but exhibitions also need to provide intellectual and cultural "hooks" that permit visitors to connect with the exhibitions.

Learning can only occur when visitors can connect to what they already know, can make an association between what they bring to the exhibition and what is presented. Thus, visitors respond favorably to art museum labels that personalize the artist and the works of art, children engage in "fantasy play" at science centers, and families reconstruct their own histories and personal connections with the events illustrated at historic sites.

Conclusion

Contrasting "world views" of research lead to different categories of answers to questions about what we know about learning in museums. But the sum total of the research carried out in this century, with increasing fervor in the past two decades, does suggest some general conclusions:

1 People "learn" in museums. Whether learning is narrowly defined as absorbing specific pedagogic messages contained in exhibits or more broadly defined to include responding to the experience of a museum visit, there can be no doubt that visitors "learn" in museums.[2] People have enriching, stimulating, rewarding, or restorative experiences in museums. They learn about themselves, the world, and specific concepts; they have aesthetic, spiritual, and "flow" experiences.

2 In order to maximize their potential to be educative, museums need first to attend to visitors' practical needs; degree of comfort influences the value of the museum experience. Comfort includes orientation, providing amenities, making the museum's agenda clear, and always maximizing the possibility that the intended interactions between the content of the museum and the visitor be as positive as possible.

3 People do attend to exhibits – they incorporate the content of museums into the agendas they bring with them, and their social interactions, attention, fantasies and feelings include, and often focus on, the content of museums.

4 People make unique, startling connections in museums.

5 Museums are not efficient places for traditional "school" education, learning specific facts and concepts, because people don't spend enough time and are not there primarily for that purpose. [& YES!]

6 Staff should never underestimate the value of wonder, exploration, expanding the mind, providing new, cognitively dissonant (intellectually shocking), and aesthetic experiences. Museums can do this well and these are an integral part of "learning."

7 For visitors to have a positive experience, their interaction with the contents of the museum must allow them to connect what they see, do and feel with what they already know, understand, and acknowledge. The new must be able to be incorporated into the old.

This connection between what visitors bring with them and new experiences is crucial and must be negotiated by each individual whenever new experiences are encountered. This is key to developing situations where learning can take place. Unless the new can be incorporated, either because the visitor already knows enough about the subject to simply include the new into existing frameworks or because the visitor has sufficient other frameworks so that the new can be accommodated by adjusting what is in the mind, the new will be rejected or not observed.

But humans also possess amazing memories and can recall events and experiences years later, although the event that initiated them may have seemed trivial or incomprehensible at the time. Thus, even an unusual or unfamiliar experience in a museum, one that is intellectually inaccessible at the time of the visit, may contribute to later enlightenment.

Constructivism provides the most comprehensive and elegant theory to consider how visitors can both use their previous beliefs and knowledge to construct new meanings and how they can actively carry out this process. How museums can go about maximizing the possibility that visitors will make rich, profitable meanings out of their museum experience is the subject of the next chapter.

8

The Constructivist Museum

We need to place hand, eye, tongue, and mind all together to work upon the real world. We need to invoke the shimmering variety of experiences that border upon and can extend the complex but well-worn patch of daily life for which the student is so well prepared by common sense.

People indeed like to know where they are; the trick may be to lead them to more agreeable places, until they recognize that they too can begin to know and to feel at home in almost any domain where other human beings have dwelt in pleasure.

(Morrison 1995: 288)

We all love to instruct, though we can teach only what is not worth knowing.

(Austen, *Pride and Prejudice*)

Introduction

If we take seriously the constructivist challenge – the implied charge that through direct instruction "we can teach only what is not worth knowing" – what does that mean for learning in museums? How can we fulfill our responsibility as teachers to lead our visitors so that "they recognize that they too can begin to know?"

What will a constructivist exhibition look like? In fact, what will the whole museum look like if it is designed along constructivist principles? No museum in the world today may fit the criteria completely, nor is it likely that some ever will do so. As is true for so many concepts included in this book, constructivism consists of a family of ideas, clustered around a few principles, but no actual exemplar may illustrate all the components. This chapter lists those components that combine to make up a constructivist position on education, and that should be considered in designing the Constructivist Museum. Each represents matters of degree, not absolute standards, and a museum can be constructivist that incorporates many of the components on the list, not necessarily all of them.

155

There are three basic ideas required in order to hold a constructivist view. Each implies specific conditions that must be met to apply the ideas to any educational setting. Museums, with their own particular opportunities and limits, provide one setting where these conditions apply in a specific way. Schools, clubs, and other institutions would have their own means for implementing a constructivist agenda. The basic questions that need to be addressed are:

- What is done to acknowledge that knowledge is constructed in the mind of the learner?

- How is learning itself made active? What is done to engage the visitor?

- How is the situation designed to make it accessible – physically, socially, and intellectually – to the visitor?

Each of these questions is involved in the considerations discussed below.

Connections to the familiar

A fundamental attribute of any constructivist position is the need for the learner to be able to associate an educational situation with what is already known. The importance of "prior knowledge" (Roschelle 1995), meaning all the ideas and concepts that the learner brings to a situation, is a major factor mediating any learning that can take place.

> A large body of findings shows that learning proceeds primarily from prior knowledge and only secondarily from the presented materials. Prior knowledge can be at odds with the presented materials, and, consequently, learners will distort the presented materials. The educator's neglect of prior knowledge can result in the learner's learning something opposed to the educator's intentions, no matter how well those intentions are executed in an exhibit, book, or lecture.
>
> (Roschelle 1995: 37)

It is not only difficult but almost impossible to learn something without making an association with familiar categories.

Adults who are suddenly able to see after having been blind all their lives, have great difficulty in making any sense out of the perceptual field that greets their eyes. They cannot distinguish the foreground from the background, the "shapes" from among the multitude of sensations; they lack the repertoire of ordered perceptions that is necessary to make visual meaning out of their environment. As we indicated in an earlier chapter on the complexity of research methods, we can carry out no research without imbuing it with our mental constructs. Even observation is not neutral.

> After the moment of the observer's birth no observation can be undertaken in all innocence. We always know something already, and this knowledge is intimately connected with what we know next,

whether by observation or in any other way. We see what we expect to see, what we believe we have every reason for seeing, and while this expectancy can make for observational error it is also responsible for veridical perception.

(Kaplan 1964: 132–3)

Likewise, in order to incorporate new ideas, new concepts, new knowledge, we need to be able to associate what we are intended to learn with what we already know. The Constructivist Museum makes a conscious effort to allow visitors to make connections between the known and the new. Possible connections range from feelings about physical space to concepts about ideas. It is worth considering separately each attribute of the museum that allows us to make such connections.

Associations with place

The first kind of connection that visitors make is with the building that they enter, its location, its appearance, and its general atmosphere. Traditionally, museums have been imposing structures, often in neo-classic style (reflecting the period in which they were built), more recently in various modern styles, but usually large, impressive, and perhaps a bit austere compared to the surroundings with which most visitors are familiar. The intention of the architecture is usually to make a grand statement, to illustrate the mighty quality of the museum and the importance of what it contains. Unfortunately, this is not necessarily the most accessible image for many visitors and potential visitors.

In describing museum buildings, Thompson (1990) comments that they changed in the early nineteenth century from being private palaces to becoming monumental public buildings, progressing to becoming aesthetic statements in their own right, such as the Museum of Modern Art or the Guggenheim. He goes on to say:

> The design of museum buildings today remains heavily dependent upon traditionally-held views of the physical environment and its relationship to people. That is, while museums built during the past forty years may look much different than the "private residential, manorial or palatial architecture" (Parr 1959; p. 313) which typified traditional museums, most of the changes reflect technological and aesthetic progress, rather than a more informed and sophisticated approach to meeting the needs of the visitor. As in the past, it often appears today as if these users were nearly forgotten during the design process, and as a result, carefully-articulated visitor-related goals for a museum are often not met in the final product.

(Thompson 1990: 74)

If museums adopt a constructivist stance, they must ask themselves what image they provide for their visitors. Even if the large, architecturally imposing building may not be an unfamiliar presence to visitors, it may suggest a bank, a courthouse, or other public building entered only when necessary, rather than a place that is desirable for learning and enjoyment.

157

Many museums occupy buildings that are specifically built to convey a cultural message, often one about the value of classical culture, about which only some groups within society have any knowledge.

> The museum building may sometimes be one that relates architecturally to the law courts, the police station, and other repressive agents of social control . . . In many cases the messages of the buildings may be enough to deter those who don't know about classical culture, who do know about the power of the law and who have not found many images of the past that have served them well.
>
> (Hooper-Greenhill 1988: 225)

John Kuo Wei Tchen (1992) suggests that an anthropologist from another culture confronted with Western museums may regard them as a manifestation of a curious form of ancestor worship carried out in special buildings.

> How can this quaint practice of these quaint people be described? These shrines exist in all shapes, materials, and sizes, but the most important of them are built in either neo-Greco-Roman style or the most modernist neo-neo design of the times. Such architectural edifices embody the parameters in which ancestor worship is practiced. The advanced hypermaterialism of the culture and the romantic exultation of the bio-individual define what they mean by modernism and freedom. They trace their lineage back to an Anglo-Puritan-Protestant capitalist work ethic of colonizers who originally settled in the northeastern corner of the United States.
>
> (Tchen 1992: 106–7)

There is a whole field of environmental psychology that has addressed this issue, as discussed previously in Chapter 7 in relation to what visitors need in order to learn. Anita Olds (1990) stresses that museum visitors need:

1   Freedom of movement: Visitors need to feel free to move in the space of the museum and the exhibitions, to have their needs met, and to know where they are.
2   Comfort: Visitors should be in an environmentally comfortable setting, one which matches the human factor needs for sensory stimulation without aggressive affront to these senses, in the presence of design that works for them.
3   Competence: In the presence of much that may be unfamiliar, visitors should feel competent, they should not be overwhelmed by so much that is new and incomprehensible that the experience exceeds their adaptive capabilities. These environmental psychological considerations intersect most directly with the pedagogic aspects of constructivist principles.
4   Control: Visitors want to feel safe. Standing with your back to an open space is not a natural activity for humans, but is often required in museums. How is the environment designed to overcome this?

Only when museums combine freedom of movement with comfort and opportunities to feel competent and in control can visitors become "fully *alive* . . . free to drop their self-consciousness, their roles and facades, their fears of knowing too little, or of needing to judge and analyze; free to allow the objects and events to become part of themselves" (Olds 1990: 10).

Others have also stressed the relationship between the environment and its influence on the meaning visitors make of the experience, often commenting negatively on museum experiences. Robert Coles, in reminiscing about museum visits with children he interviewed, comments:

> I can still, even now, [ten years later] remember the description I heard
> [from the children] of the enormous rooms, the marble floors, the
> hushed silence that threatened to envelop the children, so they felt, and
> dared them the urge to make noise as a statement of self-assertion . . .
> The enormity and splendor of many museums bears down on the eyes
> and ears, strained to see and to hear so much under such awesome and,
> yes, constrained or regulated circumstances.
>
> (Coles 1992: 16)

An attitude survey among non-visitors to museums in London (Trevelyan 1991) is entitled *Dingy Places with Different Kinds of Bits*, and concludes "a significant portion of non-visitors received a negative experience of museums as children" (Trevelyan 1991: 11).

The Getty Center focus groups (Getty Center 1991) unearthed similar responses from non-museum visitors, and a visitor survey at the Liverpool Museum and the Walker Art Gallery concluded that "the massive flights of steps and the scale of the buildings are seen as forbidding to some" (Sudbury and Russell 1995: 8–9).

About thirty years ago, a fashion in school design in the United States dictated building "open" schools (not to be confused with "open education," a pedagogic movement, not an architectural one) with few interior walls and large, common areas. Teachers and school administrators responded to this awkward and dehumanizing approach, which left little room for privacy, by designing small, enclosed shelters within the structures where a few children could gather in relative privacy to read and study, or where classes could meet without having to share space with other groups. Where this was not possible, staff complained about the noise, the inability to concentrate on work, and the generally awkward nature of the space. Similarly, museum spaces are often designed with little concern for the needs of visitors for privacy and comfort in order to learn.

Of course, most museum staff have very little choice in the building they occupy. The structure may have been built in previous generations, or the committee that determined its shape may have little connection with designers and educators who develop exhibitions and programs. Like teachers in open space classrooms, they may need to consider modifications within existing space. The internal environment can be modified and developed so that it becomes accessible to people. This usually means some way of decreasing the scale and providing human-size, familiar surroundings. The Constructivist Museum would include at least some spaces that are recognizable to visitors as settings for relaxed, engaged activity which can take time and in which the viewer would feel safe.

No matter how grandiose the overall construction, no matter how high the ceilings or vast the great hall, it is possible to humanize space, make it accessible, and make it feel comfortable (see Semper 1996).

Orientation

Orientation in museums is a powerful issue of its own, related to general comfort, but worth discussing separately from the overall impression made by the surroundings. Before visitors can even focus on the messages the museum intends to deliver, they must know where they are. The Constructivist Museum, recognizing this fundamental component of developing learning environments, is concerned with visitors' orientation. Both the physical surroundings of the building and its grounds and the orientation within those surroundings need to be considered.

Being relaxed, comfortable, not preoccupied with other concerns does not assure that people will learn, but it's a necessary condition: the opposite feelings definitely hinder learning. Describing the museum situation ten years ago, Wolf suggested that most museums had not addressed this issue:

> The element that has been missing most in achieving that connection [of engagement that can lead to a meaningful learning experience] has been the kind of orientation visitors need to maximize their chances for self-enrichment. Museum professionals have been experimenting with every teaching fad and gimmick that have been developed by the educational research community but in the process have made little significant progress in creating constituents who possess "museum literacy" so that they can capitalize on being in the museum environment.
>
> Museum literacy is just another way of describing museum orientation – that mechanism or support that visitors need in order to successfully process their (logistical and conceptual) experience.
>
> (Wolf 1986: 17)

A considerable body of visitor study research has emphasized the needs visitors bring with them to museums; needs that must be met before visitors can attend to the content of exhibitions or programs. Children on school trips need to mark out their surroundings and "take ownership" before they engage the educational programs (Balling and Falk 1980). Hayward and Brydon-Miller (1984) found that visitors to an outdoor history museum had only vague ideas about the time period portrayed and what they might find at the site. They were most interested in orienting for immediate practical needs, and only after these needs were satisfied were they willing to attend to an orientation film.

Every one of us has experienced the panic that comes from suddenly losing our bearings. Whether it is in an unfamiliar street, a public transport station, or even a once familiar setting that has been changed too much by new design, different color, or unrecognizable signage. We know that the sense of uncertainty and confusion can predominate over all other feelings.

Overcoming visitors' fears and uncertainties requires extensive orientation signage using redundant, overlapping means to let visitors know where they are, where all the services are, and where the rest of their group is likely to be. For the Constructivist Museum, this means investing heavily in explicit orientation aids – signs, maps, color codes, distinctive graphics and ideograms, as well as the most effective orientation means of all: human beings who can explain, interpret and answer mundane questions about the space and its organization. All these methods make people comfortable in their surroundings and better able to focus on making meaning at the exhibitions.

Conceptual access

Finally, there is the matter of intellectual comfort, the ability to associate the content of the museum exhibit with prior knowledge, with what is already known. Even if I feel relaxed, comfortable, and in control in a physical setting, I cannot access an exhibition that provides me with no clues to what is known to me already. A collection of totally foreign objects with labels in a language I do not understand will not only prevent me from learning what the curators intended, but will also prevent me from making coherent meanings of my own.

To make the unfamiliar more familiar, two different methods can be employed: it's possible to connect what is (presumably) familiar to the visitors with the unfamiliar content of the galleries, or it is possible to expand exhibition policy so that ordinary and therefore (presumably) familiar objects become the focus of museum exhibition. The approaches are not independent, but can be used in a variety of ways to invite, surprise, or tease the visitor.

Familiar objects Perhaps the easiest method for allowing visitors to make connections to museum exhibitions is to make sure that at least some aspect of the material on display is familiar to visitors. Alma Wittlin (1949: 237) did this in the 1940s when she added current British coins to an experimental exhibition on ancient currency. The tea kettle in the exhibit on steam power; the pocket knife among the prehistoric tools; the familiar local building illustrated next to the classic temple to give a sense of comparative scale; the garden tool mounted next to the animal claw it closely resembles are all examples of efforts to bridge the gap between the familiar and the unfamiliar.

A recent example of the addition of common objects to artifacts that may not be familiar to visitors is discussed by Cotton and Wood (1996) in connection with the new prehistoric gallery at the Museum of London. Their example of common objects in a gallery also illustrates how even simple items require interpretation when a connection with historical artifacts is attempted. What, precisely, will be the message received by the visitor? And to what extent is that association justified by the evidence available?

> Included in these cases are a number of modern items, juxtaposed with their supposed ancient equivalents, in order to allow visitors to begin connecting with the "then and now". Some of the connections make deliberately provocative assumptions and go beyond the strict limits of inference. However, we feel this is defensible if it helps visitors gain a foothold in the distant past. Thus, for instance, a modern beer glass is displayed next to a decorated pottery beaker (are the latter drinking vessels?), a pile of squashed aluminium cans alongside a hoard of scrap bronze (can our modern regard for renewable resources be equated with such a hoard?), and a Swiss army knife is displayed with flint and quartz handaxes (are such tools really "multi-purpose"?).
>
> Cotton and Wood (1996: 66–7)

Exhibiting the known A second approach is to develop exhibitions and programs that expand the museum's collection to include the "ordinary" activities and material of people's lives so that a connection can be made in the mind of the visitor between the foreign, strange objects of the older collections and their everyday material culture.

Thus, when staff at the Victoria and Albert Museum decided "to fulfil the need to make the Indian collections more accessible to a wider audience" (Akbar 1995: 84), they created a post for a South Asian Arts Officer. The incumbent, among other activities, developed a project that invited South Asian women into the museum to design and make their own textile tent hangings "on a scale equivalent to those at the V&A following visits to the gallery." Akbar's description of some of the problems they faced illustrates issues involved in providing access to a museum for non-museum attending audiences, people unfamiliar with it.

> The basic concept was well received because it touched on real experiences of real people. Of course Mughal tents are also opulent and far from the vulnerable and insecure structures of poverty and displacement, but the tent offered a form that could be embellished and decorated. The participants could use decorative motifs to express the feelings and experiences of women today, thereby combining traditional forms with modern concerns. Throughout the project we remained aware that this was essentially a museum project, that the objects were our major resource and that we had to introduce the women, many of whom had never visited museums before, to 'museum culture' and the concept of object-based learning. Most of all we had to make the learning experience an enjoyable one in order to retain the women's continued interest and to ensure further visits to the V&A and other museums, preferably undertaken independently and unsupervised.
>
> (Akbar 1995: 86)

A French museum educator (Rozé 1993) developed a multi-national museum project that brought together 1,000 children from 25 counties around the common theme of rivers, with each contingent developing an exhibition about their own local, familiar river and sharing the results.

When the Boston Children's Museum developed "Bridges," an exhibition based on the cultural differences found in the city and the ways in which various teenagers coped with them in their own lives, the museum capitalized on the common experiences of its visitors to develop an exhibition that celebrated multi-culturalism. Science centers in India often start with building a science playground, where visitors can enjoy coupled swings and other modified playground equipment that illustrate physics principles while engaging in familiar playground activities.

At the same time, the exhibitions mentioned above bring in a less-than-familiar element to provide novelty with the familiar. "Bridges" forces the visitor to recognize that many cultures exist in the city, the rivers project introduced the children to rivers in countries foreign to them, and the science center modifies typical playground equipment. The Constructivist Museum will add novel components in an effort to extend the range of visitors' understanding and allow them to link the old with the new.

The list of locally relevant exhibition themes likely to be recognizable by visitors as part of their background is increasing rapidly as museums strive to make additional connections with their public and to expand their audiences. A common aspect of front-end evaluation studies is precisely to find out what themes, concepts, and objects visitors will identify with and recognize. What can we say about dinosaurs that will resonate with our visitors? What images do they have of colonial times, Roman London, gravity, or pre-Columbian art? Examples of museum connections to new audiences (Chapter 7) and museums' expansion of their interpretive role (Chapter 1) illustrate ways for the Constructivist Museum to allow a wider range of visitors access to its exhibitions.

Museum staff also need to consider the personal connections visitors may make with modes of presentation and ways to think about exhibits. In stressing the need to recognize visitors' meaning making as the primary way in which visitors interact with exhibitions and the requirement that they be able to connect with the content of the galleries, Silverman argues (1995) that we have to fashion a "better fit" between the contents of the museum and the ways in which visitors make meanings.

> In striving to educate visitors and to develop "museum literate" people who know how to view and appreciate objects according to specific paradigms, we as museum professionals have long overfocused on the task of providing visitors with information, facilitating the traditional or "expert" discourses as aspects of visitors' meaning making processes, such as their abilities to see formal elements in artwork, or to provide historical context for artifacts from the past. In the process, the more personal and subjective ways in which visitors make meaning (such as

> through life experiences, opinions, imagination, memories, and fantasies)
> are at best ignored and more often invalidated in museums, where they
> tend to be regarded as naive and inappropriate.
>
> (Silverman 1995: 165)

What is familiar?

I started the previous section with the term "presumably" modifying familiar
to stress that particular familiarity, especially in the sense of being able to make
an intellectual connection, cannot be assumed for visitors. What will appear
familiar when placed in a museum setting can only be determined empirically.
It is a good rule of thumb to assume that you know less about your visitors
than you think you do. It is certainly better to be confirmed in your belief from
visitor studies than to be surprised as a result of your inadequate assumptions
in the absence of empirical data. The results of front-end evaluations often
come as a surprise to museum staff who are already immersed in the intended
topic of an exhibition and are startled to discover what images and ideas the
public does or does not associate with a subject.

Winter (1992: 50) points out that a pre-Columbian art exhibit intended to lure
Mexican-American visitors to a museum because it is about their culture may
instead send the message that the museum supports the destruction of their
culture from those who loot cultural sites. In an evaluation of school programs
associated with an exhibition about twentieth-century design at the Brooklyn
Museum, Hein *et al.* (1987) noted that the aesthetic elements of the exhibition
were largely ignored by many school groups, who focused on the content of the
images – New York skyscrapers, machines, and other streamlined objects – to
reinforce the purpose of their visits, studying New York City history.

Learning modalities

Recent educational theory has shifted the focus to learners and their variable
ways of learning: their learning styles. A question to ask of any gallery or
exhibit that strives to be constructivist is whether it allows viewers to engage
with it using a range of learning modalities.

One way to categorize learning modes is sensory, and how we can use them
to learn. How many of the senses can be used in the exhibition? In an effort
to make a traditional diorama exhibition more accessible to all visitors,
considering both physical limits of some and the range of intellectual modes of
all, Boston's Museum of Science added material that would engage the sense
of sound, smell and touch as well as the traditional components of dioramas –
visual material and text that engaged only the sense of sight (Davidson 1991).
After the extensive changes, not only was visitor time in the gallery doubled,
visitors demonstrated qualitatively more rich learning after the change. For
example, before and after the changes, visitors were asked to describe adaptive
characteristics of beavers (the exhibit is intended to show the range of ways

New England animals have adapted to their environment). While in the pre-test not all visitors could think of even one change, and even visitors who responded positively could mention only beavers' teeth, tail and fur as adaptive features, all visitors questioned in the post-test could mention some attribute that allowed beavers to adapt to their environment and the answers included many more features, beavers' eyelids, oil on their skin, webbed feet and other subtle attributes. Family groups also engaged with the exhibits in different ways, splitting up and following paths that utilized reading, smelling, listening or touching, to regroup and share information they had each gathered (Davidson *et al.* 1991).

Gardner's multiple intelligence theory (Gardner 1985) represents the most extensive effort to date to expand the means educators use to reach learners. He argues that there are at least seven ways to engage in thinking, each of which describes a unique cognitive style for understanding the world. These seven intelligences – linguistic, musical, logical–mathematical, spatial, bodily–kinesthetic, interpersonal and intrapersonal – are cognitive processes, ways of interpreting and organizing phenomena. More recently Gardner (1997) has suggested that there may be additional distinguishable intelligences. The end result of using each intelligence is a particular form of creativity, (for example, application of musical intelligence may lead to competence as a performer, the application of interpersonal intelligence can lead to success in vocations that require relationships with others), while their absence can often be recognized from known pathologies.

The theory of multiple intelligences directly challenges psychological conceptions of a single factor that determines intelligence which can be extrapolated from the results of various psychological tests. It suggests instead that humans have a range of unique cognitive forms for expressing thought and creativity and it argues for valuing all these forms, not only those traditionally associated with school success.

For educational practice, this theory encourages expanding educational activities beyond traditional verbal material organized to appeal to logical–mathematical thinking. All human beings possess all of the intelligences, although individuals may have preferences for particular ones. Therefore, when planning exhibitions or programs, museum staff should consider multiple ways to involve their audience by exploiting all the senses (activated for musical, spatial, and bodily–kinesthetic intelligences) as well as other learner capabilities. In discussing the application of multiple intelligence theory to classrooms, Armstrong (1994: 124) suggests ways that an educator can expand her practice beyond traditional approaches – for example, by having students draw, create 3-D objects, assemble songs, design class simulations – that take advantage of learners' multiple intelligences.

The Constructivist Museum will provide opportunities for learning using maximum possible modalities both for visitor interaction with exhibitions and for processing information.

Accessibility

Exemplary, imaginative work supporting a range of learning modalities is found in efforts to accommodate that large fraction of the visitor population classified as "disabled." The need to compensate for limitations in visitors' ability to use one sensory mode usually results in the addition of material – audio, tactile, or other – that makes the exhibit not only minimally accessible to one select group, but more accessible to all. A useful illustration for this principle is curb cuts, now found in all sidewalks in many countries.[1] Originally installed to benefit those with mobility limitations, curb cuts are routinely used by parents with strollers, bicyclists and joggers, people wheeling groceries or luggage, and all those who desire to make their path a little easier.

Further, physical accessibility is closely associated with intellectual accessibility. By acknowledging the various physical modes visitors may employ, we tacitly acknowledge their different learning styles or types of intelligences.

The opportunity for exhibitions and programs to reflect the incredible range of learning styles that visitors bring with them is limited only by imagination and, unfortunately, by the intense constraints of time, money, and space that restrict all exhibit development. Some examples of ways to expand access include:

- "Layered text" designed for various categories of visitors, so that expert knowledge, information for lay visitors and information for children can all be available. Unfortunately, this approach often degenerates into simply having too much text.
- Audio labels as well as written ones.
- The addition of drama or other live interpretation to an otherwise static gallery.
- Additional resources, such as reference books, CD-ROM computer resources, or demonstrations near the exhibition (see below).

Lessons from extreme situations   Many consider efforts to extend intellectual access to the entire population, to consider the needs of those who are designated "special," to be a modern concept. In fact, this idea goes back to the very beginnings of the scientific study of education. Our modern interest in how people learn and how to make the world accessible to them is derived from scientific study of learning of very special individuals and populations that began almost two hundred years ago.

A historically important early development in understanding learners was the attempt by a young French doctor, Jean-Marc Itard, to educate the "Wild Boy of Aveyron" at the beginning of the nineteenth century. In his effort to work with this *homme sauvage*, Itard

> created a whole new approach to education, centered on the pupil, closely adapted to his developing needs and abilities, seconded by instructional devices – an approach we have accepted so thoroughly as our ideal that we scarcely imagine any other or credit anyone with its discovery.
>
> (Lane 1976: 5)

This dramatic educational situation illustrates a recurring theme in the history of educational theory – work with special needs learners provides knowledge that is applicable to all learners. Piaget received the inspiration for his lifelong preoccupation with intellectual development from early experiences giving intelligence tests, then used to classify children in institutions. He noted that the reasons children gave for their answers appeared to be much more interesting than the answers themselves (Evans 1973).

That people with a special attribute can tell us something about everyone is evident in writings ranging from Oliver Sacks's elegant case histories to Reuben Feuerstein's (1979) clinically developed instrumental enrichment program. Feuerstein, an Israeli psychologist/educator, has devised an elaborate educational system based on Piagetian theory to enable his staff to reach the most difficult children. He and his coworkers have had success in educating children who have been given up as impossible to communicate with by others. The central concept of their system is that in order to function, the mind requires not just interaction with the external world, but some mediating influence, some person who makes possible contact between the student's internal and external worlds. All of us require this. People who have not had sufficient, developmentally appropriate mediation are incapable of making adequate connections and responding appropriately. They need more detailed and specific mediating activity. The important point, according to Feuerstein, is that such deficiency does not represent an unchangeable state; rather it is a lack that can be modified. Thus, he places major emphasis on the learning of thinking skills and on developing diagnostic instruments that are flexible and can be modified by the diagnostician to meet the current level of the learner.

An example of this approach to education, from another famous learner–teacher pair who have inspired many to broaden their view of educational possibilities, is the familiar story about how Annie Sullivan made contact with Helen Keller (Lash 1980). "Teacher" needed to find the "hook" that allowed the student to learn. In the case of Helen Keller this turned out to be the feel of water on her hand. She was able to make the connection between the symbol for water and the substance to which it referred. Once Helen Keller grasped the principle of signing, her progress was rapid. This example, like many that Feuerstein refers to, is so dramatic that we see it as an extreme case, but the concept is applicable to all learning – in all instances we need to ask: What is it that allows the learner to make a connection with what is to be learned? In the Constructivist Museum this question is constantly asked.

The learning environment: universal design An additional aspect of both the Helen Keller example and Feuerstein's work is that these are not stories about *learners* but stories about the interaction between *learners and their learning environment*. It was the dynamic interplay between Helen Keller and Anne Sullivan that resulted in growing understanding (for both of them); it is the constantly shifting, careful intervention of the trained diagnostician in response to the learner's actions that are the basis of the Feuerstein approach. Anderson (1997) has argued that

> The principal barriers to access to museums are social class, poverty, educational disadvantage, ethnic and cultural background, disability and an individual's own attitudes. These factors often operate in combination, so that a successful strategy to overcome them requires a coordinated programme.
>
> (Anderson 1997: 61)

Universal design is a relatively new expression of an idea that has been around for a long time: creating environments and artifacts that work well for *everyone*, including people with disabilities. Far from being simply an architectural or an accessibility concept, universal design in a museum is an educational concept incorporating all factors that limit access. It defines an exhibit approach that accommodates a wider population of museum visitors and, in the process, enhances the experience for all visitors.

> Technically speaking, universal design means creating environments and programs that provide opportunities for learning and enjoyment for all visitors, regardless of ability or disability, age, educational background, or preferred learning style. Practically speaking, universal design creates programs and services that are user friendly in the broadest sense.
>
> (Burda 1996: 24)

The first American Association of Museums Accessibility award, presented in 1995, was given to the Boston Museum of Fine Arts in recognition of efforts made in the imaginative installation and programming for an exhibition of Audubon watercolors. The physical space was made accessible, partly by placing objects at different heights, by careful consideration of light levels, and taking special care in developing explanatory labels. In addition, programming – including a workshop in which a speaker used cardboard wing shapes and a blind naturalist imitated bird calls – was included that made the objects accessible to people with visual impairments. The 1996 award was given to the Denver Museum of Natural History for an exhibition that employed techniques previously pioneered in the New England Habitats exhibition in Boston to make a diorama hall accessible. Not only can an inclusive exhibit engage a wider range of visitors, it can do so more attractively and at no greater cost than an exhibit with specialized access additions. Universal Design is an integral part of the Constructivist Museum.

Theater and drama in museums

Both theater (Hughes 1993) and drama (Hayes and Schindel 1994) represent ways to extend modalities for visitor learning in the museum. Drama, the use of theatre techniques that engage the learner actively (through interaction with a first person interpreter or by being drawn into a theatrical process), and theater, usually a more formal situation involving a script and a production that engage the visitor emotionally and intellectually but not necessarily physically, can help to expand the visitors' access to the content of the museum.

Drama and theater are gripping, powerful media to draw visitors into a scene, make the human connection to objects apparent to some, and allow visitors' imaginations to expand and associate rich meanings with the objects displayed. Theater and drama also provide a relatively inexpensive means to add a modern component to an outdated permanent exhibition. If women's roles or the contributions of non-dominant cultures have been neglected in an historical exhibition, theater can make amends without having to completely redesign the exhibition. The addition of a theater piece to a colonial exhibition of fine furnishings added a powerful social dimension to a traditional display of decorative arts (Munley 1982).

The Constructivist Museum, in its effort to reach all visitors and provide maximum potential for connections to its collections, will include the power and challenge of dramatic interpretation in its galleries.

Other resources

Museum exhibitions are by definition limited; they usually occupy a specific space, include only selected objects, paintings, or models, and limit themselves to a predetermined set of concepts. Museum resources on any topic covered in an exhibition often far exceed what is on display. Yet, the additional materials are seldom closely associated with a gallery.

A recent phenomenon is the addition of a computer component to a gallery. Computer screens have generally been found to attract visitors. Their holding power is less clear, especially if the computer is slow, there is no place to sit, or the screen is difficult to read. But computer resources can offer much greater options than are usually associated with exhibitions.

A particularly rich computer resource to enhance an art museum's exhibitions has been developed at the Detroit Institute of Art (Robinson *et al.* 1996). Staff have installed a Computer Hypermedia Interpretive Program (CHIP) to provide information on art, artists, art techniques and history that allows visitors to find information on both individual works of art and on the relationships between various works through historical and cultural connections.

They describe the program in terms that are compatible with and supportive of the Constructivist Museum:

> Tara Robinson proposed a program, to be built in prototype, that would represent the depth and breadth of the collections instead of dealing with individual curatorial areas or with isolated themes . . . CHIP was not planned as a virtual museum, but as a supplement to an actual gallery visit. It was to provide novice museum visitors with stimulating interpretive materials and strategies in order to help them increase their enjoyment and understanding of art. Adult visitors were to be encouraged, via CHIP and other educational strategies, to think of the museum as a resource in the process of life-long learning.
>
> (Robinson *et al.* 1996: 81–2)

Some art exhibitions include an adjacent room or a corner of the exhibition with books about the artist or period; science and children's museums have also set up resource corners to supplement exhibitions. But seldom has this strategy become an integral part of the museum experience as a whole. Are there communities where the local library and the local museum are a joint venture, and the various topics covered by the library are interspersed with the exhibitions? Are there universities that have integrated their museum and library catalogues so that each provides access to the other? Are there instances where the boxes of materials related to exhibits that are produced, marketed, or otherwise distributed by folk art, history, crafts, and science museums are directly associated with the galleries where their principles or their origins are on display?

Another approach has been to develop open storage areas: galleries where a museum's extensive collections are available to be viewed, although they may be only minimally interpreted by modern standards. But for the visitor who, having seen the exhibition, wants to study more deeply, or who came to the museum with this interest already developed, the open storage provides an opportunity to involve the new or ongoing interest, to browse at length among the eighteenth century glass, the Native American collection, or the vast array of scientific instruments or mounted sea birds.

Museums have become adept at placing a shop near the exit of a major exhibition to exploit visitors' desire to know more or, most often, to take home a souvenir of their visit. But the principle applies to a much wider range of resources associated with exhibitions; resources that might be consulted, borrowed, or bought, always related to the material in the gallery. The Constructivist Museum will provide resources of all types for those visitors who are motivated to continue their interaction with the subject of the exhibition.

Collaborations

Museums have begun to expand their associations with libraries. In a recent exchange of ideas on a museum education electronic discussion group, the following accounts appeared:

> Seattle Art Museum has been forging a strong relationship with the Seattle Public Library in a number of ways. We have been working with The Center for Technology in the Public Library, which recently became the Technology Resources Institute for Public Libraries, to develop educational materials for the World Wide Web . . . We are working with the Fine and Performing Arts Department of Seattle Public Library to offer "Internet and the Arts" trainings for teachers and students. We have also been working together in building community programming. It's been great, and has promise to get even better!
>
> (Murphy 1996)

> The Art Gallery of NSW and the State Library of NSW (which is only 5 minutes walk away, across a park) have started sharing an exhibition

called ARTEXPRESS (Outstanding works submitted for the Higher School Certificate examination in Visual Arts). This enormously popular show has been at the Art Gallery for 14 years but, starting 1996, the Library has started to mount a regular satellite show of works in series and students' "Process Diaries" at roughly the same time (January–March). Another collaboration, on a less public basis, has been in the development of a non-commercial CD-ROM based on the collection of the State Library's collection of early Australian art, for distance education students at Charles Stuart University.

(Cooper 1996)

Of course, collaborations between museums are also possible. The rain forest and its significance to our lives was recently the topic of collaborating exhibitions at three museums in Fresno, California (O'Donnell 1995a). The Fresno Metropolitan Museum, Fresno Art Museum, and Chaffee Zoological Gardens each mounted complementary exhibitions. Their purposes for doing so may have included issues distant from concerns about how visitors learn ("a trio of exhibits that is being marketed together with the help of the local convention and visitors' bureau" (O'Donnell 1995a: 21)), but the resulting displays and interactive components were likely to allow a wide range of visitors to find something that intersects with their own knowledge and interests.

Finally, museums can also collaborate with other educational institutions to make their approaches particularly appropriate for a wider range of visitors. Renewed interest in museum–school partnerships has been reviewed (Science Museum of Minnesota 1996, Hirzy 1996), as both schools and museums look for new ways to provide relevant venues for all children to learn. A novel museum–university partnership is provided in the hands-on science/learning lab at the Fort Worth Museum of Science and History (Martin and Reynolds 1996). The museum, in partnership with educators at Texas Christian University, has developed a discovery room that serves public visitors, university preservice education students, inservice teachers and school groups. The multiple use allows the collaborating partners to have selected adults and children learn "side-by-side," to carry out research on children's learning, and to increase museum service to the community.

Whether through technology (collections or other resources on CD-ROM disk), open storage, collaborative exhibitions, or partnerships with other institutions, the Constructivist Museum will make available to the visitor a much larger array of materials and objects than would be possible using only the objects of a single exhibition. And it will do so without returning to the overwhelming and alienating array of objects that characterized older museum exhibitions.

Time

It is axiomatic in any educational theory that it takes time to learn. The analogy of cooking can help here. No matter what the recipe, the mixing of ingredients to make a finished product requires the passage of time: it isn't enough to assemble the correct components in the proper amounts, nor yet to mix them as instructed. It takes a certain amount of time for the expected product to emerge. The advent of microwave ovens has made time a much less significant variable in some cooking. No parallel to microwaves has yet been discovered for learning. Ideas still need to "percolate," "simmer," or "stew" if they are to end up more than "half-baked."

All the best educational situations in the world will not lead to learning, no matter how it is defined, unless the visitor spends some time engaging with the exhibition. What have museum staffs done to extend the time that the visitor spends in the exhibition, therefore increasing the probability that something meaningful will be learned? The Constructivist Museum will do all it can to lengthen visitor time in the exhibition.

The simplest way to extend visitor time, without changing any other aspect of an exhibition, is to provide for visitor comfort – the addition of seating to a gallery will extend visitor time at the exhibition. Museums have discovered the value of stools in front of interactive exhibits; visitors settle down and are more likely to spend the period of several minutes that may be required to engage with the content of the material under the microscope, with the component parts that need to be assembled, or with the multi-minute loop projected on a screen.

A new technique to promote business efficiency is to insist that meetings be held in places without chairs; this tends to speed up the proceedings considerably. Just the opposite strategy should be the goal of museum staff; they need to do all they can to keep their visitors in the gallery.

The desire to extend visitor time does conflict with the marketing push for more and more visitors, which is often motivated by museums' increasing concern about justifying their existence. The dilemma this tension creates cannot be resolved easily. Museums need to demonstrate that visitors who stay longer have a more enriching visit.

Social interaction

Increasingly, we appreciate the central role that social interaction through language plays in learning. We also know that museum visitors come predominantly in social groups; individual visitors account for only 5–20 per cent of all visitors.

Social interaction allows learners to go beyond their individual experience, to extend their own knowledge and even their ability to learn. As Matusov and Rogoff (1995) state in discussing a perspective on the social component of learning based on Vygotsky's contributions:

> In varying communities of practice, learners participate in different
> activities explicitly or less deliberately designed for their learning. The

learners' development includes not only what they are learning how to do, but also how they are participating in the community using (and demonstrating) their developing skills and knowledge.

(Matusov and Rogoff 1995: 100–1)

One of the newer concepts developed in formal education is 'cooperative learning,' the idea that by sharing information and working together students will learn more and will learn better. Schools have embraced this idea and, among other practices, have developed seating plans that cluster children together in groups of three or four to facilitate working together.

David Uzzell (1993: 126) describes "socio-cultural" visitor studies that he and his students carried out. They devised worksheets that posed issues leading to cognitive dissonance. Various versions of the worksheets required that students work either individually or in pairs.

> In the individual condition, the children experienced cognitive conflict, whereas in the collective condition they experienced socio-cognitive conflict. It was found that group performance was significantly superior to individual performance thus supporting the hypothesis that socio-cognitive conflict is a salient factor in learning. This superiority was not attributable to modelling.
>
> (Uzzell 1993: 126)

Uzzell found similar results in exhibit situations designed to require family groups "to interact with each other in order to understand principles behind working gear wheels" (Uzzell 1993: 126). The version that required such interaction encouraged family conversational exchanges about the exhibition. "Not only did the social-interactive exhibit encourage much more social inter-action among family members, but this interaction was qualitatively different to that prompted by other interpretive media" (Uzzell 1993: 126). Matusov and Rogoff discuss findings from their research on the consequences of using social learning practices in elementary classrooms:

> in joint problem solving, third and fourth-grade children experienced with cooperative schooling built on each other's ideas in a collaborative way and embedded their instruction in collaboration more often than did children from a traditional schooling background. Children with a traditional schooling background emphasizing individual competitive performance predominantly used guidance based on withholding information, consistent with known-answer questions used by teachers in traditional schools.
>
> (Matusov and Rogoff 1995: 101)

Adult educators have long recognized the power of using students' shared experiences as an adjunct to education. A key concept in educating adults is the idea of a "learning community."

> Adults often learn most effectively in groups that they join by choice, groups characterized by discussion, interaction, and collaboration and in

173

> which participants both receive and provide academic and social
> support. Such groups value the individual; at the same time they require
> that the learner communicate and reflect within the group.
>
> (Baldwin *et al.* 1990: 7)

Elsa Feher (1996) describes how she and her colleagues developed benches for
two in order to facilitate communication at an exhibition. At the National
Museum of the Boy Scouts in Murray, Kentucky, designer Michael Sand, a long-
time advocate of the importance of social interaction to facilitate learning, built
a number of exhibit elements that require cooperation. He hoped to engage
people in a cooperative activity that would mirror the cooperative element of
scouting.

> Starting with the arrival at the Museum, visitors are invited to enter via
> a Confidence Course. I modeled the course on the high ropes challenge
> courses used throughout scouting, more recently in executive training
> and Outward Bound programs. It's easy if you cooperate, but you can't
> get through successfully alone.
>
> (Sand 1996)

The Boy Scouts Museum also contains two interactive theaters that allow
visitors collectively to influence the destiny of the audio visual presentations. In
one, visitors are presented with a scenario of a patrol looking for a lost child
and have to decide, by group vote, where to look next, with the continuing
story line depending on their vote. Another exhibition allows visitors to select
among possible options in a story that involves trusting your child.

In our observations of visitors at the Boston Museum of Science's diorama
exhibition we noted significant changes in visitor behavior after the museum
had installed additions that catered to different learning modalities. Not only
did we observe visual, oral, tactile and olfactory learners, but when members
of family groups who preferred these various learning modes reunited and
discussed their experiences they had rich conversations based on the different
modes they had employed.

Individual visitors bring their unique experiences, prior knowledge, and
preferred learning styles to the exhibition. The interaction between individual
visitors and the rich resource of the exhibition leads to unique outcomes for
each visitor. By sharing these experiences with other members of their groups,
visitors can enrich the experience for each group member. The Constructivist
Museum not only accepts the possibility of socially mediated learning, it makes
provision for social interaction and designs spaces, constructs exhibitions, and
organizes programs to deliberately capitalize on learning as a social activity.

Developmentally appropriate

No challenge may be greater than to make museum exhibitions that will
be appealing, accessible, and meaningful for the wide range of visitors who

frequent the public halls of museums. All the factors discussed above are intended to achieve this goal. But at least as important a consideration for engaging learners as culture, social background, or preferred learning styles, is the visitor's developmental level. Almost a century of research in developmental psychology has taught us that not only are children different from adults but that both children and adults go through many developmental stages.

It is not sufficient to develop exhibitions that will appeal primarily to "adults" or to "children"; we have to consider the various stages of intellectual development in our audiences, as well as the wide range of socially mediated 'developmental stages among all visitors. Marketing experts have divided the population into "segments," teenagers, twentysomethings, older adults, or low status, college graduates, high income, etc. These categories reflect a recognition that social subgroups have particular usages of language and cultural characteristics, have different tastes and interests. How can the Constructivist Museum address this immense diversity in its audience?

One approach is to provide separate venues for different groups – a children's discovery room in one gallery, a nostalgic exhibition for older visitors in another, a serious treatment for scholars in a third. Or, alternatively, the same gallery may include exhibits at different heights, with different labels for adults and children, or might incorporate material intended to interest various categories of visitors. The difficulty with this approach as an exhibition policy is usually limitations of time and money. As a programming policy, this approach can be rich and rewarding, providing services for select groups of visitors depending on their developmental stage and interests.

Another avenue for addressing the different developmental needs of visitors is to try to focus on those attributes of exhibitions that will be accessible to all. This means, for example, minimizing reliance on words, or choosing standard display characteristics – height, reading level for text, for example – that are intended to reach the largest audience.

All these efforts involve necessary compromises; there is no simple formula that will solve the problem posed by the different characteristics and developmental stages of visitors. Museums' success in engaging visitors will depend both on the quality of the presentation and the local circumstances in which particular material is used. The attitudes and expectations of visitors to a particular museum influence the readability of labels and the willingness and ability of visitors to engage with a particular presentation method.

In the Constructivist Museum, staff will have addressed the developmental needs and have empirically examined whether exhibits and programs have the ability to reach their intended audience. They will have made policy decisions and confirmed that their practice matches their decisions. They have moved away from the closed museum focused on a small group of visitors:

> The museum and gallery world is still a closed system, belonging to a very small group of people who are even more defensively protecting their territory against invasion from "outsiders." Their concept of

quality is based on a hierarchy of value, with the ideology of the industrialized West – legitimized as superior – controlling and determining this hierarchy. Concepts of progress, continuity, totality, mastery, and the universal claim to history are accepted as "true." . . .

The point is not that value judgments must be abandoned, but that they must be understood to be conditioned by who we are – our backgrounds, our educations, our interests, our positions – in the society in which we live. There is no single tradition or story, no one position, that can speak with authority and certainty to all of humanity.

(Tucker 1992: 11, 13)

The Constructivist Museum will have policies that dictate its desire to reach a wide range of visitors and will have practices that have been demonstrated to do so. One of these without the other is not sufficient. Many museums have mission statements that indicate their desire to serve minorities, communities, etc. Their practice may or may not reflect this.

Intellectual challenge

People need to connect to what is familiar, but learning, by definition, goes beyond the known; it leads to new "agreeable places." How is this accomplished? I have suggested above that one path is seduction, enticing the learner by the lure of the familiar, the comfortable, the known, to explore more deeply. But another well-recognized path is the lure of a challenge. The trick, of course, is to find just the right degree of intellectual challenge to leave the learner slightly uncomfortable but sufficiently oriented and able to recognize the challenge that she will accept it. This central dilemma of all learning, alternatively called the problem of match (Hunt 1961), cognitive dissonance (Festinger 1957/1962), disequilibrium (the Piagetian term), or, to emphasize the social aspect of learning, the Zone of Proximal Development – an intellectual "space" you can only reach with the guidance of a "teacher" (Vygotsky 1962/1978) – needs to be emphasized in every exhibition. The staff in the Constructivist Museum consistently challenge themselves and ask: Will this challenge our visitors but provide them with enough familiar context so they can rise to the challenge? Again, the answer to this question resides not in some theoretical principle, but in empirical results from trying out various exhibition components with visitors.

A special dilemma (or opportunity?) for any educator is the issue of new ideas or concepts that don't seem to make sense to the learner when first encountered but re-emerge much later, after additional reflection, exposure, or experience, to allow the learner to reach new understanding. Museums probably contribute significantly to our later enlightenment, as some of the memory research suggests. But it isn't easy to plan for delayed understanding.

Acknowledging constructivism

Embracing constructivism requires two self-conscious acts on the part of museum staff. One is to acknowledge that exhibition-making is not displaying truth, but interpretation. This issue is explored in studies of the development of exhibitions (Macdonald and Silverstone 1990, Roberts 1997). The other is to pursue aggressively the study of how visitors make meaning in the museum.

The constructed exhibition

The Constructivist Museum needs to publicly acknowledge its own role in constructing meaning when it displays objects and develops programs. It's important that this human decision-making process – full of compromise, personal views, opinions, prejudices and well-meaning efforts to provide the best possible material for the public – be opened up to view. How can this be done?

All the methods discussed above provide means to open the museum to wider interpretation and access to broader audiences. In addition, the constructivist museum will increasingly include the public in the development of exhibitions. At the Museum of London, the Peopling of London Exhibition was also a "project."

> The project sought to widen the audience to the Museum, in particular by attracting new audiences from the ethnic minority communities; to challenge the notion that immigration was a post-war phenomenon; and to change the way in which the Museum represented London's history by presenting the histories of communities of people not represented in the permanent galleries. Moreover, it was intended to encourage the Museum's staff to think about new policies and practices.
>
> (Selwood *et al.* 1996: 15)

The project included innovative means to both publicize the exhibition and gather material for it from many segments of the community. It included gathering oral histories, including community groups in the planning, and sending a mobile display van to markets, squares, and supermarket car parks throughout London to gain access to diverse voices that might otherwise not be heard. Perhaps most significant is the concept that the exhibition represents only one aspect of a larger effort to expand the museum community. At the Field Museum in Chicago, the exhibition on Africa was similarly viewed as a community building exercise.

Museums can also directly publicize the exhibition process by such methods as developing exhibitions about exhibitions, as was done at the Wadsworth Athenaeum (Lusaka 1996). Shocked that even some trustees believed that the museum's collections policy was arbitrary, the director mounted "Acquiring Art in the 90s: The Inside Story," an art exhibition that discussed acquisition policy, included quotations and pictures of the curators and handouts about various aspects of acquiring paintings for a museum. The museum curators had to be persuaded to "reveal their personal experiences to the public," and shed the impersonal tone associated with museum exhibitions. In Columbus, Ohio, the art museum director invited four community leaders to serve as guest curators and install four different galleries (O'Donnell 1995b). The result, "an installation the museum couldn't have created on its own even if it had tried" (O'Donnell 1995b: 11), was highly personal selections that emphasized the guest curators' own interests (the local zoo director chose works that featured animals, the mayor favored family scenes, and a third curator emphasized his own African-American heritage).

All exhibitions are constructed and represent the personal views of curators. These two examples illustrate that this personal factor can be made public and can provide an additional means for visitors to associate with the museum by allowing them to see the human quality of the museum itself. The Constructivist Museum will maximize the visibility of the exhibition process both to expand its connections with the larger community and to add one more layer to the many levels of meaning made available to the visitor.

The process of studying visitors

Museum staffs work hard to allow visitors to understand the contents of museums. One powerful way to improve their practice is to reflect on it by becoming involved in visitor studies. When a British Task Force designed a program for assessment of the new national curriculum in the 1990s (Black 1987), it included a comprehensive plan for teachers to get together at every level to compare their students' work and to share information about student results on the complex performance tasks they were developing. Similarly, in the United States, many argue that the most powerful inservice activity available for teachers is to come together to study children's work. The parallel activity for museum staff is to examine their visitors' engagement with museum exhibitions and programs.

Museum staff who begin to look at what visitors do and consider what visitors learn, often report this as an enormously enriching activity. Reporting on their three-year Museum Education Evaluation project at the Department of Museum Studies at the University of Leicester (Hooper-Greenhill 1996), the contributors note that they learned a great deal about how to carry on small-scale projects, about a range of approaches to evaluation, and how to improve their practice.

> In addition, and perhaps the most important result of all, we have learnt how to think critically about what we as individual professionals, and what our museums, as social cultural and educational institutions, are trying to achieve, and why.
>
> (Hooper-Greenhill 1996: 39)

The Constructivist Museum will view itself as a learning institution that constantly improves its ability to serve as an interpreter of culture by critical examination of exhibitions and programs. The most rational manner in which to do this is for the staff to become engaged in systematic examination of the visitor experience; in short, to carry out visitor studies.

Conclusion

Visitors make meaning in the museum, they learn by constructing their own understandings. The issue for museums, if they recognize this principle, is to determine what meanings visitors do make from their experience, and then to shape the experience to the extent possible by the manipulation of the environment. Every museum building will send a message (or multiple messages); every exhibition will evoke feelings, memories, and images; every encounter with an object brings about a reflection (even if it is only incomprehension and frustration); every social interaction reinforces connections, stimulates new ones, or triggers personal anxieties.

We know the range of visitor reactions to their museum experience is tremendous; we know that powerful, enriching, even life-changing moments are possible in museums. Visitors do learn in the museum. What the cumulative result of these experiences will be is up to future exhibition designers and museum educators working together and with their audience.

Notes

Introduction

1 I am told that all these resources are now on-line, available directly or through commercial services.

2 Education theory

1 Strictly speaking, "positivism" refers to the philosophy of Auguste Comte, as Miles (1993: 29) pointed out. But it has been widely used to describe the position that science provides a true picture of nature.
2 Some exhibitions, although didactic, are arranged more like "study collections" – the components are categorized and used to illustrate some subject structure, but there is no specified path through the collection.
3 The operationalism of simple S–R theory denies the existence of anything beyond the behavioral events.

3 Early visitor studies

1 I am grateful to Dr Paulette McManus for pointing out this study to me.
2 See the work of Otto Neurath, especially Chapter 7 in Neurath (1973). Neurath's significance for museum education has been discussed by Kräutler (1995).
3 See Sir Cyril Burt's work, for example, discussed at length in Gould (1981).
4 The terms "qualitative" and "quantitative" are frequently used to describe two different approaches to research, although the crucial distinction between the two does not hinge on the use (or lack) of some form of counting in the research process. The proper designation

for these two paradigms is the subject of considerable controversy. It will be discussed in the next chapter.

4 The countenance of visitor studies

1 The title of this chapter honors a seminal paper by Professor Robert Stake (1967) that helped define – and broaden – the new field of program evaluation.
2 USOE did not become a separate department of the federal government until the Carter administration, 1977–81.
3 In the United States, a post-war curriculum reform movement focused on the spiral curriculum, the possibility of teaching subjects to students at varying levels as they matured (Bruner 1960). Curriculum reform, partly inspired by efforts to keep up with apparent Soviet success in science (Goldstein 1992) also included a movement to resurrect progressive educational practices first suggested by Dewey at the turn of the century. United States educators turned to British practices of the "integrated day" (Brown and Precious 1968, Weber 1971) as models for classroom organization and instruction. In Britain, the Plowden Report (Department of Education and Science 1967) and educational reform efforts associated with the broadening of educational opportunities under post-war Labour governments took hold, leading to significant changes in education, especially in the earlier years.

5 Ladder and network theories

1 Of course, another whole field of agricultural research places particular emphasis on the variance in the results, on the behavior of the

odd or peculiar plant, rather than on the average results. In plant genetics, the efforts to find new, genetically different varieties of plants depends on looking for the unusual result, rather than on the average outcome.

2   The application of statistical means based on restricted consideration of individual differences can have serious consequences for persons who fall outside the range of applicability. Consider the example of the revelation of the lethal effects of automobile air bags on members of the population who differ from the "typical" body type of those for whom they were designed – men at least 5 ft. 8 in. (173 cm) in height. That stipulation, although (perhaps) matching the average height of American males, leaves out a shockingly large fraction of the human population.

3   Today, narrative and story telling themselves are considered appropriate forms of research, as indicated in chapter 7 (see also Coles 1987).

6   Studying visitors

1   Nielsen has been misquoted as stating that no visitors remained at an exhibit for more than 30 seconds (Falk 1982, Leichter *et al.* 1989: 38.) In fact, he reports "variations in average time of from nine seconds to one minute, and ranges from five seconds to three and one-half minutes per exhibit" (Nielsen 1942: 109).

2   She has been termed the "American doyenne of surveys" by Runyard (1994).

7   Evidence for learning in the museum

1   Earlier iterations postulated four stages plus some transition stages.

2   We need to acknowledge that some of the time the museum experience is negative from the perspective of both the visitor and the museum educator. Some museum visits teach visitors that they don't like museums, that these are boring, inappropriate or even offensive places to be avoided whenever possible.

8   The Constructivist Museum

1   Curb cuts are required by law in the United States as an accommodation for people with disabilities.

Bibliography

Akbar, S. (1993) "The Nehru Gallery National Textile Project," in Indian National Committee for ICOM, *Museums for Integration in a Multicultural Society*, Calcutta: ICOM Asia-Pacific Organization, 38.

—— (1995) "The Mughal Tent Project at the Victoria and Albert Museum," in Chadwick, A. and Stannertt, A. (eds) *Museums and the Education of Adults*, Leicester: National Institute for Adult Continuing Education, 84–91.

Alexander, E. P. (1983) *Museum Masters: Their Museums and Their Influence*, Nashville: American Association for State and Local History.

Alt, M. B. (1977) "Evaluating Didactic Exhibits: a Critical Look at Shettel's Work," *Curator*, 20(3): 241–58.

American Association of Museums (1969) *America's Museums: The Belmont Report*, Washington, DC: American Association of Museums.

—— (1984) *Museums for A New Century*, Washington, DC: American Association of Museums.

—— (1992) *Excellence and Equity: Education and the Public Dimension of Museums*, Washington, DC: American Association of Museums.

American Psychological Association (1994) "Psychology's Input Leads to Better Tests," *American Psychological Association Monitor*, 25 (June): 1.

Anderson, D. (1995) "Gradgrind Driving Queen Mab's Chariot: What Museums Have (and Have Not) Learnt from Adult Education," in

Chadwick, A. and Stannertt, A. (eds) *Museums and the Education of Adults*, Leicester: National Institute for Adult Continuing Education, 11–33.

—— (1997) *A Commonwealth: Museums and Learning in the United Kingdom*, London: Department of National Heritage.

Anderson, J. R., Reder, L. M., and Simon, H. A. (1996) "Situated Learning and Education," *Educational Researcher*, 25(4): 5–11.

—— (1997) "Situated Versus Cognitive Perspectives: Form Versus Substance," *Educational Researcher*, 26(1): 18–21.

Anderson, P. and Roe, B. C. (1993) *Museum Impact and Evaluation Study: Roles of Affect in the Museum Visit and Ways of Assessing Them*, Chicago: Museum of Science and Industry.

Anderson, S. (1968) "Nose Prints on the Glass," in Larrabee, E. (ed.) *Museums and Education*, Washington, DC: Smithsonian Press. 115–26.

Armstrong, T. (1994) *Multiple Intelligences in the Classroom*, Arlington: Association for Supervision and Curriculum Development.

Astudillo, L. (ed.) (1996) *Museums, Education and the Natural, Social and Cultural Heritage*, Cuenca.

Ausubel, D. P. (1968) *Educational Psychology: A Cognitive View*, New York: Holt, Reinhart and Winston.

Bagchi, S. K. (1993) "Museum and Community," in Indian National Committee for ICOM, *Museums for Integration in a Multicultural Society*, Calcutta: ICOM Asia-Pacific Organization, 55–6.

Bailey, E., Kelley, J., and Hein, G. E. (1996) "Summative Evaluation Report for *Investigate!*," Cambridge, Mass.: Program Evaluation and Research Group, Lesley College.

Baldwin, L., Cochrane, S., Counts, C., Dolamore, J., McKenna, M., and Vacarr, B. (1990) "Passionate and Purposeful: Adult Learning Communities," *J. Museum Ed.*, 15(1): 7–9; reprinted in *Patterns in Practice: Selections from the Journal of Museum Education* (1992) Washington, DC: Museum Education Roundtable, 162–7.

Balling, J. D. and Falk, J. H. (1980) "A Perspective on Field Trips: Environmental Effects on Learning," *Curator*, 23(4): 229–40.

Bateson, M. C. (1962/1987) "1987 Preface," in Bateson, G., *Steps Towards an Ecology of the Mind*, Northvale: Aronson.

—— (1984) *With a Daughter's Eye: A Memoir of Margaret Mead and Gregory Bateson*, New York: W. Morrow.

Belenky, M. F., Clinchy, B., Goldberger, N., and Tarule, J. (1986) *Women's Ways of Knowing: The Development of Self, Voice, and Mind*, New York: Basic Books.

Berlyne, D. (1957) "Recent Developments in Piaget's Work," *British Journal of Educational Psychology*, 27: 1–12.

Bicknell, S. (1995) "Here to Help: Evaluation and Effectiveness," in Hooper-Greenhill, E. (ed.) *Museums, Media, Message*, London: Routledge, 281–93.

Bicknell S. and Mann, P. (1993) "A Picture of Visitors of Exhibit Developers," in Thompson, D. *et al.* (eds) *Visitor Studies: Theory, Research, and Practice*, 5, Jacksonville: Visitor Studies Association, 88–98.

Bicknell, S. and Mazda, X. (1993) *Enlightening or Embarrassing? An Evaluation of Drama in the Science Museum, Volume 1*, London: National Museum of Science and Industry.

Bitgood, S., Nichols, G, Patterson, D., Pierce, M., and Conroy, P. (1987) "Designing Exhibit Labels from Experimental Research," in AAM Evaluation and Research Committee, *Current Trends in Audience Research and Evaluation*, San Francisco, 25–7.

Bitgood, S., Serrell B., and Thompson, D. (1994) "The Impact of Informal Education on Visitors to Museums," in Crane, V. *et al.*, *Informal Science Learning: What the Research Says About Television, Science Museums, and Community-Based Projects*, Dedham, Mass.: Research Communications, Ltd, 61–106.

Bitgood, S., Cleghorn, A., Cota, A., Patterson, D., and Danemeyer, C. (1996) "Enhancing the Confrontation Gallery at the Birmingham Civil Rights Institute," *Visitor Studies: Theory, Research, and Practice*, 7, Jacksonville: Visitor Studies Association, 48–56.

Black, P. (1987) *National Curriculum, Task Group on Assessment and Testing, A Report*, London: Department of Education and Science and the Welsh Office.

Bloom, B. S. (ed.) (1956) *Taxonomy of Educational Objectives: The Classification of Educational Goals, Handbook 1, The Cognitive Domain, Handbook 2, The Affective Domain*, New York: David McKay Co., Inc.

Borun, M. and Miller, M. (1980) *What's In A Name? A Study of the Effectiveness of Explanatory Labels in a Science Museum*, Philadelphia: The Franklin Institute.

Borun, M., Massey, C., and Lutter, T. (1993) "Naive Knowledge and the Design of Science Museum Exhibits," *Curator*, 36(3): 201–19.

Borun, M., Cleghorn, A., and Garfield, C. (1995) "Family Learning in Museums: A Bibliographic Review," *Curator*, 38(4): 262–70.

Borun, M., Chambers, M., and Cleghorn, A. (1996) "Families Are Learning in Science Museums," *Curator*, 39(2): 123–38.

Brooks, J. A. M. and Vernon, E. P. (1956) "A Study of Children's Interests and Comprehension at a Science Museum," *Brit. J. of Psychiatry*, 47: 175–82.

Brown, M. and Precious, N. (1968) *The Integrated Day in the Primary School*, London: Ward Lock Educational.

Bruer, J. T. (1993) *Schools for Thought: A Science of Learning in the Classroom*, Cambridge, Mass.: Massachusetts Institute of Technology Press.

Bruner, J. S. (1960) *The Process of Education*, Cambridge, Mass.: Harvard University Press.

—— (1986a) *Actual Minds, Possible Worlds*, Cambridge, Mass.: Harvard University Press.

—— (1986b) "The Inspiration of Vygotsky," *Actual Minds, Possible Worlds*, Cambridge, Mass.: Harvard University Press, Ch. 5.

Buckley, O. J. (1995) "Summative Exhibit Evaluation: Enhancing the Experience," MA thesis, Leicester: University of Leicester.

Burda, P. (1996) "Something for Everyone," *Museum News*, 75(6): 24–7.

Campbell, D. T. (1978) "Qualitative Knowing in Action Research," in Brenner, M., Marsh, P., and Brenner, M. (eds) *The Social Contexts of Method*, London: Croom Helm, 184–209.

Campbell, D. T. and Stanley, J. C. (1963) *Experimental and Quasi-experimental Design for Research*, Chicago: Rand McNally.

Champagne, A. B. (1990) "Assessment and Teaching of Thinking Skills," in Hein, G. E. (ed.) *The Assessment of Hands-on Elementary Science Programs*, Grand Forks: North Dakota Study Group, 68–82.

Chance, P. (1979) *Learning Through Play*, New York: Gardner Press.

Chandler, D. L. (1996) *Boston Globe*, April 1: 33–4.

Cizek, G. J. (1995) "Crunchy Granola and the Hegemony of the Narrative," *Educational Researcher*, 24(2): 26–8.

Cochran-Smith, M. and Lytle, S. (1990) "Research on Teaching and Teacher Research: The Issues that Divide," *Educational Researcher*, 19(2): 2–11.

—— (eds) (1993) *Inside/Outside: Teacher Research and Knowledge*, New York: Teachers College Press.

Coe, J. C. (1988) "Children's Drawings: New Tools For Zoo Exhibit Evaluation," in Bitgood, S., Benefield, A., and Patterson, D. (eds) *Visitor Studies: Theory, Research, and Practice*, 2, Jacksonville: Center for Social Design, 87–100.

Cole, M. and Scribner, S. (1974) *Culture and Thought: A Psychological Introduction*, New York: Wiley.

Coleman, L. V. (1939) *The Museum in America: A Critical Study*, Washington, DC: American Association of Museums.

Coles, R. (1987) *The Call of Stories: Teaching and the Moral Imagination*, Cambridge, Mass.: Harvard University Press.

—— (1992) "Whose Museums?" *American Art*, Winter: 11–16.

Collins, Z. W. (ed.) (1981) *Museums, Adults and the Humanities: A Guide for Educational Programming*, Washington, DC: American Association of Museums.

Conroy, P. (guest ed.) (1987) "Special Issue: Orientation and Circulation," *Visitor Behavior*, 1(4).

Cooper, J. (1996) Message on Museum-Ed Listserver: October 22.

Corwin, R., Hein, G. E., and Levin, D. (1976) "Weaving Curriculum Webs: The Structure of Nonlinear Curriculum," *Childhood Education*, 52: 248–51.

Cotton, J. and Wood, B. (1996) *Retrieving Prehistories at the Museum of London: A Gallery Case-study*, in McManus, P. M. (ed.) *Archeological Displays and the Public: Museology and Interpretation*, London: Institute of Archeology, University College London, 53–71.

Cremin, L. (1961) *The Transformation of the School: Progressivism in American Education, 1876–1957*, New York: Knopf.

Cronbach, L. J. (1966) "The Logic of Experiments in Discovery," in Shulman, L. S. and Keislar, E. R. (eds) *Learning by Discovery: A Critical Appraisal*, Chicago: Rand McNally & Co., 76–92.

Crosthwait, P. and Mask, D. L. (1994) "Can Pre and Post Drawings by Zoo Visitors be Used as a Method to Evaluate Zoo Exhibits?," in AAM Committee on Audience Research and Evaluation, *Current Trends in Audience Research and Evaluation*, 8, Seattle, 32–7.

Csikszentmihalyi, M. (1990) *Flow: The Psychology of Optimal Experience*, New York: Harper and Row, 1990.

—— (1995) "Intrinsic Motivation in Museums; Why Does One Want to Learn?," in Falk, J. H. and Dierking, L. D. (eds) *Public Institutions for Personal Learning: Establishing a Research Agenda*, Washington, DC: American Association of Museums.

Csikszentmihalyi, M. and Robinson, R. E. (1990) *The Art of Seeing: An Interpretation of the Aesthetic Encounter*, Malibou: J. Paul Getty Trust.

Cuban, L. (1993) *How Teachers Taught: Constancy and Change in American Education, 1890–1990*, Second Edition, New York: Teachers College Press.

Davidson, B. (1991) *New Dimensions for Traditional Dioramas: Multisensory Additions for Access, Interest and Learning*, Boston: Museum of Science.

Davidson, B., Heald, C. L., and Hein, G. E. (1991) "Increased Exhibit Accessibility Through Multisensory Interaction," *Curator*, 34(4): 273–90.

Davidson, M. (1989) "Information from Museum Security Personnel," in Bitgood, S., Benefield, A., and Patterson, D. (eds) *Visitor Studies: Theory, Research, and Practice*, 2, Jacksonville: Center for Social Design, 101–6.

Davis, F. (1985) "How Do Adults Learn?: A Metatheory of Learning Based on Stephen Pepper's Theory of World Hypotheses," Unpublished Ed.D. dissertation, Cambridge, Mass.: Harvard Graduate School of Education.

De Borhegyi, S. F. and Hanson, I. A. (1968) "Chronological Bibliography of Museum Visitor Surveys," in Larrabee, E. (ed.) *Museums and Education*, Washington, DC: Smithsonian Press, 239–51.

Dekvar, V. L. (1993) "Museums for Integration in a Multi-cultural Society and for Education and Cultural Action," in Indian National Committee for ICOM, *Museums for Integration in a Multicultural Society*, Calcutta: ICOM Asia-Pacific Organization, 50.

Denzin, N. K. and Lincoln, Y. S. (eds) (1994) *Handbook of Qualitative Research*, Thousand Oaks: Sage.

Department of Education and Science (1967) *Children and Their Primary Schools*, London: Her Majesty's Stationery Office.

Dewey, J. (1900/1956) *The School and Society*, Chicago: University of Chicago Press.

—— (1929/1988) *The Quest for Certainty*, Carbondale: Southern Illinois University Press.

—— (1938) *Experience and Education*, New York: Macmillan.

Dickens, C. (1854/1964) *Hard Times*, New York: Bantam Books.

Dierking, L. D. and Falk, J. H. (1994) "Family Behavior and Learning in Informal Science Settings: A Review of the Research," *Science Education*, 78(1): 57–72.

Dierking, L. and Holland, D. (1994) "Utilizing Interpretive Carts to Collect Naturalistic Data in a Natural History Museum," in AAM Committee on Audience Research and Evaluation, *Current Trends in Audience Research and Evaluation*, 8, Seattle, 38–43.

DiMaggio, P. and Ostrower, F. (1993) *Race, Ethnicity, and Participation in the Arts*, Santa Ana: Seven Locks Press.

Donawa, W. (1996) "Case Study, Designing a Gallery for Children," in Durbin, G. (ed.) *Developing Museum Exhibitions for Lifelong Learning*, Norwich: The Stationery Office, 159–62.

Duckworth, E. (1987) *"The Having of Wonderful Ideas" and Other Essays on Teaching and Learning*, New York: Teachers College Press.

Duckworth, E., Easley, J., Hawkins, D., and Henriques, A. (1990) *Science Education: A Minds-On Approach for the Elementary Years*, Hillsdale: Lawrence Erlbaum Associates.

Dufresne-Tassé, C. and A. Lefèbre, (n.d.) "Some Data on the Psychological Functioning of the Adult Visitor at the Museum and Their Implications for Museum Education," manuscript.

Durbin, G. (ed.) (1996) *Developing Museum Exhibitions for Lifelong Learning*, Norwich: The Stationery Office.

Eisner, E. W. (1991) "Taking a Second Look: Educational Connoisseurship Revisited," in McLaughlin, M. W. and Phillips, D. C., *Evaluation and Education at Quarter Century* (NSSE 96th Yearbook), Chicago: National Society for the Study of Education, 169–87.

Ellis, J. F. Jr. (1993) "Learning from Museum Exhibits: The Influence of Sequence, Verbal Ability, Field Dependence and Perspective Taking Instructions," Unpublished Doctoral dissertation, Gainsville: University of Florida.

Engel, B. S. and Hein, G. E. (1981) "Qualitative Evaluation of Cultural Institution/School Education Programs," in Lehman, S. N. and Igoe, K. (eds) *Museum School Partnerships: Plans & Programs*, Washington, DC: Center for Museum Education, 39–45.

Eoe, S. M. (1995) "Creating a National Unity: The Role of Museums," *Museums and Communities, ICOM 1995*, Oslo: Norsk ICOM, 14–15.

Ericsson, K. A. and Simon, H. A. (1993) *Protocol Analysis*, Revised Edition, Cambridge, Mass.: Massachusetts Institute of Technology Press.

Erikson, E. (1959) *Identity and the Life Cycle*, New York: International University Press.

Evans, G. W. (1995) "Learning and the Physical Environment," in Falk, J. H. and Dierking, L. D. (eds) *Public Institutions for Personal Learning: Establishing a Research Agenda*, Washington, DC: American Association of Museums, 119–26.

Evans, R. I. (1973) *Jean Piaget: The Man and his Ideas*, New York: E. P. Dutton and Co., Inc.

Falk, J. H. (1982) "The Use of Time as a Measure of Visitor Behavior and Exhibit Effectiveness," *Roundtable Reports*, 5(4): 10–13; reprinted in Nichols, S., Alexander, M, and Yellis, K. (1984) *Museum Education Anthology, 1973–1983*, Washington, DC: Museum Education Roundtable, 183–90.

—— (1983) "Time and Behavior as Predictors of Learning," *Science Education*, 67: 267–76.

—— (1993) *Leisure Decisions Influencing African American Use of Museums*, Washington, DC: American Association of Museums.

Falk J. H. and Dierking, L. D. (1991) "The Effect of Visitation Frequency on Long-Term Recollection," in Bitgood, S., Benefield, A., and Patterson, D. (eds) *Visitor Studies: Theory, Research, and Practice*, 3, Jacksonville: Center for Social Design, 94–103.

—— (1992) *The Museum Experience*, Washington, DC: Walesback Books.

—— (1994) "Assessing the Long-term Impact of School Field Trips," in AAM Committee on Audience Research and Evaluation, *Current Trends in Audience Research and Evaluation*, 8, Seattle, 71–4.

—— (1995) *Public Institutions for Personal Learning: Establishing a Research Agenda*, Washington, DC: American Association of Museums.

Farnham-Diggory, S. (1990) *Schooling*, Cambridge, Mass.: Harvard University Press.

Feher, E. (1990) "Interactive Museum Exhibits as Tools for Learning: Explorations with Light," *Int. J. of Sci. Ed.*, 12(1): 35–49.

—— (1996) "Learning Inside the Head," *ASTC Newsletter*, 24(3): 2–4.

Feher, E. and Rice, K. (1988) "Shadows and Anti-images: Children's Conceptions of Light and Vision," *Science Education*, 72(5): 637–49.

Festinger, L. (1957, reissued 1962) *A Theory of Cognitive Dissonance*, Palo Alto: Stanford University Press.

Feuerstein R. (1979) *The Dynamic Assessment of Retarded Performers: the Learning Potential Assessment Device, Theory, Instruments, and Techniques*, Baltimore: University Park Press.

Fosnot, C. T. (1996a) "Constructivism: A Psychological Theory Of Learning," in Fosnot, C. T. (ed.) *Constructivism: Theory, Perspectives, and Practice*, New York: Teachers College Press, 8–33.

—— (ed.) (1996b) *Constructivism: Theory, Perspectives, and Practice*, New York: Teachers College Press.

Freire, P. (1973) *Education for Critical Consciousness*, New York: The Seabury Press.

Frisch, M. H. and Pitcaithley, D. (1987) "Audience Expectations as Resource and Challenge: Ellis Island as Case Study," in Blatti, J. (ed.) *Past Meets Present*, Washington, DC: Smithsonian Institution Press, 153–65.

Gagné, R. (1967) "Curriculum Research and the Promotion of Learning," in Tyler. R. W., Gagné, R. M., and Scriven, M. (eds) *Perspectives of Curriculum Evaluation*, Chicago: Rand McNally.

—— (1968) "Contributions of Learning to Human Development," *Psychological Review*, 75.

—— (1977) *The Conditions of Learning*, Third Edition, New York: Holt Reinhart and Winston.

Gardner, H. (1985) *Frames of Mind: The Theory of Multiple Intelligences*, New York: Basic Books.

— (1997) "Are there Additional Intelligences? The Case for Naturalist, Spiritual, and Existential Intelligences," in Kane, J. (ed.) *Education, Information and Transformation*, Englewood Cliffs: Prentice-Hall.

Getty Center for Education in the Arts (1991) *Insights, Museum, Visitors, Attitudes, Expectations: A Focus Group Report*, A report and videotape, Los Angeles: The J. Paul Getty Trust.

Gibson, K. (1925) "An Experiment in Measuring Results of Fifth Grade Class Visits to an Art Museum," *School and Society*, XXI: 658–62.

Gilman, B. I. (1916) "Museum Fatigue," *The Scientific Monthly*, 12: 62–74.

Gino, J. (1993) "Creative Co-Existence," in Indian National Committee for ICOM, *Museums for Integration in a Multicultural Society*, Calcutta: ICOM Asia-Pacific Organization, 51–2.

Glaser, R. (1966) "Variables in Discovery Learning," in Shulman, L. S. and Keislar, E. R. (eds) *Learning by Discovery: A Critical Appraisal*, Chicago: Rand MacNally and Co., 13–26.

Glasgow Art Gallery and Museums (n.d.) *Educational Experiment, 1941–1951*, Glasgow: Corporation of the City of Glasgow.

Glass, G. V. (1977) "Integrating Findings: The Meta-analysis of Research," *Review of Research in Education*, 5: 351–79.

Goldstein, J. S. (1992) *A Different Sort of Time: The Life of Jerrold R. Zacharias*, Cambridge, Mass.: Massachusetts Institute of Technology Press.

Gottfried, J. (1981) "Do Children Learn on School Field Trips?," *Curator*, 23(3): 165–74.

Gould, S. J. (1981) *The Mismeasure of Man*, New York: Norton.

—— (1996) *Full House: The Spread of Excellence from Plato to Darwin*, New York: Harmony Books.

Gourevitch, P. (1995) "What They Saw at the Holocaust Museum," *New York Sunday Times Magazine*, Feb. 2: 44–5.

Graft, C. (1989) "Incorporating Evaluation into the Interpretive Planning Process at Colonial Williamsburg," *Visitor Studies: Theory, Research, and Practice*, 2, Jacksonville: Center for Social Design, 133–9.

Greeno, J. G. (1997) "On Claims that Answer the Wrong Question," *Educational Researcher*, 26(1): 5–17.

Greenwood, T. (1888) *Museums and Art Galleries*, London: Simpkin, Marshall and Co.

—— (1893) "The Place of Museums in Education," *Science*, XXII: 246–8.

Griggs, S. (1983) "Orienting Visitors with a Thematic Display," *Int. J. of Mus. Mang. & Curator.*, 2: 119–34.

Groys, B. (1995) "The Role of Museums When the National State Breaks Up," *Museums and Communities, ICOM 1995*, Oslo: Norsk ICOM, 8–11.

Guichard, J. (1995) "Designing Tools to Develop the Conception of Learners," *Int. J. Sci. Educ.*, 17(2): 243–53.

Hague, E. (1993) Indian National Committee for ICOM, *Museums for Integration in a Multicultural Society*, Calcutta: ICOM Asia-Pacific Organization, Report.

Hamilton, D. (1994) "Traditions, Preferences and Postures in Applied Qualitative Research," in Denizen, N. K. and Lincoln, Y. S. (eds) *Handbook of Qualitative Research*, Thousand Oaks: Sage, 60–9.

Hammond, E. H. (1995) "Politics of the War and Public History," *Bulletin of Concerned Asian Scholars*, 77: 56–9.

Harré, R. (1986) *Varieties of Realism: A Rationale for the Natural Sciences*, Oxford: Basil Blackwell.

Hawkins D. (1966) "Learning the Unteachable," in Schulman, L. S. and Keislar, E. R. (eds) *Learning by Discovery: A Critical Appraisal*, Chicago: Rand McNally and Co., 3–12.

—— (1974) "On Living in Trees," in *The Informed Vision: Essays on Learning and Human Nature*, New York: Agathon Press, 173–94.

Hayes, J. F. and Schindle, D. N. (1994) *Pioneer Journeys: Drama in Museum Education*, Charlotte: New Plays Books.

Hayward, J. and Brydon-Miller, M. L. (1984) "Spatial and Conceptual Aspects of Orientation: Visitor Experiences at an Outdoor History Museum," *J. Environmental Systems*, 13(4): 317–32.

Hayward, J. and Jensen, A. D. (1981) "Enhancing the Sense of the Past: Perceptions of Visitors and Interpreters," *The Interpreter*, XII: 4–12.

Hedge, A.(1995) "Human-Factor Considerations in the Design of Museums to Optimize Their Impact on Learning," in Falk, J. H. and Dierking, L. D. (eds) *Public Institutions for Personal Learning: Establishing a Research Agenda*, Washington, DC: American Association of Museums, 105–17.

Hein, G. E. (1975) "The Social History of Open Education," *Urban Review*, 8: 96–119.

—— (1982) "Evaluation of Museum Programs and Exhibits," in Hansen, T. H., Andersen, K.-E., and Vestergaard, P. (eds) *Museum Education*, Copenhagen: Danish ICOM/CECA, 21–6.

—— (1991) "How Children Behave in Museums," *ICOM Education, XII and XIII*: 52–7.

—— (1994a) "Constructivism and the Natural Heritage," Paper presented at ICOM/CECA, Cuenca, Ecuador.

—— (1994b) Notes on the Annapolis Conference, Unpublished.

—— (1995a) "Evaluating Teaching and Learning in Museums," in Hooper-Greenhill, E. (ed.) *Museums, Media, Message*, London: Routledge, 189–203.

—— (1995b) "The Constructivist Museum," *Journal of Education in Museums*, 15: 15–17.

—— (1996a) "Classic Papers in Visitor Studies," Unpublished bibliography.

—— (1996b) "What Can Museum Educators Learn from Constructivist Theory?" in Gesché, N. (ed.) *Study Series, Committee for Education and Cultural Action (CECA)*, Paris: ICOM, 13–15.

Hein, G. E. and Mello, R. (1993) *Summative Evaluation of Seeing the Unseen*, Cambridge, Mass.: Program Evaluation and Research Group, Lesley College.

Hein, G. E., Alberty, B., and Stein, L. (1987) *Evaluation Report: The Machine Age in America, 1918–1941*, Cambridge, Mass.: Program Evaluation and Research Group, Lesley College.

Hein, L. and Selden, M. (1997) *Living with the Bomb: American and Japanese Cultural Conflicts in the Nuclear Age*, Armonk: M. E. Sharp.

Hemming, S. (1995) "Community-based Programmes at the Geffrye Museum," in Chadwick, A. and Stannertt, A. (eds) *Museums and the Education of Adults*, Leicester: National Institute for Adult Continuing Education, 79–83.

Henry, J. (1963) *Culture Against Man*, New York: Random House.

Higgins, H. H. (1884) "Museums of Natural History," *Transactions of the Literary and Philosophical Society of Liverpool*, 183–221.

Hilke, D. D. (1988) "Strategies for Family Learning in Museums," in Bitgood, S., Roper, J. T. Jr., and Benefield A. (eds) *Visitor Studies: Theory, Research, and Practice*, Jacksonville: Center for Social Design, 121–34.

—— (1989) "The Family as Learning System: An Observational Study of Families in Museums," in Butler, B. H. and Sussman, M. B. (eds) *Museums Visits and Activities for Family Life Enrichment*, New York: Haworth Press; also published as *Marriage and Family Review* (1989) Vol. 13(3/4).

Hirzy, E. (ed.) (1996) *True Needs True Partners: Museums and Schools Transforming Education*, Washington, DC: Institute of Museum Services.

Hiss, T. (1990) *The Experience of Place*, New York: A. A. Knopf, Inc.

Holland, W. J. (1911) "Museums of Science," *The Encyclopaedia Britannica*, Eleventh Edition, XIX: 64–70.

Hood, M. G. (1983) "Staying Away – Why People Choose to Visit Museums," *Museum News*, 61(4): 50–7.

—— (1988) "Arboretum Visitor Profiles as Defined by the Four Seasons," in Bitgood, S., Roper, J. T. Jr., and Benefield, A., *Visitor Studies: Theory, Research, and Practice – 1988*, Jacksonville: Center for Social Design, 84–100.

—— (1993) "After 70 Years of Audience Research, What Have We Learned? Who Comes to Museums, Who Does Not, and Why?," in Thompson, D. *et al.* (eds) *Visitor Studies: Theory, Research, and Practice, 5*, Jacksonville: Visitor Studies Association, 16–27.

—— (1996) "A View from 'Outside' Research on Community Audiences," in Bitgood, S. C. (ed.) *Visitor Studies: Theory, Research, and Practice*, 7(1), Jacksonville: Visitor Studies Association, 77–87.

Hooper-Greenhill, E. (1988) "Counting Visitors or Visitors Who Count," in Lumley, R. (ed.) *The Museum Time Machine: Putting Culture on Display*, London: Routledge.

—— (1991) *Museum and Gallery Education*, Leicester: Leicester University Press.

—— (1994) *Museums and Their Visitors*, London: Routledge.

—— (1996) (ed.) *Improving Museum Learning*, Nottingham: East Midlands Museums Service.

House, E. R., Mathison, S., and McTaggart, R. (1989) *Educational Researcher*, 18(7): 11–15, 26.

Housen, A. (1992) "Validating a Measure of Aesthetic Development for Museums and Schools," *ILVS Review*, 2(2): 213–37.

Hudson, K. (1975) *A Social History of Museums: What the Visitors Thought*, London: Macmillan.

Hughes, C. (ed.) (1993) *Perspectives on Museum Theatre*, Washington, DC: American Association of Museums.

Hughes, C., Mello, R., and Hein G. E. (1995) *Final Evaluation Report, Heritage Of The Land Exhibit, Worcester Art Museum*, Cambridge, Mass.: Program Evaluation and Research Group, Lesley College.

Hunt, J. McV. (1961) *Intelligence and Experience*, New York: Ronald Press Co.

IBM Personal Science Laboratory (PSL) (1990) White Plains: IBM Corporation.

Indian National Committee for ICOM (1993) *Museums for Integration in a Multicultural Society*, Calcutta: ICOM Asia-Pacific Organization.

Jackson, P. (1968) *Life in Classrooms*, New York: Holt Reinhart and Winston.

Jones, J. P. (ed.) (1993) *Gallery 33: A Visitor Study*, Birmingham: Birmingham Museums and Art Gallery.

Kalloniatis, F. (1995) "Access to Museum Resources by Adult Learners," in Chadwick, A. and Stannertt, A. (eds) *Museums and the Education of Adults*, Leicester: National Institute for Adult Continuing Education, 73–8.

Kaplan, A. (1964) *The Conduct of Inquiry: Methodology for the Behavioral Sciences*, Scranton: Chandler.

Kaplan R. and Kaplan S. (1989) *The Experience of Nature: A Psychological Perspective*, New York: Cambridge University Press.

Kaplan, S., Bardwell, L. V., and Slakter, D. B. (1993) "The Museum as a Restorative Environment," *Environment and Behavior*, 25(6): 725–42.

Knowles, M. S. (1970) *The Modern Practice of Adult Education; Andragogy versus Pedagogy*, New York, Association Press.

—— (1981) "Andragogy," in Collins, Z. W. (ed.) *Museums, Adults and the Humanities: A Guide for Educational Programming*, Washington, DC: American Association of Museums, 49–78.

Koran, J. J. Jr. and Koran, M. L. (1996) "A Summary of Recent Research and Evaluation Studies in the University of Florida Program on Learning in Informal Settings," *Visitor Behavior*, 11(3): 5–8.

Korenic, M. S. (1996) "Visitor Use and Understanding of Selected Dioramas at the Milwaukee Public Museum," in AAM Committee on Audience Research and Evaluation, *Current Trends in Audience Research, and Evaluation*, 10, Minneapolis, 34–9.

Korn, R. (1992) "Evaluation Methods and Findings Shape a Junior Gallery," in Thompson, D., *et al.* (eds) *Visitor Studies: Theory, Research, and Practice*, 5, Jacksonville: Visitor Studies Association, 180–7.

—— (1995) "An Analysis of Differences Between Visitors at Natural History Museums and Science Centers," *Curator*, 38(3): 150–60.

Kräutler, H. (1995) "Observations on Semiotic Aspects in the Museum Work of Otto Neurath: Reflections on the 'Bildpädagogische Schriften' (Writings on Visual Education)," in Hooper-Greenhill, E. (ed.) *Museums, Media, Message*, London: Routledge, 59–71.

Kuhn, T. (1962) *The Structure of Scientific Revolutions*, Chicago: University of Chicago Press.

Lachapelle, R. (1994) "Aesthetic Understanding as Informed Experience: Ten Informant-made Videographic Accounts About the Process of Aesthetic Learning," unpublished Ph.D. dissertation, Montreal: Concordia University.

Laetsch W., Diamond, J., Gottfried, J. L., and Rosenfeld, S. (1980) "Children and Family Groups in Science Centers," *Science and Children*, 17(6): 14–17.

Lane, H. (1976) *The Wild Boy of Aveyron*, Cambridge, Mass.: Harvard University Press.

Lankford, S., Bitgood, S., and Cota, A. (1995) "Special Issue: Orientation and Circulation," *Visitor Behavior*, 10(2): 4–16.

Lash, J. P. (1980) *Helen and Teacher: The Story*

of *Helen Keller and Anne Sullivan Macy*, New York: Delacorte Press.

Lave, J. and Wegner, E. (1991) *Situated Learning: Legitimate Peripheral Participation*, Cambridge: Cambridge University Press.

Lawrence, G. (1991) "Rats, Street Gangs and Culture: Evaluation in Museums," in Kavanagh, G. (ed.) *Museum Languages: Objects and Texts*, Leicester: Leicester University Press, 11–32.

—— (1993) "Remembering Rats, Considering Culture: Perspectives on Museum Evaluation," in Bicknell S. and Farmelo, G. (eds) *Museum Visitor Studies in the 90s*, London: Science Museum, 117–24..

Leichter, H. J., Hensel, K., and Larsen, E. (1989) "Families and Museums: Issues and Perspectives," in Butler, B. H. and Sussman, M. B. (eds) *Museum Visits and Activities for Family Life Enrichment*, New York: Haworth Press.

Linn, M. (1980) "Free Choice Experiences: How Do They Help Children Learn?," *Science Education*, 64: 237–48.

Loomis, R. J. (1987) *Museum Visitor Evaluation: New Tool for Management*, Nashville: American Association for State and Local History.

—— (1996) "Learning in Museums: Motivation, Control and Meaningfulness," in Gesché, N. (ed.) *Study Series, Committee for Education and Cultural Action (CECA)*, Paris: ICOM, 12–13.

Low, T. L. (1942) *The Museum as a Social Instrument*, New York: The Metropolitan Museum of Art.

Lucas, A. M., McManus, P., and Thomas, G. (1986) "Investigating Learning from Informal Sources: Listening to Conversations and Observing Play in Science Museums," *Eur. J. Sci. Ed.*, 8(4): 341–53.

Luetjen, K. H. and Holmes, S. K. (1994) "Summary of Valentine Museum Educational Initiatives," in *The Sourcebook: 1994 Annual Meeting*, Washington, DC: American Association of Museums, 59–65.

Lusaka, J. (1996) "Inside the 'Inside Story'," *Museum News*, 75(2): 24–5, 72–3.

Lynch, K. (1960) *The Image of the City*, Cambridge, Mass.: Massachusetts Institute of Technology Press.

McDermott-Lewis, M. (1990) *The Denver Art Museum Interpretive Project*, Denver: The Denver Art Museum.

Macdonald, S. (1996) "Theorizing Museums: An Introduction," in Macdonald, S. and Fyfe, G. (eds) *Theorizing Museums: Representing Identity and Diversity in a Changing World*, Oxford: Blackwell, 3–18.

Macdonald, S. and Fyfe, G. (eds) (1996) *Theorizing Museums: Representing Identity and Diversity in a Changing World*, Oxford: Blackwell.

Macdonald, S. and Silverstone, R. (1990) *Food for Thought: The Sainsbury Gallery: Some Issues Involved in the Making of a Science Museum Exhibition*, Brunel University: Centre for Research into Innovation, Culture and Technology.

McLean, K. (1993) *Planning for People in Museum Exhibitions*, Washington, DC: Association of Science-Technology Centers.

McManus P. (1989a) "What People Say and How They Think in a Science Museum," in Uzzell, D. (ed.) *Heritage Interpretation*, London: Bellhaven Press, 157–65.

—— (1989b) "Oh, Yes, They Do: How Museum Visitors Read Labels and Interact with Exhibit Texts," *Curator*, 32(3): 174–89.

—— (1991) "Making Sense of Exhibits," in Kavanagh, G. (ed.) *Museum Languages, Objects as Text*, Leicester: Leicester University Press.

—— (1993a) "Thinking About the Visitors' Thinking," in Bicknell, S. and Farmelo, G. (eds) *Museum Visitor Studies in the 90s*, London: Science Museum, 108–13.

—— (1993b) "Memories as Indicators of the Impact of Museum Visits," *Museum Management and Curatorship*, 12: 367–80.

—— (1994) "Families in Museums," in Miles, R. and Savala, L. (eds) *Towards the Museum of the Future: New European Perspectives*, London: Routledge, 81–97.

MacNamara, P. A. (1987) "Visitor Participation in Formative Exhibit Evaluation," *Journal of Museum Education*, 12(1): 9–11; reprinted in *Patterns in Practice: Selections from the Journal of Museum Education* (1992) Washington, DC: Museum Education Roundtable, 204–8.

Mager, R. F. (1975) *Preparing Instructional Objectives*, Second Edition, Palo Alto: Feron.

Maikweki, J. N. (1993) "Museum Education for the Blind Children," in Indian National Committee for ICOM, *Museums for Integration in a Multicultural Society*, Calcutta: ICOM Asia-Pacific Organization, 85–6.

Martin, K. and Reynolds, S. (1996) "The Learning Laboratory: An Ongoing Conversation," *The Constructivist*, 11(1): 15–20.

Martone, M. (1984) *Alive and Dead in Indiana*, New York: Knopf.

Maslow, A. H. (1968) "Some Educational Implications of the Humanistic Psychologies," *Harvard Educational Review*, 38: 685–96.

Matusov, E. and Rogoff, B. (1995) "Evidence of Development from People's Participation in Communities of Learners," in Falk, J. D. and Dierking, L. D. (eds) *Public Institutions For Personal Learning: Establishing a Research Agenda*, Washington, DC: American Association of Museums, 97–104.

Melton, A. W. (1935, reprinted 1988) *Problems of Installation in Museums of Art*, Washington, DC: American Association of Museums.

—— (1936) "Distribution of Attention in Galleries of Science and Industry," *Museum News*, 14(3): 6–8.

Melton, A. W., Feldman, N. G., and Mason, C. W. (1936, reprinted 1988) *Experimental Studies of the Education of Children in a Museum of Science*, Washington, DC: American Association of Museums.

Menninger, M. (1990) "The Analysis of Time Data in Visitor Research and Evaluation Studies," in Bitgood, S., Benefield, A., and Patterson, D. (eds) *Visitor Studies: Theory, Research, and Practice*, 3, Jacksonville: Center for Social Design, 104–13.

Messick, S. (1989) "Meaning and Values in Test Validation: The Science and Ethics of Measurement," *Educational Researcher*, 18(2): 5–11.

Miles, M. B. and Huberman, A. M. (1994) *Qualitative Data Analysis, an Expanded Sourcebook*, Second Edition, Newbury Park: Sage.

Miles, R. S. (1993) "Grasping the Greased Pig: Evaluation of Educational Exhibits," in Bicknell, S. and Farmelo, G. (eds) *Museum Visitor Studies in the 90s*, London: Science Museum, 24–33.

Miles, R. S., Alt, M. B., Gosling, D. C., Lewis, B. N., and Tout, A. F. (1988) *The Design of Educational Exhibits*, Second Edition, London: Unwin Hyman.

Moffat, H. (1996) *Using Museums: Teachers' Guide*, Warwick: Educational Television Company Limited.

Morrison, P. (1995) "Knowing Where You Are," in *Nothing is Too Wonderful to be True*, Woodbury: American Institute of Physics, 282–8.

Morrissey, K. (1991) "Visitor Behavior and Interactive Video," *Curator*, 34(2): 109–18.

Mukhopadhyay, I. K. (1993) "Museum Education for Removing Inequalities," in Indian National Committee for ICOM, *Museums for Integration in a Multicultural Society*, Calcutta: ICOM Asia-Pacific Organization, 70–1.

Munley, M. E. (1982) *Evaluation Study of "Buyin' Freedom"*, Washington, DC: Smithsonian Institution; reprinted in Hughes, K. (ed.) (1993) *Theatre in Museums*, Washington, DC: American Association of Museums.

Murphy, A. (1996) Message on Museum-Ed Listserver: October 10.

Murray, C. H. (1932) *Museums Journal*, 31: 527–31.

Neurath, O. (1973) *Empiricism and Sociology*, edited by M. Neurath and R. S. Cohen (translated from the German by P. Foulkes and M. Neurath), Dordrecht and Boston: Reidel Publishing Company.

New York Times (1993) "Hussein Rebuilds Iraq's Economy Undeterred by the U.N. Sanctions," 24 January: 1.

Nicolopolou, A. (1993) "Play, Cognitive Development, and the Social World: Piaget, Vygotsky, and Beyond," *Human Development*, 36: 1–23.

Nielsen, L. C. (1942) "A Technique for Studying the Behavior of Museum Visitors," *The Journal of Educational Psychology*, 37: 103–10.

Novak, J. D. and Gowin, D. B. (1984) *Learning How to Learn*, New York: Cambridge University Press.

O'Donnell, S. C. (1995a) "The Rainforest in Fresno," *Museum News*, 74 (3): 21–2, 54.

—— (1995b) "Community Curators," *Museum News*, 74(5): 11–13.

Ogbu, J. U. (1992) "Understanding Cultural Diversity and Learning," *Educational Researcher*, 21(8): 5–14.

—— (1995) "The Influence of Culture on Learning and Behavior," in Falk, J. H. and Dierking, L. D. (eds) *Public Institutions and Informal Learning: Establishing a Research Agenda*, Washington, DC: American Association of Museums, 79–96.

Ohta, R. J. (1996) "Capturing the Snapshots of Experience: Continuous Experiential Reporting by Museum Visitors," in AAM Committee on Audience Research and Evaluation, *Current Trends in Audience Research and Evaluation*, 10, Minneapolis, 75–82.

Olds, A. R. (1990) "Sending Them Home Alive," *Journal of Museum Education*, 15(1): 10–12; reprinted in *Patterns in Practice: Selections from the Journal of Museum Education*, (1992) Washington, DC: Museum Education Roundtable, 174–8.

Olesen, V. (1994) "Feminisms and Models of Qualitative Research," in Denzin, N. K. and Lincoln, Y. S. (eds) *Handbook of Qualitative Research*, Thousand Oaks: Sage, 158–74.

Orosz, J. J. (1990) *Curators and Culture: The Museum Movement in America, 1740–1870*, Tuskaloosa: The University of Alabama Press.

Osborne, J. (1996) "Beyond Constructivism," *Science Education*, 80(1): 53–82.

Palumbo, D. (ed.) (1973) "The Politics of Program Evaluation," *Evaluation*, 1(3).

Parr, A. (1959) "Design for Display," *Curator*, 11(4): 313–34

Peart, B. (1984) "Impact of Exhibit Type on Knowledge Gain, Attitudes, and Behavior," *Curator*, 27(3): 220–37.

Pepper, S. (1942) *World Hypotheses: A Study in Evidence*, Berkeley: University of California Press.

Perry, D. L. (1992) "Designing Exhibits that Motivate," *Association of Science-Technology Centers, Newsletter*, 20(1): 9–10, 12.

Piaget, J. (1929) *The Child's Concept of the World*, London: Routledge and Kegan Paul, Ch. 1.

—— (1941/1965) *The Child's Conception of*

Number, New York: W. W. Norton, & Co. (English translation of *La Genèse du Nombre chez l'Enfant*).

—— (1967) "The Significance of John Amos Comenius at the Present Time," *John Amos Comenius on Education*, New York: Teachers College Press, 1–31.

Pittenger, D. J. (1993) "The Utility of the Myers–Briggs Type Indicator," *Review of Educational Research*, 63(4): 467–88.

Polanyi, M. (1958) *Personal Knowledge: Towards a Post-Critical Philosophy*, Chicago: University of Chicago Press.

Popper, K. R. (1962) *Conjectures and Refutations: The Growth of Scientific Knowledge*, New York: Basic Books.

—— (1968) "Berkeley as a Precursor to Mach and Einstein," in Martin, C. B. and Armstrong, D. M. (eds) *Locke and Berkeley, A Collection of Critical Essays*, Notre Dame: University of Notre Dame Press.

Pratt, C. K. (1933) "The Neonate," in Murchison, C. (ed.) *A Handbook of Child Psychology*, Second Edition, London: Oxford University Press.

Ramey-Gassert, L., Walberg, H. J. III, and Walberg, H. J. (1994) "Reexamining Connections: Museums as Science Learning Environments," *Science Education*, 78(4): 345–63.

Rathman, C. G. (1915) *The Educational Museum*, Washington, DC: Bureau of Education.

Rice, K. and Feher, E. (1987) "Pinholes and Images: Children's Conceptions of Light and Vision," *Science Education*, 71(14): 629–39.

Richardson, V. (1994) "Conducting Research on Practice," *Ed. Researcher*, 23(5): 5–10.

Roberts. L. (1997) *From Knowledge to Narrative: Educators and the Changing Museum*, Washington, DC: Smithsonian Press.

Robinson, E. S. (1928) *The Behavior of the Museum Visitor*, Washington, DC: American Association of Museums, New Series, No. 5.

Robinson, T., Kambouris, A., and Sikora, M. (1996) "CHIP: A Case Study in Developing a Hypermedia Program for the Detroit Institute of Arts," in *Eva '96: Electronic Imaging and the Visual Arts Conference, Exhibition,*

Tutorials and "Special Interest Group" Workshops, London: National Gallery.

Rogoff, B. (1995) "Evaluating Development in the Process of Participation: Theory, Methods, and Practice Building on Each Other," in Amstel, E. and Renninger, A. (eds) *Change and Development: Issues of Theory, Application and Method*, Hillsdale: Erlbaum.

—— (1998) "Cognition as a Collaborative Process," in Damon, W. (series ed.), Siegler, R. S. and Kuhn, D. (volume eds) *Handbook of Child Psychology, Vol. 2, Cognition, Perception and Language*, New York: Wiley.

Rogoff, B. and Lave, J. (eds) (1984) *Everyday Cognition: Its Development in Social Context*, Cambridge, Mass.: Harvard University Press.

Roschelle, J. (1995) "Learning in Interactive Environments: Prior Knowledge and New Experience," in Falk, J. H. and Dierking, L. D. (eds) *Public Institutions for Personal Learning: Establishing a Research Agenda*, Washington, DC: American Association of Museums, 37–52.

Rozé, S. (1993) "l'Europe des fleuves," in Gesché, N. (ed.) *European Museum Communication*, Brussels: ICOM–CECA, 27–9.

Runyard, S. (1994) *Low Cost Visitor Surveys: Guidance on Market Research for Small and Medium Sized Museums*, London: Museums and Galleries Association.

Sand, M. (1996) Private communication.

Sarason, S. (1971) *The Culture of the School and the Problem of Change*, Boston: Allyn and Bacon.

Sauber, C. M. (ed.) (1994) *Experiment Bench: A Workbook for Building Experimental Physics Exhibits*, St Paul: Science Museum of Minnesota.

Schmeck, R. R. (1987) *Learning Strategies and Learning Styles*, New York: Plenum Press.

School Curriculum and Assessment Authority (1995) *A Guide to the National Curriculum for Staff of Museums, Galleries, Historic Houses and Sites*, London: School Curriculum and Assessment Authority.

Science Museum of Minnesota (1996) *Museum Schools Symposium 1995: Beginning the Conversation*, St Paul: Science Museum of Minnesota.

Screven, C. G. (1986) "Exhibitions and Information Centers: Some Principles and Approaches," *Curator*, 29(2): 109–37.

Screven, C. G. and Shettel, P. (1993) *Visitor Studies Bibliography and Abstracts*, Third Edition, Shorewood: Exhibits Communication Research, Inc.

Scriven, M. (1967) "The Methodology of Evaluation," in Tyler, R., Gagné, R., and Scriven, M. (eds) *Perspectives of Curriculum Evaluation*, Chicago: Rand McNally, 39–83.

Selwood, S., Schwarz, B., and Merriman, N. (1996) *The Peopling of London: 15,000 Years of Settlement from Overseas*, London: Museum of London.

Semper, R. (1996) "The Importance of Place," *ASTC Newsletter*, 24(5): 2–5.

Serrell, B. (1993) "Using Behaviour to Define the Effectiveness of Exhibitions," in Bicknell S. and Farmelo, G. (eds) *Museum Visitor Studies in the 90s*, London: Science Museum, 140–4.

—— (1995) "The 51% Solution Research Project: A Meta-Analysis of Visitor Time/Use in Museum Exhibitions," *Visitor Behavior*, 10(3): 5–9.

—— (1996) *Exhibit Labels: An Interpretive Approach*, Walnut Creek: AltaMira Press.

Shettel, H. H. (1978) "A Critical Look at a Critical Look: A Response to Alt's Critique of Shettel's Work," *Curator*, 21(4): 329–45.

—— (1989) "Evaluation in Museums: A Short History of a Short History," in Uzzell, D. L. (ed.) *Heritage Interpretation, Vol. 2, The Visitor Experience*, London: Bellhaven Press, 129–37.

—— (1991) "Worm In My Corn: Reply #2," *Visitor Behavior*, 5(3): 12–14.

—— (1994) "What Can We Learn from 'N=1'?," *Exhibitionist*, 13(1), 12–13, as well as other articles in this issue.

—— (1995) "Should the 51% Solution Have a 'Caution' Label?," *Visitor Behavior*, 10(3): 10–13.

Shilo-Cohen, N. (1993) "Stork, Stork, How is Our Land – Works by Ethiopian Immigrant Children to Israel," in Indian National Committee for ICOM, *Museums for Integration in a Multicultural Society*, Calcutta: ICOM Asia-Pacific Organization, 84.

Shulman, L. S. and Keislar, E. R. (eds) (1966) *Learning by Discovery: A Critical Appraisal*, Chicago: Rand MacNally & Co.

Silverman, L. H. (1995) "Visitor Meaning-Making in Museums for a New Age," *Curator*, 38(3): 161–70.

Smiley, J. (1995) *Moo*, London: HarperCollins.

Springuel, M. (1996) "Analysis of Visitor Interviews Conducted by Docents in the Art Museum Galleries of The John and Mable Ringling Museum of Art," AAM Committee on Audience Research and Evaluation, *Current Trends in Audience Research and Evaluation*, 10, Minneapolis, 91–8.

St. John, M. (1991) "New Metaphors for Carrying out Evaluations in the Science Museum Setting," *Visitor Behavior*, 5(3) 4–8; reprinted as Appendix E, "Discussion papers," in Anderson, P. and Roe, B. C. (1993) *The Museum Impact and Evaluation Study, Roles of Affect in the Museum Visit and Ways of Assessing Them, Vol. 2: Composite Research Report*, Chicago: Museum of Science and Industry, 64–72.

Stake, R. E. (1967) "The Countenance of Program Evaluation," *Teachers College Record*, 68: 523–40.

—— (1986) *Quieting Reform: Social Science and Social Action in an Urban Youth Program*, Urbana: University of Illinois Press.

—— (1994) "Case Studies," in Denzin, N. K. and Lincoln, Y. S. (eds) *Handbook of Qualitative Research*, Thousand Oaks: Sage, 236–47.

Stake, R. E. and Easley, J. A. Jr. (1978) *Case Studies In Science Education*, Urbana: University of Illinois, Center for Instructional Research and Curriculum Evaluation.

Stanfield, J. H. II (1994) "Ethnic Modeling in Qualitative Research," in Denzin, N. K. and Lincoln, Y. S. (eds) *Handbook of Qualitative Research*, Thousand Oaks: Sage, 175–88.

Steffe, L. P. and Gale, G. (1995) *Constructivism in Education*, Hillsdale: Lawrence Erlbaum Associates.

Stevenson, J. (1991) "The Long-term Impact of Interactive Exhibits," *International Journal of Science Education*, 13(5): 521–31.

Sudbury, P. and Russell, T. (1995) *Evaluation of Museum and Gallery Displays*, Liverpool: Liverpool University Press.

Sykes, M. (1996) "Research Review on Museum-Based Learning in Early Childhood," *Hand to Hand*, Association of Youth Museums, Spring and Summer issues.

Tchen, J. K. W. (1992) "Ancestor Worship, Sacred Pizzerias, and the Other: A Few Conceits of Anglo-American Modernism," in Association of Art Museum Directors, *Different Voices: A Social Cultural and Historical Framework for Change in the American Art Museum*, New York: Association of Art Museum Directors, 101–16.

Thompson, D. (1990) "An Architectural View of the Visitor–Museum Experience," in Bitgood, S., Benefield, A., and Patterson, D. (eds) *Visitor Studies: Theory, Research, and Practice*, 3, Jacksonville: Center for Social Design, 72–85.

Tinbergen, N. (1974) "Ethology and Stress Diseases," *Science*, 185: 20–7.

Trevelyan, V. (ed.) (1991) *"Dingy Places with Different Kinds of Bits." An Attitudes Survey of London Museums Amongst Non-Visitors*, London: London Museum Service.

Tucker, M. (1992) "'Who's On First?' Issues of Cultural Equity in Today's Museums," in Association of Art Museum Directors, *Different Voices: A Social Cultural and Historical Framework for Change in the American Art Museum*, New York: Association of Art Museum Directors, 9–16.

Tunnicliffe, S. D. (1995) *Talking About Animals: Studies of Young Children Visiting Zoos, a Museum and a Farm*, Unpublished Ph.D. thesis, London: King's College.

United States Department of Health, Education and Welfare (1966) *Equality of Educational Opportunity Report*, Washington, DC: Government Printing Office.

Uzzell, D. (1993) "Contrasting Psychological Perspectives on Exhibition Evaluation," in Bicknell, S. and Farmelo, G. (eds) *Museum Visitor Studies in the 90s*, London: Science Museum, 125–9.

Van der Stoep, G. (1989) "Time-lapse Photography: Advantages and Disadvantages of its Application as a Research and Visitor Behavior Monitoring Tool," in Uzzell, D. L. (ed.) *Heritage Interpretation, Vol. 2, The Visitor Experience*, London: Bellhaven, 179–90.

VanLuven, P. and Miller C. (1993) "Concepts in

Context: Conceptual Frameworks, Evaluation and Exhibit Development," in Thompson, D. *et al.* (eds) *Visitor Studies: Theory, Research, and Practice, 5*, Jacksonville: Visitor Studies Association, 116–24.

Vergo, P. (ed.) (1989) *The New Museology*, London: Reaktion Books Ltd.

Veron, E. and Lavasseur, M. (1989) *Ethnographie de l'exposition: L'espace, le corp et le sens*, Paris: Centre George Pompidou.

von Glasersfeld, E. (1990) "An Exposition of Constructivism: Why Some Like it Radical," in Davis, R. B., Maher, C. A., and Noddings, N. (eds) *Constructivist Views on the Teaching and Learning of Mathematics*, Reston: National Council of Teachers of Mathematics, 19–29.

—— (1995) "A Constructivist Approach to Teaching," in Steffe, L. P. and Gale, J. (eds) *Constructivism in Education*, Hillsdale: Lawrence Erlbaum Associates, 3–15.

Vukelich, R. (1984) "Time Language for Interpreting History Collections to Children," *Museum Studies Journal*, 1(4): 43–50.

Vygotsky, L. (1962) *Thought and Language*, Cambridge, Mass.: Harvard University Press.

—— (1962/1978) *Mind in Society: The Development of Higher Psychological Processes*, Cole, M., Scribner, S., John-Steiner, V., and Souderman, E. (eds), Cambridge, Mass.: Harvard University Press.

Watson, J. B. (1930) *Behaviorism*, Revised Edition, New York: Norton, 12–13: 158–61. (He reports that the original work appeared in Rayner, R. and Watson, J. B. (1921) "Conditioned Emotional Reactions," *Scientific Monthly*: 493).

Webb, E. J., Campbell, D. T., Schwartz, R. D., and Sechrest, L. (1966) *Unobtrusive Measures: Nonreactive Research in the Social Sciences*, Chicago: Rand McNally & Co.

Weber, L. (1971) *The English Infant School and Informal Education*, Englewood Cliffs: Prentice-Hall.

Weiss, C. H. (1973) "Where Politics and Evaluation Research Meet," *Evaluation*, 1(3).

—— (1991) "Evaluation Research in the Political Context: Sixteen Years and Four Administrations Later," in McLaughlin, M. W. and Phillips, D. C., *Evaluation and Education at Quarter Century* (NSSE 96th Yearbook),

Chicago: National Society for the Study of Education, 211–31.

Weiss, R. and Boutourline, S. (1963) "The Communication Value of Exhibits," *Museum News*, 42(3): 23–7.

Wertsch, J. V. (1991) *Voices of the Mind: A Socio-cultural Approach to Mediated Action*, Cambridge, Mass.: Harvard University Press.

White, J. and Barry, S. (1984) *Families, Frogs, and Fun: Developing a Family Learning Lab in a Zoo HERPlab: A Case Study*, Washington, DC: Smithsonian Institution.

Whittel, G. (1996) "Crime Buster," *The Times* (London), Monday, May 6: 13.

Winter, I. J. (1992) "Change in the American Art Museum: The (An) Art Historian's Voice," in Association of Art Museum Directors, *Different Voices: A Social Cultural and Historical Framework for Change in the American Art Museum*, New York: Association of Art Museum Directors, 30–57.

Wittlin, A. S. (1949) *The Museum, Its History and Its Tasks in Education*, London: Routledge and Keagan Paul.

—— (1971) *Museums for a Usable Future*, Cambridge, Mass.: Massachusetts Institute of Technology Press.

Wizevich, K. J. (1994) "Use of Annotated Floor Plans in Evaluation," in AAM Committee on Audience Research and Evaluation, *Current Trends in Audience Research and Evaluation*, 8, Seattle, 49–53.

Wolf, R. L. (1979) *Strategies for Conducting Naturalistic Interviews*, Kalamazoo: Evaluation Center, Western Michigan University.

—— (1986) "The Missing Link: the Role of Orientation in Enriching the Museum Experience," *Journal of Museum Ed.*, 11(1) Winter: 17–21; reprinted in *Patterns in Practice: Selections from the Journal of Museum Education* (1992) Washington, DC: Museum Education Roundtable, 134–43.

Wolf, R. L. and Tymitz, B. (1978a) *A Preliminary Guide for Studying Museum Environments*, Washington, DC: Smithsonian Institution, Office of Museum Programs.

—— (1978b) *Whatever Happened to the Giant Wombat: An Investigation of the Impact of the Ice Age Mammals and Emergence of Man Exhibit, National Museum of Natural History,*

Smithsonian Institution, Washington, DC: Smithsonian Institution.

Worts, D. (1993) "Making Meaning in Museums: There's a Lot to Learn," *Pathways to Partnerships, MEAA & MEANZ 1993*

Conference Proceedings, MEAA (Victorian Branch), 39–83.

Yorath, J. (ed.) (1995) *Learning About Science and Technology in Museums*, London: South Eastern Museum Service.

Index

Lightning Source UK Ltd.
Milton Keynes UK
11 December 2009

147385UK00010B/20/A

9 780415 097765